Treaties

on

Trial

TREATIES
ON
TRIAL

The Continuing Controversy
over Northwest Indian Fishing Rights

FAY G. COHEN

With contributions by
Joan La France and Vivian L. Bowden

Introduction by Andy Fernando

A REPORT PREPARED FOR THE
American Friends Service Committee

UNIVERSITY OF WASHINGTON PRESS

SEATTLE AND LONDON

Library of Congress Cataloging-in-Publication Data
Cohen, Fay G.
    Treaties on trial.

    "A report prepared for the American Friends Service Committee."
    Includes index.
    1. Indians of North America—Washington (State)—Fishing—Law and legislation.   I. La France, Joan.
II. Bowden, Vivian L.   III. American Friends Service Committee.   IV. Title.
KFW505.6.H85C64   1986   343.797'07692'08997   85-40396
ISBN 0-295-96263-1 (cloth)   347.9703769208997
ISBN 0-295-96268-2 (pbk.)

THIS IS MY LAND

This is my land
From the time of the first moon
Till the time of the last sun
It was given to my people.
Wha-neh Wha-neh, the great giver of life
Made me out of the earth of this land
He said, "You are the land, and the land is you."
I take good care of this land,
For I am part of it.
I take good care of the animals,
For they are my brothers and sisters.
I take care of the streams and rivers,
For they clean my land.
I honor Ocean as my father,
For he gives me food and a means of travel.
Ocean knows everything, for he is everywhere.
Ocean is wise, for he is old.
Listen to Ocean, for he speaks wisdom.
He sees much, and knows more.
He says, "Take care of my sister, Earth,
She is young and has little wisdom, but much kindness."
"When she smiles, it is springtime."
"Scar not her beauty, for she is beautiful beyond all things."
"Her face looks eternally upward to the beauty of sky and stars,
Where once she lived with her father, Sky."
I am forever grateful for this beautiful and bountiful earth.
God gave it to me
This is my land.

Clarence Pickernell
Quinault, Taholah
from *Uncommon Controversy*

Contents

Illustrations

Preface

The controversy described in this book has its roots in encounters between the Northwest tribes who reaped abundant salmon from the rivers at their doorways and the white settlers who began entering the region in the mid-nineteenth century. When the United States government negotiated treaties with the tribes to permit white settlement, the Indians retained their all-important rights to the fish. Treaty negotiators told the tribes, "This paper secures your fish." [1]

Yet in the years that followed, increasing population, industrialization, environmental degradation, and state regulations combined to restrict Indian fishing. After many years of struggling against these obstacles, the Indians initiated new court cases and "fish-ins"—fishing in defiance of state law but in accord with Indian interpretations of the treaties—in an effort to assert their rights. Their efforts were strongly opposed by state agencies and non-Indian fishermen.

Thus, a century after the treaties were signed, Indian fishing rights became a highly volatile issue in the Pacific Northwest. In 1965, the American Friends Service Committee (AFSC) in Seattle formed a study group to examine the issue. AFSC is a peace and social justice organization established by members of the Religious Society of Friends (Quakers) in 1917. Awarded the Nobel Peace Prize in 1947, AFSC reflects the Friends' quest for nonviolent resolution to conflict and their concern for human rights. The Seattle Regional Office of AFSC had worked with Indian communities for nearly twenty years when its study group, comprised of Indian and non-Indian volunteers, began its investigation. Its efforts produced a mimeographed report, issued by the National Congress of American Indians in 1967, and subsequently published as *Uncommon Controversy: Fishing Rights of the Muckleshoot, Puyallup, and Nisqually Indians* by the University of Washington Press in 1970.

Uncommon Controversy argued that the restriction of Indian fishing reflected the failure of contemporary society to live with and accept diversity. It advocated a coordinated system of management that would allocate fish to the Indians and would include them in making decisions about the resource. *Uncommon Controversy* called for increased public awareness and concern for the human element of the controversy. It urged everyone who cared about fish to "come to terms on allocation and unite to devote their attention to the environmental threats."[2]

Uncommon Controversy was widely circulated and well received. Described as "uncommonly comprehensive,"[3] the book clearly conveyed the message that "the survival of men and fish are inextricably linked to the problems of the total environment."[4] The University of Washington Press reprinted the book four times, twice adding new prefaces that described how the basic controversy continued to command public attention while remaining essentially unresolved.

On February 12, 1974, Judge George Boldt of the United States District Court of Western Washington issued his decision in the case of *U.S.* v. *Washington*. His ruling clarified the basic issues of the treaty right to fish, the nature of the Indian allocation and the role of the tribes within the management system. Following the decision, the controversy intensified. The 1970s were a tumultuous period for Northwest Indian fishing rights, and it became increasingly clear that a new report was needed. AFSC thus commissioned a study that could build upon *Uncommon Controversy* and bring its story up to date. This book is the result.

Treaties on Trial extends the time under consideration from 1970 until 1984, and extends the scope to all of the Northwest tribes engaged in treaty fishing in western Washington and along the Columbia River. Although some material from *Uncommon Controversy* is incorporated, this book is neither a revision nor a sequel; it is an entirely new work.

Treaties on Trial is based primarily on research conducted between February 1979 and August 1981 in the Northwest and in Washington, D.C. It draws upon interviews with more than a hundred persons directly involved with the Indian fishing rights controversy: tribal leaders, tribal biologists, and Indian fishermen; state officials and biologists; attorneys on both sides of the issue; federal officials; and non-Indian commercial and sports fishermen. Government documents, newspaper accounts, public opinion data, legal records, and historical and anthropological references also were important sources of information for the book. Additional information was collected by attendance at legal proceedings, government hearings, Indian gatherings, and open meetings of agencies involved with fisheries regulations. The material obtained during this period was updated in subsequent years by correspondence, telephone interviews, and trips to Seattle in July 1982 and May 1984.

A book of this nature can never be completely up to date. Significant events continue to unfold. For example, in March 1985, the United States and Canada signed the Pacific Salmon Treaty. After decades of negotiations, this new agreement provides a comprehensive framework for cooperative management of the stocks shared by fishermen of both nations. Northwest Indian tribes are represented on the United States section of the commission established to implement the treaty. Furthermore, tribal and state fisheries management agencies increasingly have become involved in the joint management of the Northwest fishery. Currently, they are working together on long-range watershed planning. Such developments represent a continuation of the trend toward cooperation described in the closing chapters of the book.

Fay G. Cohen
Institute for Resource and Environmental Studies
Dalhousie University
Halifax, Nova Scotia

December 1985

Acknowledgments

Treaties on Trial is the result of many minds, hearts, and hands. I wish to acknowledge the American Friends Service Committee's National and Northwest Regional Office for their confidence in the project and their financial support over many years. Ed Nakawatase of the National Office, Warren Witte, Gretchen Smith, and Linda Jones of the Regional Office, and Romayne Watt, Gary Peterson, Martha Smyser, Ellie Menzies, Jon Bell, and Mary Parks of the Pacific Northwest Regional Indian Committee played a particularly important role in the process of developing, reviewing, and producing the book. Sandra Osawa participated in interviews and gathered information during her work as a member of the AFSC Research Staff in 1979–80. Charles Broches prepared several background papers for AFSC. Maureen di Giacomo, Kate Campbell, Barbara Fritzmeier, and Craig Brown assisted on the project by verifying information and collecting photographs. I also wish to thank Joe Ryan, Indian Program Director since 1982, who performed many tasks necessary for the completion of the book.

I am grateful as well to the Institute for Resource and Environmental Studies, Dalhousie University, Halifax, Nova Scotia, where the book took on most of its present shape and form between 1981 and 1985. I wish to thank Arthur J. Hanson, Director, for financial support for preparing the manuscript at IRES and for the encouragement that he, Susan Guppy, and Pierre Taschereau offered during this period. I also acknowledge Susan Macdonald's administrative assistance, Judy Reade's consultations on bibliography, and Brenda Finn, Gina MacPhail, and Christine Ritchie's secretarial support.

Tribal management agencies made significant contributions to this project. The Northwest Indian Fisheries Commission, the Columbia River Inter-Tribal Fish Commission, the Skagit System Cooperative, and the Point No Point Treaty Council as well as many tribal fisheries biologists and managers offered information and responded helpfully to frequent queries.

State and federal government officials and agencies cooperated fully with this study. The assistance of the Washington Department of Fisheries, the Washington Department of Game, the Washington Attorney General's Office, the U.S. Bureau of Indian Affairs, congressional members and staff, and the U.S. Commission on Civil Rights is gratefully acknowledged.

Legal firms and attorneys were very helpful in clarifying the complex legal issues discussed in this book. I appreciate the assistance of the firm of Ziontz, Pirtle, Chestnut, Ernstoff, and Morisset and of the Evergreen Legal Services of Seattle, the Chambers and Sasche firm in Washington, D.C., George Dysart of the U.S. Department of Justice, Portland, Oregon, Sue Hvalsoe of Olympia, and Michael Thorpe of Tacoma, Washington, for providing information and for facilitating the use of legal documents.

I also thank Øystein Gaasholt, University of Aarhus, Denmark for our collaboration on issues of public opinion surrounding treaty rights, which he undertook as part of his research supported by the Danish Social Science Research Council.

I am grateful as well to all the individuals who were interviewed and who provided so much of the information on which the book is based. I wish to mention Hank Adams, Bill Frank, Jr., Jim Heckman, Russel Barsh, Cecelia Carpenter, and the fishermen of Cook's Landing and Frank's Landing, and also the other fishermen—Indian and non-Indian alike—who shared their experiences and viewpoints. I also wish to thank Van Chase for sharing her perspectives on Indian issues with me over many years.

Treaties on Trial benefited from an extensive academic and community review process. Reviewers included Laura Berg, Elsie Dennis, Andy Fernando, Mike Grayum, Ralph Johnson, Phil Katzen, Nick Lampsakis, Cynthia Lamson, Barbara Lane, Gary

Morishima, Lee Cunninggim Neff, Gary Peterson, Martha Smyser, Charles Sneatlum, Richard Whitney, and Bruce Wildsmith. They lent their expertise in tribal fisheries, fisheries biology and management, community perceptions, philosophy, anthropology, and law; their comments were extremely valuable. Because of the diversity of views expressed, not every suggestion was accommodated, but a significant proportion were utilized to revise and improve the text.

The relationship between the American Friends Service Committee and the University of Washington Press has now spanned more than a decade, first with the publication of *Uncommon Controversy* and now with *Treaties on Trial*. Julidta Tarver, Managing Editor of the press, who worked on both books, and Lane Morgan and Veronica Seyd, who provided assistance on this book, are sincerely acknowledged.

I wish to express my appreciation to the contributors to *Treaties on Trial*. Joan La France, a member of the original study group involved in *Uncommon Controversy*, contributed to the formulation and research for this book during her work as AFSC Indian Program Director from 1978–81. Some of the information which we collected during this period was included in her MPA degree project at the University of Washington entitled "Salmon Resource Management: Contributions from Tribal Management" (1981). Following her departure from AFSC, she continued to serve the project by providing critiques of several drafts of the manuscript. Vivian Bowden contributed valuable editorial assistance in developing the structure of the narrative and ensuring clear, well-polished prose. I am also grateful to Andy Fernando for his Introduction—a first-hand account of the meaning of treaty fishing rights for Indian people and their communities.

Members of the Northwest tribes provided continual encouragement for this project and it is with respect for their ongoing efforts to secure the fish that this book is offered.

Introduction

In the clear light of morning, a young Indian girl casts a small flat stone from the riverbank. It skips across the smooth water slowly circling in a broad eddy. As the stone dances on the water's surface, the ripples it creates break the mirrored reflection of the girl's mother and father pulling a net across the bow of their fourteen-foot river skiff. Wisps of fog rise from the river surface. Gently pushed by a light late-spring breeze blowing from the far shore, the fog spins and swirls into the tall evergreen trees. The river, called Skagit, is wide here—200 yards across: the sparrows darting and gliding along the opposite bank seem no larger than insects to the small girl. The new day sun, just rising above the mountain tops, has already warmed the air, yet the river is cold. The stream has been chilled by melting ancient glaciers and the previous winter's snow. Only a few miles downstream the Skagit will empty into Puget Sound, the river's clean, fresh waters joining the brine that leads to the Pacific Ocean.

The flat stone skips a final time and sinks to the river bottom, joining a thousand other stones thrown by a thousand other children for a thousand years. As the ripples disappear, the girl resumes watching her parents at work, the work she has watched for as long as she can remember. The task is well rehearsed, practiced by each generation, and, according to tradition, taught to the

xv

children by example on the river. This morning she is watching the end of a lesson begun the day before, a lesson that was months in preparation.

The previous evening, the young girl's parents, Skagit Indians, had tied one end of their thirty-five-fathom (210-foot) gill net to the riverbank, and carefully piled the rest of the net into the bow of the flat-bottom boat. The wooden skiff, hand-tooled to remove any sharp edges and worn smooth by years of use, is made especially for river net fishing. While it has modern contours, its shape and purpose is reminiscent of the forty-foot, flat-bottom river canoes used by countless Indian ancestors. While her father slowly rowed the skiff backwards from the bank, her mother guided the net off the bow, releasing its length along the edge of the river eddy until the last fathom slipped off the boat. A rope fastened to the end of the net followed, and, last, the mother pushed a fifty-pound rock, bound and tied to the rope, into the water to anchor the net.

When they were finished, the gill net bowed in a gentle arc on the water. Even extended, it stretched less than a third of the way across the river, and would allow most of the returning fish to pass upstream. Supporting the net were three dozen small floats, no larger than the girl's hand, spaced evenly along a strong rope and held fast by firmly-tied twine, which also bound the net webbing to the rope. Months earlier, the girl had counted the floats as she helped her father slide the rope through the hole in each one, then watched as he tied the floats a fathom apart. With the same stout twine, he tied the net to lead-weighted rope, which now rested on the river gravels almost thirty feet below. Between the buoyed and leaded ropes, thousands of diamond-shaped webs billowed loosely in the eddy current. The webs were measured to catch fish of a certain size. Travelling upstream from the ocean, a fish would sense and strive to reach the river eddy, where it could pause and rest from its fight against the current. On the edge of the eddy, it would encounter the net in its path. In an effort to escape, the fish would push its head through a web opening, only to catch the gill plates behind its head in the net. A fish too small could pass through the web; too large a fish might break the web, free to continue upstream to spawn.

Last night, the anchor rock thrown, the net freed from tangles, the parents had rowed the skiff back to shore, and walked through a small group of tents and camper trailers to join a discussion around the campfire. There the girl's uncles and aunts, cousins and grandparents were making optimistic talk over expectations for the new fishing season, about where and how each of them had set their nets, about how generations before had laughed and talked much the same way at the same campsite. The happy conversation lasted well into the night, and shortly before her mother tucked her into a sleeping bag, the girl heard the murmur of small outboard motors as her uncles and aunts travelled off to their net sites, and she listened to the clatter of oars against wood as her mother and father also rowed their boat out from the bank. Three times during the night the adults would clear the twigs, leaves and branches from their nets and lift the webbing to see if their effort had been rewarded with a fish or two.

There had been no fish that night.

In the morning, the girl woke to the sounds of her grandparents cooking breakfast over the campfire. The sun had not yet risen, but her parents were already at the riverbank, preparing the boat for setting a second floating net to fish upriver. The girl turned in her sleeping bag, lulled by the familiar stir of morning activity. But at the sound of a loud splash she had jumped up and hurriedly dressed. Outside, the grandparents, too, responded to the sound, stopping at mid-task to search out the source of commotion, then setting aside their firewood and frypans to walk to the river's edge. By the time the girl had pulled on her rubber boots and run from the tent, her parents had already rowed the skiff from the bank toward the net. Joining her grandparents, the girl reached down to pick up a stone to throw across the water. They all knew—child, parents and grandparents alike—what had made the splash. All had heard the same sound many times, but this was the first time each had heard it this season.

The young girl's parents are pulling the net, their backs straining against its weight. Pulling the net across the bow, they remove branches and leaves as they go, returning the previous length of net to the water as they draw the next length into the boat. The sun breaks over the jagged mountain peaks to the east to bathe the scene in a rich golden glow. The dainty fog wisps dance around the boat and disappear, and steam rises from the dew-speckled wool coats worn by the girl's parents. Their backs warmed by the sun and their own effort, the adults pull the heavily leaded line and webbing. The splashing persists near the far end of the net. They resist the temptation to work too quickly, for the entire length of the net must be checked for branches and the possibility of another fish caught during the night.

At last, the girl's parents reach the focus of the commotion. The struggle of the thrashing prey is intense: it takes both adults' weight and strength to pull the catch into the boat. In its fight against the net, the fish has torn a hole three feet wide; sun-drenched beads of water dangle from the ragged strands of webbing. Normally the parents would take time to repair the tear before returning to shore, but they, too, are excited about their first catch of the season. Carefully, they grasp the fish by the tail and remove it from the net by the same direction it entered, the mother stretching back the webbing over the fish's gills.

As the girl's parents row their boat back to shore, aunts and uncles return by boat from net sites up and down stream. Their nets were empty. The boats land simultaneously, and the girl scampers down the beach to meet them, followed closely by her grandparents. Her parents' catch is held high; everyone beams smiles of approval. It is a king salmon, four feet long and 57 pounds—almost as tall as the girl, and heavier than her slight eight-year-old body. Bright scales flash in the sunlight as the salmon is laid back down in the boat and continues to thrash, refusing to end its struggle, its broad tail slapping the floor of the skiff with a loud thumping sound. The king salmon is a large male, and has begun its physical transformation in the journey from saltwater to freshwater, where it would have spawned and died. Its snout is assuming a hook-shape, where before it was round, and its back has begun to arch slightly. Its silver-colored scales, which would have disappeared by the time the salmon spawned, have just begun to darken and recede. Still, this is a prime salmon, worth $1.50 or more a pound to the girl's parents from the commercial salmon buyers who will arrive at their camp later in the day.

But this salmon will not be sold.

According to a centuries-old, Northwest coastal Indian tradition, carried on by the girl's family, this first salmon will neither be sold nor traded nor even preserved for eating later in the year. The many generations born before the girl's grandparents and great-grandparents had each celebrated the same first catch in the late spring of the year. During the long winter months, Indian families mostly remained indoors in their great cedar longhouses along the banks of the river, subsisting on stores of dried salmon, berries, roots, and game. Fresh food, particularly their staple diet of salmon, was scarce during these months. By the spring months of "pedhweywats"—the time of robins whistling—the stocks of food were depleted or spoiled, well-fed game was scarce, and edible plants and berries were not yet ready to harvest. But in those spring months king salmon would return to the river, completing their four-year cycle from river-hatched eggs to ocean-dwelling juveniles to mature adults ready to spawn their progeny. The spring salmon were few in number, but they returned earlier than other salmon to seek the colder snow-fed streams, and their larger size and firmer flesh made them a fine prize. The entire village would gather together and appoint fishermen to each catch one salmon—no more.

In fine regalia, accompanied by a fanfare of deerskin drum and special village songs, the first salmon caught would be carried from the riverbank to the gathered villagers. A village leader, or shaman, would carefully clean and save the salmon's entrails, then carve away the meat until a carcass of head, bones, and tail was left, still connected. The entrails would be placed in the skeleton, and the framework of bones from the flashing bright salmon laid on a mat of fresh, spring-green ferns. Meanwhile, the villagers would have raised a fire of alderwood, the smoke thick from the new sap filling the wood. The wood's low blaze would cook the salmon slowly, and leave a mild smoke taste in the meat. The pieces of salmon meat would then be skewered on thin sticks carved from small ironwood trees growing along the riverbank; the end of each stick had been sharpened so it could be staked into the ground near the fire. Nearly an hour would pass before the salmon was fully cooked, but the villagers would gladly wait, perhaps speculating to each other about the upcoming season; or talking of where and how they would set their nets, or build their fish traps, or spear their salmon; or reminiscing over the generations before who had gathered in the same campsite to perform the first salmon ceremony.

When the salmon was cooked, everyone would gather to eat. It mattered not whether there were ten villagers or a hundred: each would share equally in the fruit of the first catch. The meal finished, leaders would recount the village stories of great fishermen and hunters of fact, legend, and myth—or all three combined. The headmen and women would speak of the importance of the first salmon ceremony, of sharing the first catch, harvest, or kill, of the high status bestowed to those villagers who were given the gift and the power to provide food for the village.

In the end, the headmen would lift the fern mat cradling the remains of the salmon, and, followed by villagers, walk to the riverbank. The drums would sound and songs ring around the valley, echoes from the steep slopes above singing praise back to the gathering. Placing the fern mat on the water with the salmon's head pointed downstream, the headman would release the mat to float on the river toward the sea, signifying the completion of the salmon cycle. The villagers and the salmon had fulfilled their duty, prescribed by the great spirit. The salmon had returned to the appointed time and place; the villagers had faithfully honored the salmon in sharing and ceremony. The people thereby assured themselves of a good season, and the harvest could begin.

The young girl finishes her portion of the first salmon. Her grandparents have cooked the fish well on thin ironwood stakes over the green alderwood boughs. The last morsels are still warm, full of juices from the fat king salmon, and taste of mild alderwood smoke. Her parents, uncles, aunts and cousins have eaten their fill, too; there is plenty of salmon to go around. The girl doesn't understand the stories her grandparents tell as they eat, about great hunters and fishermen with special powers. She knows only that the juicy red meat of the king salmon is far better than the canned, frozen and hardsmoked salmon her family ate during the past winter. In a few years, at the age of 14, she can receive her own permit from her tribe and fish with her parents. Perhaps then, she says to herself, I will catch the first salmon and share it with my family. She had heard that good fishermen are respected in the tribe, and that long ago those who provided for the people were known as high-class persons. She has heard that if the first salmon is shared and eaten, she will have good luck and good fishing.

The meal finished, the girl begins to help her grandparents gather the plates for washing, while her parents, aunts and uncles return to the riverbank to again prepare their nets for drift fishing. They have shared the first salmon together, and they laugh and joke with each other, warmed by the friendly feel of fresh-cooked salmon in their stomachs. They have fulfilled their duty, as has the salmon, and each person knows that this promises a good fishing season ahead.

Suddenly, their conversation stops short. A familiar sound

breaks through the voices, snaps each mind and eye to attention. In the direction of the net, a splash is heard.

Only a few changes in technology separate this scene in 1983 from 1883. In different settings, through the eyes of different children, the scene is repeated today along the river valleys throughout western Washington and Oregon. But the truth is, without the benefit of the court decision which the following chapters describe, there might not have been a traditional first salmon ceremony for the young Indian girl to witness. Instead of fishing for salmon by the light of day, the girl's parents would only be setting their gill net at night, fearing arrest by state fisheries police for violating state laws that long prohibited gillnetting, spearing, and other traditional Indian salmon-harvesting techniques in the rivers and bays off-reservation.

Northwest Indian families have for centuries gathered along the riverbanks and saltwater bays to stake their gill nets, to erect wooden fish traps, or to poise long spears in search of salmon. They cherished this part of their lives so that, even as they signed away their traditional lands in treaties with the United States government in 1854–55, the Indian people retained the right to fish at their traditional grounds and waters, regardless of where those places were, on-reservation or off. Since they were written, these treaties have been treated as worthless paper by the Washington and Oregon state governments. As the states prevented the Indians from fishing at their traditional places, a strong and important part of Indian culture began to disappear. If not for the court decision, quite possibly the scene of a young girl at the riverbank would soon vanish, and so also vanish one of the few remnants of traditional Northwest Indian society.

But this has not happened. On February 12, 1974, George H. Boldt, senior federal judge for western Washington, emphatically and comprehensively affirmed the right of most Washington Indian tribes to fish for salmon in accordance with federal treaties they had signed 119 years before. The ruling in *U.S.* v. *Washington,* known throughout the Pacific Northwest as the "Boldt deci-

sion," was by no means the first court case to deal with t|
of treaty salmon-fishing rights. It was, in fact, the culmin
eighty-seven years of nearly continuous court battles se
either restore or prevent traditional Indian fishing for salmon.

The Boldt decision was a milestone, indeed. To the grandparents of the young Indian girl, the decision reaffirms the sanctity of
the contract between people and their governments that the treaties
signified. The ruling to restore recognition for Indian treaty-
fishing rights has been long in coming, and many grandfathers
and grandmothers have waited many years for its arrival. To our
elders, the court decision is a tribute to the resiliency and tenacity
of their ancestors. It is a vindication of the federal government's
promise that "the right to fish in usual and accustomed places"—
a term central to the treaties—stands for more than fading words
on crumbling paper.

Many Indian grandfathers and grandmothers, such as my own,
have reminded us that the treaties of 1854–55, made a pledge.
Indian elders placed great stock in promises, and remembered
well when promises were broken. I recall listening to my grandfather, who often reminded me, as a twelve-year-old spearfisher-
man, of a right guaranteed by a piece of paper. My grandfather's
words were echoed by another elder, Si James, a great orator of
the Tulalip Reservation, who said: "My grandfather once told me,
for as long as the sun comes up in the east and sets in the west,
the word shall be good. For as long as the water comes down from
the mountains and goes out to the sound, the word shall be good.
For as long as the tide comes to the shore and goes back out again,
the word shall be good."

Then Si observed: "The sun still comes up and goes down. The
water still comes out of the mountains and goes into the sound.
The tide comes to the shore and goes back out again. . . ."

The old man's voice grew silent. He did not finish the story.
The word had not been good, and on his face the disappointment
was chiselled as sharply as the furrows in his brow.

Our grandfathers and grandmothers remembered how state laws
had made fishing by gill net, trap and spear illegal in many rivers

and bays, illegal in those ancestral places the treaties called "usual and accustomed." In defiance, our grandparents set their nets by moonlight and withstood harassment and arrest by state police, only to return to fish the rivers again. More than one hundred years ago, our ancestors of many tribes gave up control of tens of thousands of acres in what is now Washington, Oregon, and Idaho in exchange for keeping a few limited rights, including the right to fish in traditional places. To the elders, a promise made was a promise kept, and those who have lived to see the Boldt decision believe now that both parties to the treaty can keep their part of the bargain.

To the parents of the young girl, the court decree would mean return to a traditional vocation and to new opportunities that vocation supports. The parents would carry out a livelihood and lifestyle, through traditional forms of fishing, that retains the best parts of their Indian culture, and permits them to attain that level of respect in the Indian community bestowed upon good fishermen and women.

Decades of decay in many Indian communities have given succeeding generations fewer reasons to follow the traditions and to remain active in tribal society. The Boldt decision has acted as a catalyst to change that. In years past, most talented Indian people left the reservations. Driven away by lack of jobs or a future, they fled to opportunities in the cities. Their exodus sapped strength from the reservations. The fishing right assured by the Boldt decision has reversed the trend. The elation and positive feeling of pulling a fifty-pound salmon into the boat is being translated into social change and activity in more than two dozen Indian communities. Following the 1974 decision, many young Indian people returned to their tribes at first only to fish. But now they stay on because they see renewed activity in their tribal communities. Those people bringing skills have found welcoming tribal councils and communities eager to tap their knowledge and experience. Those willing to learn have found new opportunities, training, and employment in tribally-operated housing, health, and service programs, in the many tribally-owned businesses that have emerged in recent years, and in the tribal salmon management programs created under the Boldt decision. No one is suggesting that the Boldt decision has solved all the problems in Indian country, but the opportunities created directly or indirectly from the legally-secured right to fish are the difference between staying and leaving for many young Indian families. Today, when young Indians leave the reservation for college or to learn a skill, most intend to return and use their knowledge close to home. And many of those young people will return, to stay and build a future.

Even more important than the legal milestone or vocational opportunity the Boldt decision represents for the grandparents and parents in our scene, the judgment holds its greatest promise and value for the young girl, and her children's children. For young Indian boys and girls, the Boldt decision shapes a new image of self. Many of their parents, as children, had watched the adults having to fish by cover of darkness, concealing their nets and boats, furtive glances alert to the arrival of state police. Those children grew to know fishing as a surreptitious, almost embarrassing activity from a diminishing culture, better forgotten in the pursuit of more conventional occupations in the larger non-Indian society.

Today's Indian children form a different impression from the hours and days of long, hard work to earn a rightful, though modest, income from salmon fishing. They learn that salmon fishing is truly a family activity, with every member taking part. Mothers, fathers, grandparents, aunts, uncles, and cousins gather together in family fishing camps on dozens of rivers and bays to share the work and the enjoyment of fishing. Whether the family is earning its income from fishing or simply stocking a home smokehouse or freezer, the children can see firsthand the benefit of its labor. The child learns that the fisherman or woman is a respected member of the tribal community—a person who carries on an honorable tradition. In small measures and unspoken lessons, the Indian child shapes an identity that many elders were never able to savor. The child is learning that, as Indians, the people form a strong community. As a fisherman or woman, the child will one day find self-respect and be respected. As a future parent, this child will have a heritage to give his or her children.

Having this sense of community, respect, and heritage will be very important to our children as they become adults and assume the reins of leadership in their respective Indian communities. For Indian people, this is the key to the Boldt decision, this is its true value. When Judge Boldt died on March 18, 1984, he left his legacy in the strength of the Northwest Indian communities which are drawing new energy and life from the return of the salmon. To appreciate that legacy, the citizens of this nation, Indian and non-Indian, must understand the reasons the treaty rights have met resistance for so long. The ultimate benefits these rights confer—moral, cultural, ecological, and economic—upon the larger society have long been argued away for more immediate and narrow interests. The chapters which follow seek to explain these benefits and their implications, not just for Indian people, but also for the salmon itself, and for the future health of all the region's inhabitants. A legacy neglected bears no harvest.

We, as Indian leaders, have a responsibility to preserve our right, now that it has been secured, just as our elders fought to preserve it. We must preserve that right, for more than the value it carries today, for more even than the value of saving the past. Our obligation is to preserve the right to fish for our future, for the many Indian children who will wake to the far-off sound of the first splash of the first salmon of the season.

ANDY FERNANDO
Former Chairman
Upper Skagit Tribal Community
Sedro Woolley, Washington

Indian fisherman
Reporter, *Bellingham Herald*

May 1984

Treaties

on

Trial

Chapter 1

The Boldt Decision:
Desecration or Affirmation?

"It is doubtful if any future case on fishing rights will see such a mass of evidence put forward in support of a legal question."[1]
—Vine Deloria, Jr., Indian lawyer and historian

"What Judge Boldt did that had never been done before was to calculate with some precision just what the Indian treaty fishing rights were."[2]
—Fred Brack, reporter, *Seattle Post-Intelligencer*

EXPECTATIONS

On August 27, 1973, the United States, representing fourteen Indian tribes, sued the State of Washington. From the start people expected a landmark case. "Battle for Indian Fishing Rights Joined," a local paper headlined the news.[3] Three years of pretrial preparation stood complete. Now George H. Boldt, senior judge of the Federal District Court in Tacoma, Washington, sat down to hear the evidence.

Judge with Determination. Judge Boldt, a balding man whose face was framed with heavy dark-rimmed glasses, was approaching his seventieth birthday. He had spent two decades as a federal judge and was well equipped to hear the case. An Eisenhower appointee to the bench, he was a respected jurist with a reputation for firmness. He was known for his tough treatment not only of racketeers and gangsters, but also of antiwar protesters, whose disruptive courtroom tactics he refused to tolerate. He was also recognized as a scholar who had coauthored and edited the federal court system's *Manual for Complex and Multidistrict Litigation,* the guidebook for managing complicated cases.

U.S. v. *Washington* was indeed a complicated case, and, in considering it, the judge described his goal in ambitious terms. He intended "to determine every issue of fact and law presented and, at long last, thereby settle, either in this decision or on appeal thereof, as many as possible of the divisive problems of treaty right fishing which for so long have plagued all the citizens of the area and still do."[4]

Issue with a Past. The way of life the judge would examine was thousands of years old. Long before written history began, Indians were living and fishing along the rivers and streams of what is now western Washington. Their lives centered about the salmon, the magnificent vagabond fish that hatches in freshwater shallows, slips past its foes on the voyage out, and grazes for years through the great ocean pastures, only to snap about at a silent summons and beat itself ragged climbing miles of water and rock back to its natal stream. There it spawns . . . and dies. The Indians also depended upon the steelhead, an oceangoing trout with habits similar to the salmon, along with a fighting spirit that was later to entrance the rod-and-reel sportsman.

Conflict between non-Indian culture and the needs of both salmon and Indian created the issue before the court, an issue more than a century old. It grew out of a series of treaties, six in all, that western Washington tribes and the United States government had negotiated in 1854 and 1855. So important did Indians consider the salmon that in signing these treaties they knowingly ceded vast quantities of land but were determined not to give up their right to continue harvesting fish. The white negotiators, however, did not offer to *exchange* fishing rights for land. As the United States Supreme Court has stated, whites were powerless to *grant* any such rights. The tribes possessed these rights already, just as they possessed the land they were now handing over. What the negotiators signed was a guarantee to protect fishing rights: the treaties *reserved* and *secured* those rights for the tribes.[5]

In subsequent years more and more newcomers demanded a share of the salmon harvest. More and more developers found competing—and destructive—uses for the salmon's freshwater nursery. Early explorers and immigrants had called the abundance of the salmon runs "astonishing."[6] Now overfishing and environmental damage worked as a grim team decimating the fish runs. State agencies, pressed to divide the spoils, pushed the tribes aside, and Indians saw their fishing rights increasingly eroded. Finally, in culmination of many lawsuits that had borne them round about from county court to state court to U.S. Supreme Court and back, the Indians had come before Judge Boldt for a definitive ruling on the substance and force of their treaty rights.

Decision in Two Phases. As a first step in clarifying the issue, Judge Boldt divided *U.S.* v. *Washington* into two phases. He would hear Phase I of the case in 1973. This phase would question whether Indians had *treaty* rights to fish *off* their reservations. (The Indians' exclusive rights to fish *on* their reservation were not in dispute here. Neither did anyone dispute their rights to fish off-reservation as ordinary citizens did, subject to the same state regulations restricting time, location, and extent of harvest as other nontreaty fishermen encountered.) The answer being sought to the question of *off-reservation treaty rights* would depend on Judge Boldt's interpretation of twenty-eight key words contained in almost identical form in the six treaties. The passage says: "The right of taking fish, at all usual and accustomed grounds and stations, is further secured to said Indians, in common with all citizens of the United States."[7] A "yes" answer would lead to another question: did these words also reserve the tribes a specific *portion* of the salmon and steelhead swimming through such "usual and accustomed" fishing places?

Phase II of the case, to be decided subsequently, would of course hinge upon the determinations in Phase I. It would ask the following:

1. Do the fish allocated to Indians include hatchery-bred fish and artificially propagated fish?

2. Do the treaties guarantee the continued protection of the salmon against destruction of its habitat?[8]

Volumes of material concerned with Phase I lay before the judge. At the outset he had invited all groups having any interest in the case to participate directly as parties, or indirectly as *amicus curiae,* "friends of the court" who have no legal right to participate in a case but who are permitted to introduce information and arguments to support their interests.

Extensive anthropological reports were presented by Dr. Barbara Lane, engaged by the federal government and by several of the tribes, and by Dr. Carroll Riley, hired by the state of Washington. State and federal agencies, prepared to agree on certain facts concerning the fishery, worked together on a thick report entitled "Joint Statement Regarding the Biology, Status, Management, and Harvest of the Salmon and Steelhead Resources of the Puget Sound and Olympic Peninsular Drainage Areas of Western Washington."[9] Some 350 documents were entered into the record as exhibits, and attorneys for the different sides presented the judge with proposals for over 500 factual and legal conclusions.

The collected information before the court ranged broad and deep, from a 120-year history of Indian-white relations to the most intricate details of the timing and movement patterns of each salmon run. Thorough descriptions of the nature of the tribes, of salmon and, perhaps most critical, of the essential cultural and legal relationship between them, confronted the judge when he began to consider the positions advanced by the disputing sides.

ARGUMENTS: FOR AND AGAINST, BETWIXT AND BETWEEN

The positions before the court were not limited simply to those of two adversaries who were diametrically opposed. Rather, the court had to consider several different sides presenting an array of positions. Attorney General Slade Gorton represented the state of

Washington. Separate deputy and assistant attorneys general argued for the state Department of Game (which regulates steelhead fishing) and the Department of Fisheries (which regulates salmon fishing). The Washington Reefnet Owners Association, a commercial fishermen's group, was also represented in the case. While not parties to the case, several organizations of sportsmen and commercial fishermen—Northwest Steelheaders Inc., Committee to Save our Fish, Tacoma Sportsmen's Club, Tacoma Poggie Club Inc., Purse Seine Vessel Owners Association, Idaho Fish and Game Association, and the Washington State Sportsmen's Council—submitted friend-of-the-court briefs opposing Indian treaty fishing.

On behalf of the tribes, government attorneys from the U.S. Attorney's Office of the Justice Department and George Dysart, the Assistant Regional Solicitor of the Department of the Interior, presented the federal case. Then there were the positions presented by attorneys retained by eleven separate tribes on their own behalf. (The plaintiff tribes and their treaties are listed in table 1.1; see fig. 6.1 for a map of the treaty areas.)

These were the major viewpoints that were before the court:

No Right to Any. The Washington Department of Game argued that the treaties did not entitle Indians to any privileges or rights greater than those that non-Indians had. It particularly objected to Indian net-fishing for steelhead, which the state defined and managed as "game fish," and which it only permitted to be caught with a hook and line. In its management of steelhead, the department and the Game Commission, the body that sets department policy, saw the department's purpose as conservation of the resource—defined as "wise or prudent use," provision for the sports harvest, and prevention of commercial sale of steelhead. The department director, Carl Crouse, and the head of the department's fisheries program, Clifford Millenbach, argued that an Indian net-fishery—from which fish might be sold—would be detrimental to recreational use and that it should not be permitted.[10]

Arthur Coffin, chairman of the state Game Commission, ex-

TABLE 1.1

Plaintiff Tribes in U.S. v. Washington (1974)

Hoh Indian Tribe	Treaty with Quinault et al. (Treaty of Olympia)
Lummi Tribe of Indians	Treaty of Point Elliott
Makah Indian Tribe	Treaty with the Makah (Treaty of Neah Bay)
Muckleshoot Indian Tribe	Treaty of Point Elliott and Treaty of Medicine Creek
Nisqually Indian Community of the Nisqually Reservation	Treaty of Medicine Creek
Puyallup Tribe of the Puyallup Reservation	Treaty of Medicine Creek
Quileute Tribe of the Quileute Reservation	Treaty of Quinault
Quinault Tribe of Indians	Treaty of Quinault
Sauk-Suiattle Indian Tribe	Treaty of Point Elliott
Skokomish Indian Tribe	Treaty of Point No Point
Squaxin Island Tribe of Indians	Treaty of Medicine Creek
Stillaguamish Indian Tribe	Treaty of Point Elliott
Upper Skagit River Tribe	Treaty of Point Elliott
Confederated Tribes and Bands of the Yakima Indian Nation	Treaty with the Yakimas

SOURCE: *U.S.* v. *Wash.*, 384 F. Supp. 312 (1974), p. 349.

plained that "the Department always considers the (sports) license-holders as the one they represent . . . It's their money that permits the department to propagate the resource."[11]

The Game Department brought in witnesses to testify in favor of sport. The vice president of the Steelhead Trout Club of Washington, Garland Morrison, described his feeling for "the thrill and tug of a giant-sized rainbow trout! If you have ever made love, I guess that's about the nearest I can express it."[12] The Game Department and its supporters, the sportsfishermen, seemed unwilling to give an inch. For them, treaty fishing rights to net-fish for steelhead simply did not exist.

Perhaps One-Third. The Washington Department of Fisheries (WDF) did not dispute that a treaty fishing right existed. An earlier court case in Oregon, which dealt with similar treaty rights of tribes fishing the Columbia River, had ruled that the Indians were entitled to a fair and equitable portion of the fish going through their usual and accustomed places, and WDF wanted quantification of what such a portion would be.[13] At one point, fisheries spokesmen even proposed a specific formula: of the fish originating in the rivers where Indians fish, one-third would go to the Indians as their "fair share," while one-third would go to commercial fishermen and one-third to the sportsmen.[14]

Enough to Live By. The tribal positions contrasted sharply with that of both agencies of the state of Washington. One major argument insisted that the intent of the treaty was to preserve the Indians' right to make their living by fishing. The Indians' share should be based, the tribes argued, on the quantity of fish necessary to meet their needs. Economic deprivation among Indians was well-known, and thus the need for the fish was high. "I think that we should be given a chance to build our economic base around our fisheries, and we have never been given this chance in the state of Washington," testified Forrest "Dutch" Kinley of the Lummi tribe. "We have been harassed in our accustomed fishing grounds . . . we need no training to make a livelihood in fishing. Our people, this is their way of life."[15]

Some tribes also said that the state had no power to regulate

Indian fishing at all. They reasoned that their treaty right to fish could only be modified by Congress—which had not done so. Professor of law Ralph Johnson has argued that the notion that states had authority to regulate Indian fishing crept erroneously into early fishing rights cases and was then elaborated upon in subsequent cases, but without real legal justification.[16]

An Equal Share. The federal government's position focused on affirming the Indians' right to fish under the treaties. It asked the court to require the state of Washington to recognize the treaty-signing tribes as a separate fishing group. Essentially, the government argued to extend the "fair and equitable" doctrine of the earlier Oregon case to the *U.S.* v. *Washington* case area in western Washington. However, the government believed the concept of *a fair and equitable share* was vague and subject to too many differing interpretations. Government attorneys suggested instead the Indians be entitled to *an equal share.*[17]

DELIBERATION

Judge Boldt posed critical questions at several points in the testimony. The authoritative evidence presented by the federal government's anthropologist, Dr. Barbara Lane, seemed to impress him strongly. The judge asked both Indian and non-Indian witnesses how the fish should be allocated. Responses ranged from zero (the Game Department's refusal for any allotment) to 100 percent (an Indian fisherman's view that Indians were entitled to all the fish swimming through their traditional fishing places since Indians had caught nearly all the fish harvested at the time of the treaties).[18] The judge was searching for a way to divide the fish fairly, in line with the meaning of the treaties.

Judge Boldt heard forty-nine witnesses in all and held court six days a week including Labor Day to expedite the case. When all witnesses had been heard and the record completed with exhibits and depositions, he congratulated the lawyers on the thoroughness with which they had handled the case. He promised them that after hearing final arguments, he would "do no judicial work, excepting open the mail or routine matters, other than to prepare my opinion and decision in this case."[19]

Judge Boldt deliberated for several months. He studied the exhibits, the testimony, the treaties, the attorneys' briefs, and the long line of treaty fishing rights cases that preceded this one. In a front-page banner headline on 12 February 1974 the *Seattle Times* announced his decision: "Indian Tribes Win Fishing Rights Case."[20]

DECISION

Judge Boldt reaffirmed an earlier government's solemn pledge to secure the fish so central to the treaty-making process. In all, some fourteen tribes were considered qualified to share in the decision as treaty tribes. Three more could participate upon federal approval. (By 1984, a total of twenty tribes were included.[21]) The judge held that these tribes did indeed have definable rights to salmon, steelhead, and other fish. These rights had to be considered separately from the rights of other users.

The judge interpreted the tribes' right to take fish "in common with" non-Indian citizens to mean "sharing equally." The treaty tribes, he said, were entitled to an opportunity to catch 50 percent of the harvestable fish that were destined to pass through their usual and accustomed fishing grounds and stations. As most of these traditional places were situated along the rivers—the endpoint of the salmon's migratory journey—the decision meant that authorities would have to limit those fishing farther out, either on Puget Sound or on the ocean, so as to permit enough fish to reach the Indian fishermen.

The judge also ruled that tribes themselves were entitled to regulate and manage their share of the fishery.

In Common Means 50–50. Judge Boldt based his interpretation upon dictionary definitions used at the time of the treaties and also upon his sense of how the Indians had understood the meaning of the terms in the treaties. He agreed with federal attorneys and with the state department of fisheries on the need for a more precise definition of the treaty right than "a fair and equitable share." He defined the right as "an equal share."

The 50–50 sharing formula he set out is more complex than it might appear. For one thing, it requires a definition of "harvestable fish." Judge Boldt excluded the following categories of fish from his definition:

1. Those fish that Indians catch on reservations.

2. Those that Indians catch to meet ceremonial and subsistence needs.

3. Those that are necessary for escapement, i.e. which must be permitted to reach their home rivers to spawn and perpetuate the species.[22]

The population in these categories must be subtracted from the total run *before* the "harvestable fish" that remain can be divided.

The judge also took care to spell out the breadth of the tribal right: "The right secured by the treaties to the Plaintiff tribes is not limited as to species of fish, the origin of fish, the purpose or use, or the time or manner of taking, except to the extent necessary to achieve preservation of the resource and to allow non-Indians to fish in common with treaty right fishermen outside reservation boundaries."[23]

Guidelines for State and Tribal Management. Judge Boldt was especially precise in delineating just how, when, and why the state could regulate the treaty right to fish. He required the state to meet specific standards before it could enforce any regulations it claimed necessary for conservation. Conservation regulations to preserve and maintain the resource had to be designed "so as to carry out the purposes of the treaty provision securing to the tribe the right to take fish."[24] Regulations could not discriminate against the treaty tribes' right to fish: the state had to show that its conservation objective could not be met by restricting non-Indian fishermen. The regulations also had to be subject to open hearings and public review.

The judge ruled that in the past the state had unlawfully re-stricted Indian fishing under the guise of "conservation regula-tions." He declared that many of these regulations did not meet either the standards he was establishing or the provisions of fed-eral law. He ruled that restrictions on types of gear and on times and places for fishing would be illegal unless issued according to guidelines he set. He also declared unlawful the seizure and con-fiscation of gear that had occurred when the state enforced its illegal regulations. He set out procedures for the return of many Indian boats and nets taken over the years.

Judge Boldt ruled that all of the tribes were entitled to regulate off-reservation fishing by their members; the state could regulate them only for clearly shown conservation purposes. In addition, some tribes were considered completely self-regulating. A self-regulating tribe was required to meet certain qualifications, including competent and responsible leadership, an officially ap-proved tribal membership roll, personnel to enforce its regula-tions, and provision for tribal membership certification cards. The conditions for self-regulation required the tribes to discuss their fishing regulations with the state before final adoption, and to inform the state about fishing activities and harvests. The Quinault and Yakima tribes were deemed to meet most of these standards at the time the decision and the judge accorded them self-regulating status.[25] The recognition that Indian tribes could man-age their share of the fishery was an important part of the ruling. For years, sportsmen and state officials had pictured the Indian as a threat to the resource. Judge Boldt helped debunk this propa-ganda, noting that "with a single exception testified to by a highly interested witness, and not otherwise substantiated, notwithstand-ing three years of exhaustive trial preparation, neither Game nor Fisheries has discovered and produced any credible evidence showing any instance, remote or recent, when a definitely identi-fied member of any plaintiff tribe exercised his off-reservation treaty rights by any conduct or means detrimental to the perpetua-tion of any species of andromadous fish."[26]

The court's examination of the evidence in *U.S.* v. *Washington* failed to uncover a single valid case of treaty tribes' endangering fish runs, thus dismissing one of the persistent myths of the controversy.

The New Math. The court's requirements for allocating and managing the fishery were going to require some significant changes. While Judge Boldt told the parties that he would not require mathematical precision at the outset,[27] better data gathering clearly was going to be needed to make the system work equitably for treaty and nontreaty fishermen. State and tribal fisheries managers would need to be able to figure with some accuracy the number of species of fish expected to return, the number needed for escapement, and the number being caught en route to tribal fishing grounds by various categories of fishermen. The managers also needed to know how many fishermen using various types of gear would be in each area. The treaty and nontreaty catches had to be tallied as the season progressed in order to know how much additional fishing time could safely be permitted.

There would be a number of variables to account for in making these estimates. For example, the areas to which the estimates pertain are of two types: management districts set up and assigned a number by the Department of Fisheries, and Indian treaty-fishing areas as defined by each tribe's usual and accustomed fishing sites. The two kinds of areas may overlap. The categories of fishermen could include non-Indians fishing with a Department of Fisheries license; nontreaty Indians with a department license; or treaty Indians with the right to catch fish swimming through their area on the way to another tribe's fishing grounds.

Judge Boldt recognized that his decision required a new approach to fisheries management.[28] A clear-cut plan of allocation between treaty and nontreaty fishermen, better and more precise data to aid management, and the recognition of the tribes' right to regulate—all these were to force radical changes upon the old system. Judge Boldt therefore retained jurisdiction in the case so as to answer the questions that were certain to follow. He appointed a Special Master and a Technical Adviser to assist him in resolving future controversies.

In his ruling the judge expressed optimism that the principles he set out would be accepted and respected by the people: "This Court is confident that the vast majority of residents of this state, whether of Indian heritage or otherwise, and regardless of personal interest in fishing, are fair, reasonable, and law-abiding people. They expect that kind of solution to all adjudicated controversies, including those pertaining to treaty right fishing, and they will accept and abide by those decisions even if adverse to interests of their occupational or recreational activities."[29]

In fact, the Boldt decision—as *U.S.* v. *Washington* came to be called—set off a new round of controversy in the media, in the corridors of the state capitol, in the courts, and on the waters. The association of Judge Boldt's name with the case reflects the intense reaction to his ruling. Rarely is a case called by the name of its presiding trial judge.[30] Use of his name has persisted even through review by higher courts, although the correct title remains *U.S.* v. *Washington*.

Following the ruling, steelheaders fought to regain their monopoly on these fish. Non-Indian commercial fishermen mounted an especially vigorous campaign against the decision. They initiated additional court tests, staged protests, and fished illegally in defiance of Fisheries Department regulations issued to implement the decision. Bumper stickers appeared: "Nuts to Boldt." "Can Judge Boldt—Not Salmon." Three years later non-Indian fishermen were still resisting, going so far as to hang the judge in effigy in 1977.[31] In 1981 two non-Indian fishermen drowned at sea during foul weather. Some fishermen blamed their deaths on the Boldt decision, claiming that having to fish in such a restricted season caused the victims to risk venturing further out to sea in bad weather.[32]

Some Indians were disappointed that the court had not gone further. They wanted the fish apportioned on the basis of need, which they felt should award Indians a greater-than-equal share. All Indians found that it was going to be a long uphill battle even to establish the equal-sharing formula as reality. Now there was a new dimension to the controversy. Added to the years of ill-founded belief that Indians posed a danger to the fish was a perhaps even more threatening view that the Indian treaty right, as affirmed by *U.S.* v. *Washington,* presented a danger to the fishing economy of the Northwest. Soon the decision itself came to be blamed for what was really a long-standing problem of too many fishermen chasing too few fish.

CONCLUSION: A SHOCKING DECISION?

The charge persists that the ruling in *U.S.* v. *Washington* was truly a shock—a decree hurled down upon unsuspecting commercial fishermen, state agencies, and sportsmen. This complaint, so frequent and so outraged, makes it absolutely essential to grasp the forces and events that led up to the decision. What makes the charge of judgment without warning so puzzling is that Judge Boldt's determination was so much the culmination of a process. The process had evolved logically from culture, from history, and from biology. It had also evolved from law, for it was reached only after the United States Supreme Court had affirmed Indian treaty fishing rights on not one, but several occasions. Given the developments that precipitated it, a definitive ruling could hardly have been avoided.

Chapters 2 through 5 describe the evolution leading up to Judge Boldt's ruling. Chapters 6 and 7 tell of the additional legal affirmation which followed, and the problems of implementing the ruling. Chapter 8 describes the Indian fishing controversy on the Columbia River and examines how negotiation rather than litigation was used in attempting to resolve the problems there. Chapter 9 explores the issue of environmental threats to the salmon resource. Chapter 10 considers how the tribes and the fish are faring one decade after Judge Boldt's ruling. These final chapters also take a look at treaty tribes in two emerging roles: as protectors attempting to secure a healthy environment for everyone's fish, and as managers of the traditional fishing grounds and full participants in the fishery.

Chapter 11 examines the significance of the controversy and its implications for the Indians, the salmon, the society, and the environment in which they must coexist. From that vantage point, readers can assess the validity of this book's premise: By affirming Northwest Indian treaty rights, *U.S.* v. *Washington* not only honors this nation's legal commitment to Indian tribes, but also holds promise for beneficial use of the resource by Indians and all other citizens.

Chapter 2

Before the Treaties

For thousands of years, native people have made their homes along the northwest coast of North America. From what is now southeast Alaska down the Pacific coast to Northern California, the climate is mild, modulated by the warmwater Japanese Current. Prevailing winds carry ocean vapors eastward, bumping them against the coastal mountains where they let fall their burden of rain. As the winter season advances, snow creeps down from the peaks. On the ocean side of the lower slopes, in both winter and summer, the boughs of fir and cedar trees comb moisture from the low-lying clouds and drip gently onto the ferns and moss below. Weary of the mist that permeates Northwest days, the region's Indians sang appeals to the sun:

> Don't you ever,
> You up in the sky,
> Don't you ever get tired
> Of having clouds
> Between you and us.[1]

Washington state has two north-south mountain ranges. The coastal mountains, called the Olympics, are younger and craggier. The inland mountains, a chain of volcanoes which include Mount St. Helens, are called the Cascades. The Cascades form a barrier that keeps the moist air within western Washington.

18

At the northwest tip of Washington state, the Pacific finds a break in the coast and flows inland through a passage called the Strait of Juan de Fuca. The incoming tide sweeps down the strait into a vast inland sea called Puget Sound, which extends south between the two ranges of mountains. Fed by the rains and by snow melting off the mountains each spring, streams and rivers form a laybrinth of waterways within the area's dense woods. These waters flow into the sound and mingle there with salt water from the Pacific.

South, beyond the sound's farthest reach, the Columbia River separates the states of Washington and Oregon. A mighty river 1,200 miles long, the Columbia begins in Canada and bends south and west, swelling to a six-mile width near its mouth on the Pacific. Western Washington and the Columbia, its banks and its watershed, provide the setting for this book.

THE HARVESTERS—THE LIFE OF SALMON-FISHING TRIBES

The harvest of plants and animals from this region was once one of plenty.[2] With food so abundant, Indians clustered more densely in the Pacific Northwest than anywhere else in North America. They lived along the waters in relatively permanent villages in winter. In most cases they moved frequently throughout the spring and summer and established temporary summer houses at the best food-producing sites.[3] Although whites who came to settle in the region sought to deal with Indian governors, no heavy-handed chief or leader ruled these groups. Within each village some people ranked higher than others, ranging from those who were most highly respected through what could be thought of as the middle rank and down to those unfortunates captured in war and enslaved.

Indians of this region are still known for their potlatches—the social gatherings where special events are commemorated and where a leader can affirm his position by a great sharing of his goods and possessions. Native peoples are also admired as workers of wood, especially the durable and versatile cedar, from which they have made cedar-bark clothing, hats, baskets, sculptures, and engravings, and built large-planked longhouses. From cedar they also fashioned canoes to pursue fish into the rivers and even out onto the ocean.

They spoke in dialects of several languages and followed customs with many local variations. Some paddled with zest in rough ocean waters while others stayed close to rivers or kept to inland prairies and the Columbia River plateaus. Some tribes raided each other and were enemies, while others maintained friendly relations. Still the tribes of this region had much in common. They gave gifts and traded goods, such as baskets, and delicacies, such as dried fish from their home rivers. Young men and women of various tribes intermarried so that some people spoke not only their own language but that of other groups. But what the tribes shared most significantly was a life pattern centered on fish. To these people, it was explained to the justices of the U.S. Supreme Court in 1905, "fish were . . . not much less necessary than the atmosphere they breathed."[4] Fishing, then and now, figured strongly in all areas of subsistence, technology, art, mythology, and ritual. Many species of fish were harvested, including smelt, sturgeon, halibut, herring, flounder, and trout.

The most important fish taken—and the mainstay of the regional diet—were the five species of Pacific salmon and the salmon-like steelhead trout. The salmon are *anadromous*—born in fresh water, migrating out to mature in the ocean, then returning to their birthplace to spawn and die. The steelhead also follow this migratory pattern, but, like Atlantic salmon, a small proportion may enact the cycle more than once. Neither Indians nor early white settlers saw the steelhead as essentially different from salmon. People depended upon these fish—fresh, smoked, or dried—as the staple article of the year-round diet. Salmon were so important to the individual that, according to a Chinook man at the time of early contact with whites, "if he was three days without (it), his heart failed him."[5]

Home Is the River. Native fishermen poised themselves—as they do still—along the many rivers of this region to await the homecoming salmon. At the northwestern tip of the Olympic Peninsula lived Makahs, who fished both ocean and rivers. Southward along the Pacific Coast, tribes like the Quinault and Quileute made their home. Near Washington's northern border with Canada dwelt the Nooksack, Lummi, Swinomish, Sauk-Suiattle, and Skagit tribes. Further south, on the shore and islands of Puget Sound where the Seattle-Tacoma metropolis sprawls now, were the many small ancestral villages of today's Nisqually, Muckleshoot, Puyallup, and Suquamish Indians. To the west across the sound and around the bend of Hood Canal live the Twana, now generally known as Skokomish. South of them along the Columbia River dwelt such groups as Chinook, Umatilla, and Yakima. Others, such as the Nez Perce, spread throughout the interior of the region but came to the Columbia to fish. All these tribes, who continue to live in what have become the states of Washington, Oregon, and Idaho, asked enforcement of their rights in one or the other of two famous cases tried before federal district courts. Tribes fishing the Columbia River brought suit in the case of *Sohappy* v. *Smith*, decided by Judge Robert C. Belloni in 1969. Western Washington tribes took the stand in the related case of *United States* v. *Washington*, Phase I of which was decided by Judge George H. Boldt in 1974.

Indians were very much aware of the region's character as a great watershed. Anthropologist Marian Smith observes that Indians from southeastern Puget Sound derived their major concept of social unity from the geographical concept of the drainage system.[6]

Often the names of a village site and the area that fed its river were the same. For example, the Puyallup River above its fork with the Carbon River was called "ts'uwa," as was the village at that spot. The Indians living there called themselves "the people of ts'uwa.": "ts'uwadiabc."[7]

Indians had individual rights to fish in the rivers near their winter villages and shared rights with people from other villages at spring and summer fishing camps. A person might also have rights to catch fish in the fishing territory of the village where he or she had been born or had relatives.[8] Property concepts about ownership rights to specific fishing areas were well developed in western Washington Indian cultures.[9] For example, when the Skagit Indians fished in bays, harbors, channels, and rivers, where they built dams, weirs, and traps, they strictly controlled who could fish and at which sites. They also exercised close supervision when large numbers of persons were involved in drying the fish. When they went to traditional areas further out from shore, supervision was less strict, but they permitted only persons of their part of the coast or nearby friendly tribes to fish with them.[10]

When the salmon were leaping upstream, everyone was busy. All in the community who were able spent hours and hours catching, preparing, and storing the fish. They utilized an intricate technology employing many kinds of spears, gaffs, dipnets, hooks and lines, and traps and weirs.[11] Women cleaned the fish. Some fish might be boiled while others were split and either spread open for broiling or laid on wooden racks to be smoked, dried, and stored in wooden boxes for later use. Children gathered wood and helped clean fish.[12]

Salmon at the Heart of Life. Salmon figured prominently in the thoughts, beliefs, and rituals of the Indian people. For example, when the Quileute on the Pacific coast divided up the year, they named four of the twelve portions for runs of fish.[13] The periods and their approximate equivalents in today's calendar were:

1. "Beginning of the spawning of the steelhead salmon." (January).

2. "Regular or strong spawning time of salmon" (February). Steelhead were caught then.

3. "The time for getting cow-cabbages" (March).

4. "The time for getting salmonberry sprouts" (April).

5. "The time for getting salmonberries" (May).

6. "The time for getting elderberries" (June).

7. "The time for getting salal berries" (July).

8. "The time of no berries" (August).

9. "The time for black (chinook) salmon" (September).

10. "The time for silver salmon" (October).
11. "The bad weather month" (November).
12. "The time for frosty weather" (December).

When the Nisqually at the southern end of Puget Sound looked skyward at night, they thought of stellar configurations of fish. According to ethnologist George Gibbs, who kept a journal of his experiences with the Indians during the mid-nineteenth century treaty-making period, Nisqually astronomy was permeated with images of fish. One constellation, for which Gibbs did not know the European name, was termed "edad," meaning "fish weir" in the Nisqually language. Orion's belt was seen as three Indians catching small schools of fish and his sword as the fish. The Pleiades—seven stars in the constellation Taurus—were envisioned as a species of fish which had large heads and small tails. Gibbs also reported that the Nisqually regarded the northern lights as schools of herring turning up their white bellies.[14]

Tribal legends speak of the salmon world and the tribal world as closely connected and similar in structure. The Twana (today's Skokomish) considered each of the five species of salmon returning to their streams to be separate groups of salmon people which lived to the west in homes beyond the ocean. A leader guided his own group from its village to the waters of the Twana country. Once the fish were caught, the souls of the salmon people returned to the salmon country, where they would once again become fish for the following year's run.[15]

The Columbia River tribes tell how Coyote, an important culture hero, made salmon and humans interdependent. Coyote was said to have "created the Columbia River and the fish by making an outlet to a pond where two women kept fish." Coyote told the two women to share the fish, which was to be the food of the people who would be coming to the region. To these people, he gave mouths and instructions for catching and preparing salmon with which to feed themselves.[16]

Reverence and Responsibility. Each season, beginning with the taking of the first salmon, religious ceremonies celebrate renewal of life and express thanks, both for the spirit of fish and for the people who are fortunate enough to be given the use of the salmon's flesh. Religious attitudes and rites require that harvesters never waste fish wantonly or permit streams to be polluted. Because the "salmon people" are beings with supernatural power, their arrival must be greeted with respect and ceremony. Beliefs warn that improper treatment of the salmon will cause them to return disgruntled to their villages under the sea, not to return until the situation is corrected. First Salmon ceremonies, performed by almost all Northwest tribes, continue to be practiced today. The ceremonies differ in detail, but in most rituals the normal handling of the fish is elaborately reenacted.[17] Those persons who can catch, carry, and cut the fish are precisely designated and the rules for cutting, cooking, and consuming the fish are carefully described.

In 1964, a Puyallup Indian told a Congressional subcommittee how his elders conducted the ceremony. "They barbecued the first salmon of the run over an open fire. It is then parcelled out to all, in small morsels or portions so all can participate. Doing this, all bones are saved intact. Then in a torchbearing, dancing, chanting, and singing procession, they proceeded to the river where they cast the skeleton of the salmon into the stream with its head pointing upstream, symbolic of a spawning salmon, so the run of salmon will return a thousand-fold."[18]

The tribes observed the coming of the salmon both by ritually "opening the season" and also by preparing the environment so that it would not be offensive to the salmon. The river had to be prepared in advance of the run. Among the Skokomish, for example, people were prohibited from throwing rubbish or food scraps into the river and canoes could not be baled into it. Menstruating women could not swim in the river. The purpose of these rules was to make the river inviting to the salmon.[19]

Indian practice, enforced by belief, would not permit fishermen to catch more salmon than they needed. When the fish were running, the fishermen periodically opened their traps and weirs to let spawners escape upstream. Traps sometimes washed out, as well, allowing more fish through.[20] Perhaps most important, once the Indians had met their needs, they stopped fishing.

THE HARVESTED—THE LIFE OF A SALMON AND STEELHEAD

Like the Indian people, the salmon are intimately dependent upon freshwater rivers and their tributaries. Although salmon spend the greater part of their lives swimming in salt water, all the most critical events of life—birth, mating, reproduction, and natural death—occur in rivers, lakes and streams. The intricate network of freshwater river systems provides them with their roadways to and from the open sea: their survival is thus fundamentally tied to fresh water.

There are five species of salmon: the *chinook,* the largest, often called king, tyee, or quinnat salmon; the *coho,* or silver salmon; the *chum,* which earned its popular name, dog salmon, from its use as food for sled dogs in the far North, and its snout shaped like that of a snarling dog; *pinks,* the smallest, commonly called humpbacks or humpies; and *sockeye,* also called blueback or red salmon, which are considered by many to be the choicest of all.

A sixth species, the steelhead, while biologically similar to salmon, is an ocean-going trout. The tribes did not distinguish it from salmon, because its life pattern is so similar.[21]

Just as Indian customs and dialects vary locally, each species of salmon contains within it distinctive local groups. Fisheries specialists call these groups, adapted to particular environments, *stocks. Stock* refers to fish that interbreed in a particular river or lake at a particular time.[22] Fish from a common stock on their way to breed in their freshwater home are called a *run.*[23]

Mystery Navigators. Each stock will eventually swim hundreds, even thousands of miles away from its place of origin. During this impressive migration it will mix with stocks and species from river systems in other states and nations. Yet each will respond to the relationship it has with its place of birth and will return to this homewater to reproduce and die. Thus as each stock nears the end of its return journey it separates itself from others and swims almost exclusively with natives of its own birthplace. How the fish navigate their intricate course is still to be explained. There is evidence that a combination of factors provide a map: odor characteristics of their freshwater environment imprinted upon them as juveniles; electromagnetic cues from ocean currents; and direction cues from the sun.[24] The fish have grown to full adult size, which varies with the species from an average weight of three to four pounds for pinks to an average of twenty to twenty-five pounds for chinook. The long swim in open seas also varies with the species from one to five years. Some early maturing salmon, known as "jacks," may return ahead of schedule. During this time the fish have stored the food energy necessary for the homeward journey. Salmon may swim as much as twenty-two hours a day to reach fresh water[25] and slow down briefly when they get there. Once beginning their return to the rivers, few species feed, but the fish still must gain the spawning grounds and reproduce before their energy fails. The pressure to return is intense, explaining the feats of enormous jumps that prompted the Romans to name such fish "salmo—the leaper."[26]

Renewing the Cycle. Those who have mastered all the hurdles will reach their place of birth to spawn. There they begin an intricate courting, mating, and nest-building ritual.[27] The female will explore the gravelly streambed, seeking out ideal areas for her nest, which is called a "redd." She constructs the redd by turning on her side and sweeping the gravel with her tail. This behavior triggers the males' courtship, as they compete with one another to mate with the female.

To form his partnership, the dominant male takes his position beside the female, and trembles as he moves forward alongside her. He crosses back and forth over her, sometimes interrupting his courtship to fend off intruders. In the last phase of nest construction, the female probes the depths of the pocket she has dug in the gravel. This action excites the male and intensifies his trembling. Both male and female align themselves side by side over the nest and release eggs and sperm simultaneously. The orange-red eggs drift downward, surrounded and fertilized by clouds of milky-white sperm, into the carefully dug nest. The female lays between 500 and 1,000 eggs in each of a succession of nests, one next to the other.

Once the eggs have settled to the bottom of the nest, the female begins to cover them with loose gravel. Her first efforts are quite gentle, her objective not so much to move the gravel over the eggs as to create gentle currents which will lodge the eggs between the larger pieces of gravel. Gradually, her motion becomes more vigorous, and she begins to cover the nest. She will guard the nest until she dies, a few days after spawning. Only as she weakens does she begin to drift away downstream.

After courtship and spawning, all species of Pacific salmon rapidly age and deteriorate. (Steelhead, being trout, are the only exception; some may survive, go back to sea, and then return to spawn a second or even a third time.) As glandular activity speeds up, the spawning streams fill with dead and dying salmon, to the delight of numerous eagles overhead.

Within an hour of fertilization, the new egg hardens into an incubator of amazing strength. Even so, in its first month the egg can easily be shocked by movement. As the embryo grows, it needs more oxygen. When it demands more than can reach it through the membrane of the egg, the embryo hatches. Now an *alevin*, it burrows into the gravel bed and feeds from the yolk sac attached to its body.

If all its needs are met, it will evolve into its next stage and be a *fry*. The growth and development from egg to fry requires ninety to 150 days, depending on water temperatures. The fry no longer has a yolk sac and so must leave its home in the gravel to find food in the flowing stream. This is the period leading to salmon migration, which differs among species. However, even under normal conditions few fry grow big enough for ocean migration. Predators, inadequate food, and insufficient resting and hiding places greatly diminish their numbers.

The chum and pink salmon begin their migration to sea immediately upon emergence from their eggs. Chinook remain in fresh water from several months to a year; sockeye, coho, and steelhead stay one to two years in fresh water. Sockeye spend much of this time in lakes.

Scientists today call the youngest fry still in fresh water *fingerlings* and their older siblings *yearlings*. Ready for entrance into salt water, fry on their way to the ocean are called *smolts*. These juvenile salmon stop briefly in the estuaries, where fresh water meets salt water. There they adapt to seawater and grow rapidly, feeding on the area's fish, insects, and abundant microorganisms.

The ocean itself provides a gigantic pasture for the arriving adolescent salmon. They intermingle with other species as they feed and store energy. The length of time spent in salt water varies by species. Chinook average a three-year stay, but coho stay only from one summer through the next. Pinks never go very far out to sea, always returning in their second year of life. Pink runs return to Washington only in odd-numbered years.[28] The pattern and distance of migration varies by stock, some staying relatively close to home and some ranging far out to sea. Upon maturity, individual salmon stocks break away from the shared feeding grounds and swim landward, schooling for their return to the stream of origin, where the cycle of death and birth will occur again.

Requirements for Survival. Salmon are noted for their endurance, persistence, and strength. Yet for all their hardiness, they are extremely vulnerable. At each point in their life cycle, many die. Only 10 to 20 percent survive the fry and fingerling stage.[29] To propagate and migrate successfully, salmon must have certain conditions including: unimpeded access to and from the sea; enough water of a high quality (proper temperature, clarity, and flow); adequate beds for spawning and hatching; sufficient food; and protective cover.[30]

For example, if natural or man-made structures block their way, young salmon cannot reach salt water in time to obtain nutrients vital to their adult weight. Similarly, if the temperature of the stream water is too high, if it lacks sufficient oxygen, or if it is laden with pollutants, eggs fail to hatch or young fry die. Seasonal flow patterns cue the onset of freshwater phases, so that dams that hold back too much or that spill water suddenly play havoc with water levels downstream and throw off a synchrony salmon have developed over thousands of generations. Too sluggish a flow means the salmon will not lay their eggs. Neither will they nest without proper beds of gravel. Gravel buried under silt won't do either. The fish also need nutrients from sources like aquatic insects. And they need shelter from predators. Because these conditions act upon one another, the complete set must be present for the fish to maintain their life cycle.[31]

CONCLUSION: A LONG-LASTING PARTNERSHIP

For centuries before Europeans came upon North America, the rivers met the needs of the salmon and the salmon met the needs of the Indian. The tribes and the salmon had benefited from this partnership, secure in their adaptation to the environment and to each other. The Indians knew they had to protect the quality of the rivers. Under conditions of abundance, their religious and technological precautions ensured the perpetuation of the fish.

In the eighteenth century, European explorers began to visit the Northwest coast. They sailed forth first to search for the elusive Northwest Passage believed to link the Pacific and Atlantic oceans. Later they came for lucrative sea otter pelts. Early in the nineteenth century British and American companies sent representatives travelling overland to compete for trade with the tribes. Christian missionaries arrived to convert the Indians not long after. The Europeans brought new tools, foods and beliefs; they also carried diseases against which Indians had no immunity. Measles, ague (malaria), and smallpox took a terrible toll in the years following contact with Europeans.

Explorers also noted the Pacific salmon, reporting that the fish returned each year by the thousands. The American explorers Meriwether Lewis and William Clark travelled along the Columbia River in October 1805. Along one stretch of river they found some 100 Indian lodges with every member busy catching, dry-ing, or pounding the fish into thin strips to make pemmican for future use.

"The multitudes of this fish are almost inconceivable," Clark reported. "The water is so clear that they can readily be seen at the depth of fifteen or twenty feet, but at this season they float in such quantities down the stream, and are drifted ashore, the Indians have only to collect, split and dry them on the scaffolds."[32] According to a later estimate, 50,000 Indians along the Columbia caught some 18 million pounds of salmon a year.[33]

The last wave of white newcomers were the settlers. Some years after Lewis and Clark's journey, the settler Ezra Meeker, who lived north of the Columbia River on Puget Sound, described a salmon run at the headwaters of a short creek emptying into the Puyallup River:

"I have seen the salmon so numerous . . . as to literally touch each other. It was utterly impossible to wade across without touching the fish."[34]

These latest newcomers, the white settlers, were the most dis-ruptive: neither Indians nor salmon were to continue their friend-ship undisturbed.

Chapter 3

Clash

The right of taking fish at all usual and accustomed places is further secured to said Indians in common with all citizens of the United States. . . .

Treaty of Point No Point, 1855[1]

The United States and Great Britain had agreed to a northern international boundary in 1846. Now settlers came in increasing numbers to find a living on the land. Following the Oregon Donation Act in 1850, which offered each settler 320 acres of land, newcomers encroached more and more upon Indian lands. To maintain peace and assist white settlers, the federal government began to negotiate land settlements with the tribes. Its major instrument was the *treaty*, which is a formal agreement between nations and which continues to define Indian rights.

DEALING WITH THE TRIBES

European Theories. By the mid-nineteenth century when federal officials sat with Northwest Indians in the treaty councils, the United States already had worked out many principles of its Indian policy. Primary sources for these principles were the theories that Europeans used to justify their occupation of the New World. Europeans argued that the doctrine of discovery gave the first country to "discover" lands unoccupied by Europeans the right to acquire those lands. However, as early as 1537 the Spanish theologian Franciscus de Vitoria, adviser to the Emperor of Spain, stated that Indians retained their rights to the land. He concluded that "the aborigines in question were true owners, before the Spaniards came among them, both from the public and the private point of view."[2] The Indians occupying the land had sovereignty and the "discoverers" needed to follow legal procedures to acquire these holdings. Treaties became the vehicle for negotiating title to the land; they are legal contracts that established political and property relationships between the Indian and the non-Indian nations.[3] The process, however, required a system of European legal concepts, such as transferable title to land, that was in many respects alien to the Indians' well-defined concepts of property ownership and use rights.

The American Way: Aiming High. Derived from these European doctrines, United States policy was set forth in the new nation's Constitution under the Commerce Clause and the Supremacy Clause. The Commerce Clause (Article 1, Section 8) provided Congress with the power "to regulate Commerce with foreign Nations, and among the several States, and with the Indian Tribes."[4] The Supremacy Clause (Article 6) provided that "all treaties made, or which shall be made, under the authority of the United States, shall be the supreme law of the land; and the judges in every state shall be bound thereby, anything in the constitution or laws of any state to the contrary notwithstanding."[5] Many treaties between Indian nations and the Confederation already existed at the time the Constitution was ratified. These and subsequent Indian treaties are the law of the land, supreme over state law.

Most treaties negotiated with North American Indian nations were treaties of peace, not conquest; the tribes retained powers of self-government over their internal affairs. Under the treaties, the tribes *reserved* certain rights for themselves and their descendants, and *granted* specific rights and resources to the United States.[6] In exchange for rights granted, the tribes typically received a federal guarantee that the rights they had reserved would be protected from attack by non-Indians. These rights would be reserved in perpetuity, or, as Si James of the Puget Sound region's Tulalip Reservation said, "for as long as the sun comes up in the east and sets in the west . . . for as long as the water comes down from the mountains and goes out to the sound . . . for as long as the tide comes to the shore and goes back out again."[7]

A series of federal enactments—the Northwest Ordinance of 1787 and the various Trade and Intercourse Acts—had made it increasingly clear that only the federal government, not the states, had the responsibility and the legal power to deal with the tribes. From the outset the federal government stated a high ideal for Indian policy. The Northwest Ordinance of 1787 provided the classic example of this philosophy:

> The utmost good faith shall always be observed towards the Indians; their land and property shall never be taken from them without their consent; and in their property, rights, and liberty they shall never be invaded or disturbed, unless in just and lawful wars authorized by Congress; but laws founded in justice and humanity shall from time to time be made, for preventing wrongs being done to them, and for preserving peace and friendship with them.[8]

Federal policy would, many times, do just the opposite.

Furthermore, two important Supreme Court cases had defined tribes as "domestic dependent nations"[9] (in 1831), and as "distinct political communities having territories within which their authority is exclusive and having a right to the lands within those boundaries"[10] (in 1832). In these cases and their successors[11] the Supreme Court recognized the threat that states, as their nearest neighbors, posed to Indians. It also recognized that the federal government had a special duty to protect the rights of the tribes.

Treaties, federal legislation, and court decisions set the foundation for what has been called the "trust relationship": the special obligations that the federal government has with respect to the tribes.[12] The federal government also developed a bureaucracy to administer Indian matters. The Bureau of Indian Affairs was founded in 1824 within the Department of War, and transferred in 1849 to the Department of Interior.

A special political and legal association thus was evolving between tribes and the federal government. This relationship was quite different from that with any other portion of the nation's population. The federal government was seen as having "plenary"—or full—power over Indian affairs, and this power let Congress establish Indian policy and pass legislation which had far-reaching effects on Indian life.[13]

Falling Short. Despite its treaty obligations, the federal government very early began to violate its promises. It forced populous eastern tribes to leave homes and farms and travel to "Indian Territory" west of the Mississippi River. President Andrew Jackson's Indian Removal Act of 1830 authorized the forced removal of thousands of Southeastern Indians—Cherokees, Choctaws, Chickasaws, Creeks, and others—who suffered the long and arduous journey west that has come to be known as the "Trail of Tears." Once removed, they still had to face continuing incursions of white settlers. The federal government's promise to protect the tribes, already difficult to carry out, became even more necessary in the face of strong opposition and prejudice on the local frontier.[14]

During the 1800s and up until the mid-1930s, the Indian affairs were administered by federal Indian commissioners and agents, who saw their mission as the carrying out of the federal government's "assimilation policy."[15] This policy, which sought to make Indians more like white Americans, guided the negotiation of treaties and the settling of Indians on reservations in the Northwest as well as other parts of the country. It was reflected in educational policies as well: government agents believed that it was "indispensible to their improvement" to take children away from their parents and compel them to go to schools where English would be the only language permitted.[16] The policy justified measures such as the establishment of boarding schools for young children in many parts of the country, measures that today appear unduly harsh.

The attitudes surrounding the assimilation policy placed no value on Indian traditions, but sought only to replace them with white ways of life. As the Commissioner of Indian Affairs said in 1889, "this civilization may not be the best possible, but it is the best the Indians can get. They cannot escape it, and must either conform to it or be crushed by it."[17] The assimilation policy also encouraged the Indians to take up farming, which was seen as a "civilized" way of making a living. Yet in the Northwest it was fishing, not farming, that was the concern of Indians as they entered treaty negotiations with federal representatives.

PROMISES ON PAPER: TREATY-SIGNING IN THE NORTHWEST

When the Oregon Territory was established in 1848, it included the Puget Sound region. The act establishing the territory echoed federal ideals for fair dealings with the tribes. It preserved "rights to person or property now pertaining to the Indians" and made the provisions of the Northwest Ordinance applicable to the new territory.[18] Two years later the Oregon Donation Land Act provided free acreage to American citizens, even though federal policy recognized Indian rights to this land. The ground was laid for trouble as settlers streamed into the territory.[19]

Quickly, Congress passed an Indian Treaty Act to authorize purchase of the lands from the various Northwest tribes and to remove the occupants to areas the settlers did not want. Anson Dart was appointed to negotiate with the Oregon tribes, but Congress failed to ratify the Oregon treaties and violence erupted.[20] Joel Palmer, an Oregon settler said to be respected by both Indians and whites, was appointed to succeed Dart. He set in motion the reservation policy subsequently used throughout the Northwest.[21] Its main purpose was to place Indians on reservations, protecting them by separating them from white settlers. Although the government did not expect them to give up fishing, it wanted the Indians to "settle

down" in these domains—preferably in centralized locations—
and become farmers. Federal policymakers asserted that encouraging the Indians to become agriculturalists as well as fishermen
would help "civilize" them, and ultimately encourage their assimilation into American society.

Joel Palmer made treaties with several Oregon tribes, including
those which had fished at the most important of the traditional
sites, a narrow channel over rapids called "The Dalles" on the
Columbia River where for centuries Indians had gathered to fish
and trade. According to the treaty that dealt with Indian claims,
these Indians were to be settled in Warm Springs, an isolated area
some seventy-five miles south.[22] When Washington became a
separate territory in 1853, similar pressures urged a speedy process of extinguishing Indian title to the land. Military officials
stationed in the territory sent reports back to Washington, D.C.,
that whites were unjustly taking Indian lands around Puget Sound
and that similar actions east of the Cascade Mountains threatened
to precipitate an Indian war.[23]

Isaac, Open the Territory! Newly elected President Franklin
Pierce rewarded one of his eager young supporters, Isaac Ingalls
Stevens, by appointing him governor of Washington Territory.[24]
An officer in the Army Corps of Engineers and a graduate of West
Point, Stevens was also given two other major tasks: to survey the
northernmost of the possible transcontinental railway routes and
to serve as Superintendent of Indian Affairs. Stevens had the re-
quired drive, as historian Alvin Josephy's description attests:

> Still a man of thirty-five, a dynamo of energy who moved with
> speed and decisiveness, Stevens saw all three of his jobs comple-
> menting each other toward a single grand end. As a governor who
> would build up the population and prosperity of this territory, he
> was intent on winning Congressional approval for a railroad that
> would terminate at Puget Sound . . . He bore no ill will against
> Indians, and even fancied that he admired and respected them. But
> as an instrument of advancing American civilization, he had a job
> to carry out, and with a flair for publicity he expected to win notice
> in the East for what he would achieve. As Superintendent of Indian

Affairs, he would try to treat the Indians justly and peaceably, but he was determined to bend them to his wishes.[25]

Stevens pushed treaties with the Indians with remarkable speed. In just a few months, he involved 6,000 Puget Sound Indians. In this region where no traditional centralized authority represented all the Indians, Stevens appointed "chiefs" and "subchiefs" to sign for their people. Later, the authority of those signers was disputed by their villagers. Some Indians boycotted the talks and stayed away in the mountains, and others refused to sign.

In December 1854, Stevens negotiated the Treaty of Medicine Creek for south Puget Sound; in January 1855, the Treaty of Point Elliott for the region to the north, the Treaty of Point No Point for the Hood Canal and Kitsap Peninsula tribes on the sound's west shore, and the Treaty of Neah Bay for the northwest tip of the Olympic Peninsula. In June 1855, after the tribes' considerable resistance, he and Palmer also negotiated the Yakima Treaty for tribes east of the Cascade Mountains. In July 1855, the coastal tribes signed the Treaty of Olympia, which included the Quinault, Hoh, and Quileute groups on the Olympic Peninsula.

The treaty negotiations were held in the Chinook jargon, which Northwest tribes and whites used as a trade language. It contained only about 300 words and simply lacked equivalents for many key English words in the treaty. Cultural differences compounded communication problems. For example, the Indians used a system of ownership rights that the white negotiators probably did not fully understand.

This Paper Secures Your Fish. In the case of the Northwest treaties, retaining the right to fish was what the Indians wanted and what they believed they were getting. The treaty negotiators knew how much Indians needed fish. George Gibbs, a lawyer-ethnologist present at the negotiations, reported that "what is necessary for them, and just in itself, is . . . the use of their customary fisheries."[26]

Even more impressive was Isaac Stevens' own promise as he

showed the treaty to the Indians assembled at Point No Point: "This paper secures your fish."[27]

In nearly identical terms, all treaties stated: "The right of taking fish at usual and accustomed grounds and stations is further secured to said Indians in common with all citizens of the United States and of erecting temporary houses for the purpose of curing, together with the privilege of hunting and gathering roots and berries on open and unclaimed lands; provided, however, that they shall not take shell fish from any beds staked or cultivated by citizens."[28]

The fish that the Indians needed—and had been promised—were to be used not only for personal requirements but also for intertribal commerce. Furthermore, the Indians supplied most of the fish upon which white settlers and traders depended. As Isaac Stevens wrote to the Commissioner of Indian Affairs on December 30, 1854: "The Indians on Puget Sound have been for a considerable time in contact with the whites . . . they form a very considerable proportion of the trade of the sound . . . they catch most of our fish, supplying not only our people with clams and oysters but salmon to those who cure and export it."[29]

In only a few years, Governor Stevens negotiated treaties in the Northwest with "more than seventeen thousand Indians and in doing so had extinguished the Indian title to more than one hundred thousand square miles (64 million acres) of land now making up much of the territory of Washington, Idaho, and Montana."[30] The Indians gave up vast quantities of land, but they retained their key holding—their right to make a living by fishing.[31] The treaties secured their rights not only on the rivers running through the reservations, but also to all other places at which they were accustomed to fish. Their only concession was that they would share these off-reservation fishing grounds with the white settlers.

The treaties worked no cure-all for problems arising from white settlement of the territory. Indians were forced to move onto reservations even before the treaties were ratified. Although Stevens originally would have preferred to shift all the tribes off their land to areas east of the Cascades, in the end he realized that they would never agree to this. But even the land the Indians retained—the reservations—proved difficult to defend against settlers. Once treaties were indeed signed and ratified and the Indians settled on reservations, the tribes were to receive annual payments ("annuities") as well as instruction and tools for farming, despite the fact that much of the land was not suitable for crops. These reservations were in some cases extremely inadequate. For tribes like the Swinomish, insufficient land was set aside to permit self-sufficient farming and the government delayed providing the assistance it had promised to make more land suitable for crops.[32] Some reservation boundaries were later changed.

Many of the Indians probably would have preferred to practice their traditional fishing, hunting, and gathering exclusively. As an agent for the Makah later observed, "The Makahs are not, nor are they likely ever to become to any extent, an agricultural people. Their location at the mouth of the Strait of Juan de Fuca, the character of their climate incident to their close proximity to the Pacific, and their habits, are all of such a nature as to preclude it."[33] Dissatisfaction with the treaties was severe among some of the Indians and hostilities broke out. The village of Seattle suffered an attack on January 25, 1856, and eastern Washington tribes fought fiercely for several years following the treaties.[34]

Although the treaty period wrought severe changes in Indian life, white settlement had yet to affect the fish in ways equally damaging. The fish runs were still abundant. During the 1860s, salmon resources in Puget Sound and on the Columbia River[35] amply met Indian needs for family and ritual use and for trade with the whites, who continued to depend upon the Indians to supply them with fish. This situation was soon to change.

SALMON MEET THE SETTLERS

When it arrived, change struck the salmon with blows as rapid and hard as those that had sent the Indians reeling. As the American Friends Service Committee pointed out in the 1970 edition of *Uncommon Controversy*:

. . . salmon seem in many respects to be among the most special-
ized of fish, and their "simple requirements" actually to be quite
complex. The nuances of the river are built into their movement.
The rivers and the land have a set of relationships with each other,
a series of delicate balances, each river with its own watershed;
and the salmon, over thousands and thousands of fish generations,
have become interwoven into those relationships. Small changes
and adjustments occur constantly, but what happens when the
changes are drastic and fundamental?[36]

The first drastic and fundamental change in the life of the
salmon came from the new methods of commercial preservation.
Indians preserved salmon by drying and smoking, techniques that
met their needs for food and local trade. Initially whites attempted
to market salmon more extensively by salting it and shipping it
overseas, but their methods of preserving it were inadequate and
they met with little success.[37] When Europeans invented the canning process in the early nineteenth century, the trade in Northwest salmon and steelhead boomed.

Canneries Make Fishing Big Business. Salmon canning was
introduced at Eagle Cliff on the Columbia River by Hapgood,
Hume and Company in 1866.[38] By 1883 there were fifty-five canneries on the Columbia and its tributaries.[39] Puget Sound had canneries by 1877, and by the end of the century more salmon were
canned on Puget Sound than on the Columbia.[40] Cannery production became increasingly efficient with the invention of a mechan-
ical cutting machine and the sanitary tin can. In three decades the
odds changed remarkably: a salmon bound for its native stream
was much more likely to end up packed in a can before it could
reach either the nets of the Indians or its birthplace.

In some areas Indians fished for the canneries. In others, non-
Indians caught the salmon, usually with gill nets which snare the
fish by entangling their gills in the mesh of nets which have one
end attached to a boat and the other to a buoy. Non-Indians also
used purse seines, sac-like nets whose opening could be drawn
together to surround and capture schools of fish like the action of
a drawstring on a purse. Cannery-owned fishwheels and traps

came to dot the banks of the Columbia and river mouths on Puget
Sound. These traps were costly but very effective. On the Columbia, the famous Seufert No. 5 wheel captured 209 tons in its highest yearly catch (1906) and ten tons in its lowest (1913).[41] Puget
Sound traps could harvest as much as forty tons, returning $2.50
for every dollar invested. The state enacted regulations that specified depth, length, spacing, and mesh standards for traps. In addition, the regulations required that the highly efficient traps be
removed periodically so that fish could escape.[42] As more and
more people were drawn to the Northwest fishing industry, newly
arrived fishermen using boats and nets fought against the established and often wealthy local trapmen and their stationary gear.
Competing techniques of fish-catching soon came to be associated
with ethnic and political competition for the fish. The losers in the
competition were the Indians, who were pushed aside by the
traps, wheels, and immigrant white fishermen, and the fish, which
were dangerously overharvested.

On the Columbia, gill nets were used primarily by Scandinavi-
ans, who fished as they had done back home.[43] Austrians introduced purse seines on the Columbia and Croatians used them on
Puget Sound.[44] When marine gasoline engines became available
in the early 1900s, fishing with these nets became more efficient
because the boats could quickly stake their owners in front of the
traps where the fish were running. Engines also powered troll
boats, which used several lines, each barbed with as many as six
hooks, to catch coho and chinook.

New Settlers Want Their Share. Fishermen who had recently
immigrated from Europe competed against each other and against
the trap owners and cannerymen, whom they saw as wealthy cap-
italists able to afford trapsites costing an average of almost
$20,000 at the turn of the century.[45] Pressure mounted against the
trap users in Puget Sound[46] and fights over fish broke out along
the Columbia between gillnetters and trapmen and later between
gillnetters and seiners.[47]

Competing fishermen eagerly sought advantage by fishing further from shore than the rest. For example, gillnetters would in-

tercept fish before they could reach the traps; trollers would go further out to sea—beyond the reach of state regulation—and intercept fish before they could reach the gill nets. A pattern of leapfrogging evolved. Each leap oceanward involved more cost to the fishermen in time and fuel, as they chased after fish which would eventually have returned home on their own. Fishermen far from shore also preyed upon immature fish which swam in groups of many intermingled stocks that had yet to separate and head for their own rivers. Fewer and fewer fish reached the Indians waiting at the end of the salmon's journey.

States Attempt to Regulate Fishing. The states of Oregon and Washington, concerned about the impact on the fish runs, tried to control the burgeoning industry. In 1898, the Washington Annual Report noted that "in the history of the salmon fisheries of the Atlantic Coast there is a warning against the extravagant manner in which our Pacific Coast salmon fisheries have been carried on for many years."[48] Similarly, the first report of the Oregon Fish Protector in 1894 summarized the situation in stark terms:

> It does not require a study of statistics to convince one that the salmon industry has suffered a great decline during the past decade, and that it is only a matter of a few years under present conditions when the chinook of the Columbia will be as scarce as the beaver that once was so plentiful in our streams. Common observance is amply able to apprehend a fact so plain. For a third of a century, Oregon has drawn wealth from her streams, but now, by reason of her wastefulness and lack of intelligent provision for the future, the source of that wealth is disappearing and is threatened with annihilation.[49]

At first Washington attempted to control the industry by limiting times and places that fishing could take place. The territorial legislature instituted a closed season, i.e. a period during which fishing was prohibited, in 1877, as did Oregon the year following.[50] By the turn of the century, Washington had restricted fishing severely in the places where Indians traditionally fished—in rivers and tributaries. In 1897, again in 1899, and nearly every year thereafter the legislature prohibited fishing in each Puget Sound tributary and in salt water within three miles of them.[51] In 1915, state government passed its first fisheries code restricting certain methods, such as spearing and snaring.[52] It is unlikely that these early attempts at regulation gave much protection to the resource. Fisheries economists Crutchfield and Pontecorvo have observed that in Washington "there was no technical staff to guide the legislature, nor does the record suggest that its deliberations were based on more than a cursory knowledge of the life history of the Pacific salmon. It does not appear that the regulations were influenced in any significant way by the work of the few scientists then interested in salmon research. . . ."[53] By the 1920s Oregon and Washington each had developed a fisheries management agency and agreed by compact to jointly manage the Columbia River fishery.

Spreading the Catch. At this time, however, another group of fishermen offered growing competition to commercial fishermen. These were the sportsmen. In search of relaxation and the thrill of catching a fish that would challenge their skill, they took to the rivers with hooks and lines. Sportsmen especially liked the steelhead, said to be among the most spirited fish alive.

These fishermen demonstrated their political clout in 1925 when the Washington State Legislature declared their favorite fish, the steelhead, to be a "game fish" upon reaching fresh waters. (Prior to that time, the state, like the Indians, had not distinguished salmon from steelhead in its management of the fishery.) The government forbade net fishing for steelhead to everyone except Indians fishing on reservation rivers and streams. Two years later it extended the ban to those Indians as well. To coastal tribes, for whom the winter steelhead runs supplied nearly half their annual food and a proportion of their trade, the ban was a severe blow.[54] To serve sportsmen's interests and enforce steelhead and other game regulations, the Legislature in 1933 established a Department of Game separate from the Department of Fisheries. License fees supplied a significant proportion of the

Game Department's budget and thus subjected the new department to more direct pressure from sports fishermen than from any other citizens.

As Russel Barsh, on the faculty of the University of Washington School of Business Administration, observed in 1979, "the Northwest commercial fishery has been managed by myths, symbols, and ethnic politics, not by science."[55] In both Washington and Oregon, sportsfishermen joined in support of commercial fishermen's attempts to outlaw traps and fishwheels. These battles were fought largely in ethnic terms, by the many immigrant groups who had left their native lands in hopes of finding a better life in America. These newcomers resented the competition of the wealthy, more established trapmen. An Oregon citizens' initiative, pitting upriver trapmen against downriver fishermen, outlawed fixed traps, wheels, and seines in 1926, only to be overturned by the legislature eight years later.[56]

In Washington state a similar initiative, sponsored by sportsfishermen and Puget Sound commercial fishermen, passed in 1934: Initiative 77 eliminated all fixed gear, such as traps, fishwheels, beach seines, and set nets. It also described a line that closed the interior of Puget Sound to all commercial fishermen except Indians fishing reservation rivers. What this initiative did was redistribute the harvest formerly caught in fish traps: the trollers caught more, then the gillnetters, and then the purse seiners.[57] The initiative also eliminated fishwheels, trap sites, set nets, and drag seines on Washington's side of the Columbia River.[58]

As the fishing fleet grew, unrestricted competition among fishermen continued. State agencies tried to "spread the catch" by adding more regulations.[59] Frequently the point of the regulations was to shorten the time the more efficient boats, such as purse seiners, could fish. This crowded the waters during the legal seasons and reduced what an individual commercial fisherman could earn. As each group saw its income decline, it blamed the others for its woes. All this time the battle was over how to divide the catch, rather than how to protect the fish themselves. Meanwhile environmental changes began depleting salmon runs in other ways.

The changes which accompanied the Northwest's growth in population threatened almost every aspect of the salmon life cycle. Beginning in the late nineteenth century and continuing ever since, dam-building, logging, farming, and industrial development have all placed increasing pressures on the environment.

Dams Block the Fish Runs. Dam-building has caused the most dramatic change in the salmon's natural environment. The danger presented by dams was recognized at the outset in 1894 when Hugh Smith of the U.S. Fish Commission stated that a dam on the Clackamas River in Oregon represented "one of the greatest evils affecting fisheries of the Columbia Basin."[60] By 1948 some 300 dams from the tiny to the megalithic had been built in the Columbia Basin, both by private utility companies and by the federal government.[61] The detrimental impact of these structures has been well documented. Anthropologist Courtland Smith, in his book *Salmon Fishers of the Columbia,* calculated that between 1880 and 1930, before the major impact of the dams, an average of 33.9 million pounds of fish were caught each year. In contrast, as the effects of the dams began to be felt between 1931 and 1948, only 23.8 million pounds were caught on average, indicating a decline of 294,000 pounds per year.[62]

Getting fish over the dams has been a major problem both for adult fish returning upstream to spawn and young fish on their way downstream to feed in the ocean. Grand Coulee Dam, for example, was completed in 1941. It forms a 350-foot-high barrier above the river, yet no fish passage facilities were built. Although some attempts to relocate the runs were made by trapping fish downstream, removing them to holding ponds, and then incubating the eggs in hatcheries, they were not very successful and it is estimated that Grand Coulee effectively closed 40 percent of the

Columbia River watershed to fish migration.[63] Some 1,100 river miles of upper Columbia River spawning habitat became inaccessible. Of the passageways provided on other dams (and the fish now have to surmount nine on the Columbia River), each kills an estimated 15 percent of young fish on their way downstream. A major culprit is gas supersaturation (particularly nitrogen) which occurs at the spillways created behind the dams, and induces "gas bubble disease" in the fish. In addition, the dams may adversely affect the fish downstream as well, for example, by causing fluctuations in water flow.[64]

Celilo Falls on the Columbia River was an ancient and productive fishing site and gathering place for Indians, some of whom came all the way from the Rocky Mountains to trade. The falls were just east of The Dalles, the western end of the Oregon Trail. At The Dalles the river was no more than 200 feet wide and "turned sideways and rushed between two narrow, rockribbed walls," according to an early account.[65] When the government was about to inundate Celilo Falls behind The Dalles Dam in 1956, the Indians held the last of their First Salmon ceremonies there. The United States compensated the tribes that fished at Celilo Falls for their loss—in 1955 an annual catch estimated to be some two million pounds. But as Courtland Smith, in his 1979 chronicle of Columbia River salmon fishermen, asks: "How can a group of people be compensated for a renewable resource which is an intimate part of their culture?"[66]

Fell a Tree, Lose a Fish. Logging practices have affected almost every aquatic condition basic to salmon survival. In the early days of white settlement on Puget Sound, for example, the most economical means of transporting logs from forest to mill was to float them along the river systems. Timber companies constructed series of log dams to hold logs and to manipulate streamflow so that the logs would be pushed downstream. Those great log jams prevented adult salmon from reaching their spawning grounds and prevented young salmon from migrating oceanward. When the timber companies substituted rail for water transport, many abandoned their log dams. The dams remained until they rotted away, were washed out, or were removed by the Washington Department of Fisheries.[67]

Wood wastes from the logs decayed in the water, releasing nutrients which encouraged algae and plant growth. This process robbed oxygen from the upper water layer and left precious little to reach the gravel beds below. Incubating salmon died for lack of oxygen. In addition, algae sometimes formed mats over the streambed, impeding the natural flow of water over the gravel and making the area unsuitable for a nursery. When the related pulp and paper industry came along, it augmented the increasing damage to the resource. Decaying wood wastes poured into the water and exhausted the oxygen needed by the fish. Chemical wastes from wood processing poisoned the young salmon.[68] Sewage, agricultural pesticide sprays, and discharges from food processors began to pollute the streams. Pollution itself did not necessarily kill fish directly, but it could make streams uninhabitable. If fish cannot spawn in a stream for several years, there will be few or none to return to perpetuate that particular run. The U.S. Public Health Service warned that water pollution "exerts its great toll on the fishery not because of individual kills but by destroying habitat. Serious fish kills seldom occur in badly polluted water because there are usually few or no fish left in the stream to die."[69]

Clearcutting a forest, which means felling every tree in the area, also affected the fish. Removing forest cover accelerated the run-off from the abundant Northwest rainfall and increased stream-flows. Snow-melt and heavy rainfall led to flash floods, which in turn altered stream courses and left spawning beds either inhospitable or dry. Often such floods dumped so much sand and silt in the streams that the spawning beds were completely destroyed. Construction of logging roads was also a major source of sedimentation in streams.

Clearcutting the trees alongside a stream exposed the water to the sun's heat. Salmon eggs and fry tolerate very little fluctuation in temperature: they became overheated and died. Cutting trees and shrubs also could cause a decline in insects which the fish needed as food.

Housing the Northwest's new population and building roads to reach the houses often meant construction near creeks. In many cases the builders cut shoreline trees that had shaded the creek, or felled trees further back, which had formerly absorbed the run-off from the rains and moderated the creek's flow. Even today, Seattle residents are startled to see an occasional salmon making its way through a backyard stream.

Farmers Channel the Waters. Farming practices affected the habitat as well.[70] The Northwest's farmers rely heavily on streams and rivers to feed their irrigation ditches. Diverting this water to the fields slowed the stream flows and let the streams warm to temperatures beyond the tolerance of the young fish. Fertilizers running into a stream may cause aquatic plants to bloom and decay, decreasing the amount of oxygen available to the fish. Many of the survivors become confused, as they set out for sea, by the maze of irrigation ditches. Some reach the sea late; some never find it.

SALMON HATCHERIES

Observers in Washington and Oregon duly noted the changes both fish and fishermen were experiencing. Instead of protecting the wild salmon, state governments sought artificial means to assist nature's salmon production. In 1887 the first hatchery in Oregon was built on the Clackamas River (part of the Columbia River watershed). In 1895 Washington opened its first hatchery, the Kalama, on the Columbia itself. These hatcheries were founded upon the belief that the natural runs, overfished and depleted by environmental damage, could be replaced by fish produced in hatcheries. Washington's first Fish Commissioner, James Crawford, asserted in 1890 that "to foster and replenish the streams . . . the establishment of a hatchery is a positive necessity, for although much can be done by regulation of fishing, still, as has been demonstrated in the older states, without the aid of artificial propagation the stock of fish will eventually become exhausted."[71]

Hatchery production was in full swing in both states by the 1890s, but results were uncertain. The early hatcheries, despite rhetoric about scientific management, were but crude ponds. They were neither designed nor managed in a scientific fashion. As historian Howard Droker noted in his study of the hatchery system in Washington state, "the early methodology of the hatchery program was simple and totally lacking in scientific verification, due to the lack of money and scientific personnel." "Success" was not scientifically measured, and those few successes which could indeed be verified "misled the Department of Fisheries into thinking failures were due to outside factors."[72] In fact, major problems came from releasing salmon too early, when they were vulnerable to disease and predators. In addition, the diet fed baby salmon—an unsavory mix of such cannery and packing house wastes as fish scrap, eyes and tail, pork, and horse hearts—was inadequate.[73] Hatcheries sometimes appeared instead to be breeding grounds for disease, as in 1952, when Bonneville hatchery fish on the Columbia River became infected.[74]

In Technology We Trust. Relying upon hatcheries as an antidote to the problem of habitat destruction and overfishing was both politically expedient and a logical extension of the growing American faith in the wonders of human technology. Washington Fish Commissioner L. H. Darwin was a most ardent supporter of the belief that hatcheries could mitigate the natural resource destruction caused by development. In 1915 he promoted a law which enabled dam-builders to construct hatcheries in lieu of fishways over their dams. Most of the early "in lieu" hatcheries failed within eight years of their construction.[75] Significant improvements in hatchery technology occurred only recently. The use of holding ponds in the 1930s to protect the fish until they were better equipped for release was one such improvement. Even more important was the development in 1959 of the Oregon Moist Pellet which combines food and medication for juvenile salmon.[76] (In the Northwest today, hatcheries are major producers of salmon, contributing over half of some species of salmon currently caught in Washington.[77])

Not everyone has shared the enthusiasts' faith in hatcheries, past or present. In 1934, John N. Cobb, founder of the College of Fisheries at the University of Washington, saw reliance on artificial propagation as a sign of "an idolatrous faith in the efficacy of artificial culture for replenishing the ravages of man and animals."[78] Fisheries biologists today express concern about genetic alterations that hatchery-bred fish may introduce into wild runs. Wild salmon are creatures that have, over thousands and thousands of years, adapted to conditions of their particular river or stream. In contrast, hatchery salmon sometimes are introduced into waters where they are not native.

An abundance of hatchery stock may overcrowd the stream and push the wild stock aside. Overabundant smolt from predator species (such as steelhead) may wreak havoc on other fry. Hatchery fish and wild fish may interbreed. The hatchery fish, having been protected in early life, may be less hardy, or have other undesirable traits, which they may introduce to the wild stock. The loss of wild stock may ultimately decrease the genetic diversity believed to be important for the success of future adaptation.[79] These issues make the careful placement, planning, and operation of hatcheries very important.

CONCLUSION: HARD TIMES FOR INDIANS AND SALMON

The scramble to develop the Northwest severely affected both salmon and Indians. Difficult times for salmon were equally difficult for the Indian people who depended upon them. State law forbade them to fish at almost all of their usual and accustomed grounds and stations. Where they could fish, they were forbidden to use traditional gear.

The salmon were subjected to the onslaught of commercial and recreational fishermen and, at the same time, were forced to spend their freshwater existence in an increasingly inhospitable environment. Thus the process of developing the Northwest, which established Indian reservations and attempted to assimilate Indians into modern society, also began confining young salmon to hatcheries away from their native streams, and attempted to tame the fish for society's own uses.

Both the tribes and the fish became increasingly imperiled during the century between the treaty-making of the 1850s and the treaty-rights struggles that began in the 1950s. In the next chapter, we will explore how the tribes and their fishing rights guarantor, the federal government, responded to the exclusion of Indians from their traditional fishing during this period. We will also examine the evolution of major battles to secure Indian fishing rights anew.

Chapter 4

Fishing "In Common"?

In the late nineteenth century, Washington and Oregon began attempting to distribute the dwindling harvest among a swelling population of vociferous immigrant fishermen. The Indians tried to exercise their treaty right and pursue their way of life, continuing to fish with traditional methods at their accustomed fishing sites, "in common with" the settlers. This chapter recounts how two developments—increased state restriction and a federal policy bent on "assimilating" Indians—caught tribes in the grip of hunger, fear, and prison. The chapter also describes the tribes' appeal to the courts and the mounting frustration which led them to political activism in the 1960s and the decisive 1973 confrontation in federal district court before Judge George Boldt.

The treaties that Territorial Governor Isaac Stevens had negotiated with Northwest salmon-fishing tribes in the 1850s contained a federal guarantee that the treaty tribes and their descendants would be able to fish as always. By the 1880s, however, non-Indians claimed that Indian fishing interfered with the fishing of citizens with whom Indians held rights "in common." In 1889, the same year Washington became a state, S.C. Davidson, a lawyer and U.S. Commissioner in Ellensburg, Washington, wrote to Indian Agent F. L. Simcoe:

Dear Sir:

There is some trouble about Indians fishing in some of the streams in this country. The local authorities claim that the Indians have no right to use traps, etc. Will you please send me a copy of the treaty with the Yakima Indians so that the matter can be settled without further trouble. The Indians have appealed to me to know what to do knowing I am a commissioner.[1]

It seems likely that Simcoe failed to resolve the problem, because the same issue would arise repeatedly in the decades that followed.

THE FEDERAL SOLUTION—ASSIMILATION

Tribes had retained their powers of self-government in internal affairs under the treaties, but they had difficulty exerting such powers in the face of unremitting federal pressure to give up Indian ways and become assimilated into white culture.[2] Nowhere was this policy used to assault tribal self-government more harshly than in the development of allotment programs, culminating in the Dawes Allotment Act of 1887, which eliminated the traditional practice of communal or tribal ownership.[3]

This legislation divided reservations into plots of limited size for distribution to individual Indians who would receive title to the land. Those Indians holding allotments would become U.S. citizens. Proponents of the act argued that Indians would benefit from this privately-held property and the "civilizing" effects of the farming life. Once allotments had been assigned, all unallotted parcels were to be declared "surplus" and could then be sold to whites.[4] The Dawes Act thus made available vast amounts of "surplus" Indian land for white settlement. It is estimated that as a result of the Dawes Act, the nation's Indian tribes lost more than 90 million acres and saw their reservations assume the checkerboard pattern of Indian and non-Indian ownership that persists today.[5] As a direct result of similar legislation, for example, the Puyallup Tribe saw much of its land directly bordering the Puyallup River pass out of Indian hands.

The federal government's treaty guarantees of Indian fishing rights should have afforded some protection against incursions on Indian fishing by white settlers and fishermen in Washington and Oregon, but they did not. Federal officials wanted Indians to give up old ways and become farmers. When state agencies and courts restricted Indian fishing, federal protection of the Indian right was not generally forthcoming. The difficult encounters that occurred when Indians continued to fish are reflected in early court cases, in the bureaucratic record, and in the memories of Indian people.

THE INDIAN SOLUTION—APPEAL TO THE COURTS

Even before Washington became a state, Indians who continued to fish and encounter white hostility were seeking a solution in court. The legal battles over Indian fishing rights have spanned a century. The account of these cases is important. Although the cases may be complex and the outcomes inconsistent, the chronicle of confrontation in court tells a great deal about the nature of the growing conflict between Indian and non-Indian fishermen. A close look at these cases explains how the conflict occurred, the terms in which it was framed, the rights that courts recognized, and the remedies they imposed. For, as the late Roscoe Pound, professor of law at Harvard University, put it: "The law is an attempt to reconcile, to harmonize, to compromise . . . overlapping or conflicting interests. The American system is an adversarial one in which each side pits its position against that of the opposing side. This process brings the issues into bold relief; the legal principles that emerge are like prescriptions for resolving the conflict. The process, however, does not unfold in a vacuum; it is part of the political and social context of the time and place where it occurs."[6]

The Fence Case: Yes. The earliest Northwest Indian fishing rights case on record occurred in 1887, when Washington was still a territory. Frank Taylor, a homesteader, had acquired some land along the Columbia River near Tumwater where the fish gathered. To protect his crops, he built a fence around the site. The fence blocked access for the Yakima Indians, who had always fished at this place. The federal Indian agent and the Yakima Tribe first went to the District Court to restrain Taylor from keeping out Yakima fishermen. When that court ruled for Taylor, the tribe took the case to the Supreme Court of Washington Territory. The judges were to decide which had legal superiority: Indian treaty rights or Taylor's rights as a homesteader.[7] The judges ruled in favor of the Indians. They ordered Taylor to remove the obstruction because the treaty expressly protected the Yakima's right to fish at all usual and accustomed places.

The Wheel Case: Yes, Qualified. In 1905, the Yakima Nation faced a similar situation in *U.S.* v. *Winans,* the first of seven fishing rights cases to reach the United States Supreme Court.[8] Mr. Winans, a white citizen, also owned land along the Columbia and operated a state-licensed fish wheel at one of the Yakima Nation's usual and accustomed fishing places. Winans' attorneys argued that his way of catching fish using the sophisticated fish wheel was superior to the Indians' techniques and therefore gave him superior rights.

Justice Joseph McKenna stated in his 1905 majority opinion that the Indians held the right to cross the land, to fish in the river, and to erect temporary houses for curing their catch. He rejected arguments that the technical advancement of the fish wheel conferred such superiority that Winans could exclude the Indians as "inferior." He also refused to buy Winans' argument that as Washington was now a state, the treaty between the federal government and the Yakima Tribe was no longer binding.

McKenna said further that the treaty (because it was written in white man's language and legal terminology) had to be interpreted in the way that the Indians would have understood it. Moreover, the judges had to be guided by justice and reason rather than by technical rules, because the United States government exerted greater power than the tribes and owed them care and protection.[9] These rules of treaty interpretation were to be very important in the future.

Two other important principles arose in the Winans case:

1. The decision clarified the nature of the treaty by putting forth what came to be called the "reserved rights doctrine." The court explained that "the treaty was not a grant of rights *to* the Indians, but a grant of rights *from* them—a reservation of those (rights) not granted."[10] That is, the treaty documented certain rights the Indians were granting *to* non-Indians, as well as certain other rights the Indians chose to reserve for themselves.

2. In a general comment not directly related to the issue at hand, the court suggested that the state might have some role in regulating the tribes. The decision said that the United States was competent (i.e. had the authority) to secure the Indians' off-reservation fishing rights, and that it did not "restrain the State unreasonably in the regulation of the right."[11]

Thus, on the one hand, the justices in the Winans case affirmed the Yakimas' continuing right of access to the fish. (This right was later extended beyond the Yakima treaty by the U.S. Supreme Court in *Seufert Brothers* v. *United States* in 1919.[12]) On the other hand, the justices opened the door to state regulation of that right.[13]

Towessnute and Alexis: No. Federal courts were not the only arbiters of fishing rights. State courts also heard a series of Indian fishing rights cases at the turn of the century. When these cases reached the Washington State Supreme Court, the decisions dealt setbacks to the tribes. An especially crushing blow was struck by the Towessnute[14] and the Alexis[15] cases in 1916. Towessnute was a Yakima Indian arrested for fishing without a license, for snagging salmon with a gaff hook, and for catching fish without hook or line within a mile of a dam—all contrary to state regulation. Alexis, a Lummi Indian, had also been charged with violating state fishing laws. In both cases the state Supreme Court ruled against the Indians. The judges saw Towessnute and Alexis as subject to the same state laws as all other citizens. In the court's view, the only treaty right held by the Indians was an easement over private land to reach a traditional fishing place.[16] In unrestrained candor, state Supreme Court Justice Bausman wrote:

The premise of Indian sovereignty we reject. The treaty is not to be interpreted in that light. At no time did our ancestors in getting title to this continent ever regard the aborigines as other than mere occupants, and incompetent occupants, of the soil. Any title that could be had from them was always disdained. . . . Only that title was esteemed which came from white men. . . .

The Indian was a child, and a dangerous child of nature, to be both protected and restrained. In his nomadic life, he was to be left, as long as civilization did not demand his region. When it did demand that region, he was to be allotted a more confined area with permanent subsistence. . . .

These arrangements were but the announcement of our benevolence which, notwithstanding our frequent frailties, has been continuously displayed. Neither Rome nor sagacious Britain ever dealt more liberally with their subject races than we with these savage tribes, whom it was generally tempting and always easy to destroy and whom we have so often permitted to squander vast areas of fertile land before our eyes.[17]

The decision diminished the Indians' right to fish off-reservation as it subjected that right to state regulation and the state forbade traditional methods of fishing like snaring and spearing.

The early court cases had thus focused on two questions which would determine Indian *access* to the fish, in the Taylor and Winans cases, and *state regulation* of Indian fishing, in the Alexis and Towessnute cases. The questions and their outcomes were these:

1. Should Indians have access to the fish at traditional sites off as well as on their reservations?

The tribes secured their right of access in these cases.

2. Could the state regulate Indian fishing?

The state won the right to regulate Indians in these cases.

THE FEDERAL REACTION—NO ACTION

During these first decades of the new century, the United States did little to support treaty fishing rights. Although the Commissioner of Indian Affairs wrote the Secretary of Interior urging that an appeal of the Towessnute and Alexis cases be made, his request was not granted.[18] The U.S. Supreme Court had recently decided that New York state could regulate the Seneca Indians' fishing.[19] Although the facts in that case differed significantly from those in the Alexis and Towessnute cases, the Interior Department secretary may have figured an appeal held little promise.[20] The predominant government policy of promoting assimilation through agriculture may have blinded government decision-makers to the important implications of the treaty fishing rights issue.

To Indian agents closer to the scene, the effect of the Towessnute and Alexis cases was immediately apparent: the state stepped up enforcement against Indians who were fishing off-reservation in their usual and accustomed places contrary to state-set seasons or gear restrictions. One superintendent wrote back to Washington that some Indian families would starve were help not obtained.[21] Help was not forthcoming.

Malcolm McDowell, a member of the federal Board of Indian Commissioners, lamented over the way tribes were suffering because they were being pushed out of the fishery. He charged the state with yielding to economic and political pressures exerted by whites at the expense of the Indians. "The larger fishing companies, the canneries, the deep-sea fishing interests and other groups send their representatives to Olympia to fight legislation proposed by the State (Fisheries) Commission," he said in his 1921 report to the board chairman. "In this conflict between the white men and the State authorities, the Indians are ignored, for no one has undertaken to protect their interests."[22] To remedy this situation, he called for the federal government to conduct a complete study of "the fishing problem in its relation to the Indians." The study was never conducted.

THE INDIAN REMEDY

It became harder and harder for the Indians to fish. Fishing on the reservation often failed to supply Indian needs and fishing at traditional off-reservation sites was frequently prohibited. One Indian fisherman still actively fishing today recalled how in the early

1900s his grandparents from the Port Gamble Klallam group used to go south, up the Hood Canal, to the area near the town of Brinnon to catch fish for the winter, until the state stopped them. A Nisqually woman who grew up during the 1930s recalled how her father risked arrest fishing in a stream above the Nisqually River. He continued to fish because he had thirteen children to feed. "He was fishing," she explained, "for us to exist."[23]

It was a story retold on many reservations. People did the best they could under difficult circumstances. Hattie Cross, a Puyallup tribal elder, was born in 1893. In a 1967 fishing rights case she recalled the difficulties she, her husband, and other Puyallups encountered. Here is her testimony as she answered questions the tribal attorney put to her before the court:

> Q. Now, did you see any fishing activities that took place by the Puyallups, say, from 1911 on?
> A. Well, my own family did quite a bit of fishing, and everybody, all the Indians that lived on the river fished. And the other people that lived close to the creeks, like Wapato Creek, they all fished in the creeks. They were closer to their homes.
> Q. Now, you say they fished in their creek. How long did they continue to do this fishing?
> A. Oh, they continued until they, the game wardens, came after them.
> Q. And after the game warden came after them, did that terminate the fishing?
> A. Not exactly.
> Q. Well, let's put it in another manner; did it discourage daylight fishing after that?
> A. Yes, it discouraged them from fishing there. They would have to be fishing on the sly.[24]

Many Indians can still recount the difficulties they faced when they tried to fish in the 1920s and 1930s. The lack of support from the federal Bureau of Indian Affairs and the threat of arrest by state fisheries wardens intimidated many people. Indians could sell fish openly only when Washington's regular fishing seasons were open. Other times they used circumspect practices and circuitous routes to sell their fish to the processors in Seattle.

Even during the most difficult times, however, Indians refused to give up fishing altogether. They would not sever their relationship with the salmon. Beginning late in the 1920s and continuing throughout the 1930s, new national policies were evolving that would encourage Indians to challenge the states once again. These changes involved federal Indian policy and also tribal structure and awareness.

THE NEW FEDERAL SOLUTIONS

After World War I there had been increased public concern about the conditions faced by Indians, who, contrary to non-Indian expectations, had neither vanished nor been assimilated into the non-Indian culture. The Citizenship Act of 1924 conferred citizenship upon all Indians who had not previously attained it by one of several routes, such as accepting an allotment of tribal land or serving in the Army. (The act passed despite a 1915 study commissioned by Congress that reported the Indians generally didn't want citizenship.[25]) The Citizenship Act modified neither treaty rights nor tribal status. Indians are citizens of the United States and of a tribe at the same time. In somewhat the same way, non-Indian Americans can claim citizenship in a city, county, state, and nation, and vote and participate in these respective governments all at the same time. Indians vote in their tribal elections as well as in elections held by the other political jurisdictions of which they are residents.

Survey Them. A few years later the federal government commissioned a comprehensive survey of conditions among Indians throughout the country. Issued in 1928, the Meriam Report, named after the head of the survey team, Dr. Lewis Meriam, detailed the dismal economic and health status of the tribes:[26] "An overwhelming majority of the Indians are poor, even extremely poor, and they are not adjusted to the economics and social system of the dominant white civilization."[27]

The assimilation policy had not accomplished its goals after all. The report described how disease was rampant, living conditions inadequate, and suffering and discontent prevalent. Individual ownership through allotment had *not* made farmers out of Indians. The Indian Service, following its practice of removing Indian children from their homes, had engendered the disintegration of Indian families because it had "failed to appreciate the fundamental importance of family life and community activities in the social and economic development of a people."[28] The Meriam Report did not recommend abandoning the assimilation policy: instead it suggested improving its realization for those Indians who would accept assimilation. However, the report also called for assisting those Indians who preferred to retain their old ways in making a decent living at them.[29]

Recognize Self-Rule. The interest stimulated by the Meriam Report and the national programs being developed under President Franklin D. Roosevelt's New Deal made the time ripe for a change in Indian policy. In 1934, Congress passed the Indian Reorganization Act (IRA)—the first major federal legislation in Indian affairs since the Dawes Allotment Act some fifty years earlier. The IRA, also known as the Wheeler-Howard Act, ended the allotting of Indian lands and set out procedures for regaining previously-held land. It recognized the tribes' right to formulate constitutions and to reorganize their governments, as well as to set up business corporations.[30] Thus it held potential for strengthening tribal self-government and for returning more responsibility to the tribes for managing their own affairs. It also established procedures to give Indians preference for positions in the Bureau of Indian Affairs.

Many Indian governments were fully functioning before passage of the IRA and continued to operate independent of the act. Tribes organized under the IRA operated within the limits of a continuing federal presence. For example, IRA tribal constitutions have had to be approved by the Secretary of the Interior. The act further required that newly reorganized Indian governments seek the secretary's approval for many actions.

Some tribes had established fishing regulations well before passage of the IRA. The Quinault on the Washington coast, for example, had written a series of twenty rules in 1915, including requirements that an open channel be maintained for fish to escape for spawning and penalties for regulation violators.[31] The newly-established IRA governments created similar sets of regulations. The Yakima, the Tulalip, and the Confederated Tribes of Warm Springs in Oregon were among those tribes which drew up rules for stating who could fish, what types of gear they could use, and when and where they could fish.[32]

THE INDIAN SOLUTION—RETURN TO COURT

Tulee: Yes . . . and No. As time went by, Indian challenges to state regulation increased. In 1939 Sampson Tulee was able to enlist federal support when he risked arrest for catching salmon with a dip net and selling it commercially without a state license. He had been fishing under the same Yakima Treaty of 1855[33] that had caused the early confrontations in the Taylor case, the Winans case, and the Towessnute case. Some fifty years of controversy had preceded his challenge. Not surprisingly, he lost his case in the county court and the state Supreme Court. When the U.S. Supreme Court finally considered his case in 1942, results were mixed. The Supreme Court held:

> The license fees prescribed are regulatory as well as revenue pro-
> ducing. But it is clear that their regulatory purpose could be accom-
> plished otherwise, that the imposition of license fees is not indis-
> pensable to the effectiveness of a state conservation program. Even
> though this method may be both convenient and, in its general
> impact fair, it acts upon the Indians as a charge for exercising the
> very right their ancestors intended to reserve. We believe that such
> exaction of fees as a prerequisite to the enjoyment of fishing in the
> "usual and accustomed places" cannot be reconciled with a fair
> construction of the treaty. We therefore hold the state statute in-
> valid as applied in this case.[34]

This decision indicated that the state could still regulate, but not by imposing license fees. The criteria appeared to be that regulations should be necessary and "indispensable to the effectiveness of a state conservation program."

Makah: Yes. Now another case, this time brought by the Makah Tribe to prevent state interference with Indians who were net fishing—in their usual and accustomed off-reservation fishing ground on the Hoko River—found its way through the appeals process to the Ninth Circuit Court of Appeals. The judges evaluated the state regulations in terms of their necessity for conservation.[35] The court did not view the ban on net fishing as essential for conservation, and so in 1951 struck it down, admonishing the state to work more cooperatively with the Makah in the future.

THE *NEW,* NEW FEDERAL SOLUTION—TERMINATE THEM

Many Indians served in World War II. They returned home only to find their rights abridged in the very country for which they had fought. During the 1950s the controversy surrounding Indian fishing increased as Indians continued to challenge state restrictions. A new, postwar Indian policy was developing as the federal government shifted its stance from tribal development, encouraged by the Indian Reorganization Act, to tribal dissolution, under the policy aptly named "termination."

Severing Federal-Tribal Ties. The termination policy was designed to sever the longstanding ties between the tribes and the federal government. Congress saw it as a way of getting the federal government "out of the Indian business" by cutting its ties with the tribes.[36] Those tribes that were eventually terminated, for example the Klamaths of Oregon and Menominees of Wisconsin, saw their tribal assets divided and distributed to individuals, and their tribal structure dismantled.[37] Klamath and Menominee property became subject to state taxation. The Indian residents had to seek services from the state that had previously been provided by the federal and tribal governments. Another facet of the termination policy was embodied in Public Law 280. In a number of states this law transferred—without tribal consent—criminal and civil jurisdiction over the reservations from federal to state government.

The Indians viewed termination with alarm: it threatened their land base—the reservation—as well as the tribe's political status. As ambivalent as many Indians were toward their uneven relationship with the federal government, they were extremely wary of the treatment they were likely to receive at the hands of the states. States had been the prime instigators of the removal policy that had sent so many Indians away from their homelands in the East. The U.S. Supreme Court had described the states as the Indian's "deadliest enemies."[38] Termination manifested the vulnerability of Indians. They saw again how Congressional fiat could take away the guarantee that the federal government would protect those rights for which they had given so much.

THE *NEW*, NEW INDIAN SOLUTION—A STRONG PUBLIC APPEAL

The effect of these threats was to increase awareness among Indians of the precarious position their people shared. The National Congress of American Indians, founded in 1944, lobbied vigorously against the termination policy.[39] The *Washington Post* reported that "Congress has run into a storm of protest against some of the Indian bills it has under consideration. When hearings on the so-called termination bills were held recently, tribes from 21 states and Alaska are said to have sent to Washington the largest gathering of Indians ever to appear here. Complaints are continuing to flow in by mail and telephone and personal visits."[40]

The Indians' resistance to termination was supported by such organizations as the Indian Rights Association and the American Friends Service Committee.[41] Congress, however, forged ahead, terminating a significant number of tribes and threatening to terminate others.

Going Public: The Fish-In. During this same time, Indians became increasingly aware of the growing post-World War II concern with minority rights in their own country. Much of this national concern focused on the struggle for black civil rights in the

South. As Indian historian and lawyer Vine Deloria, Jr., has observed, Indian people saw the impressive gains being made by nonviolent demonstrations, such as bus boycotts and "sit-ins" to challenge state laws that segregated public places.[42] Although the problems Indians faced were quite different from the grievances of blacks, Indians adapted some forms of civil rights social protest to fit their own, quite specific needs. In the Northwest a new method of challenging state regulation evolved: it was called the "fish-in." This effort, in turn, was an inspiration to Indians struggling for their rights elsewhere in the nation.[43]

In the fish-ins, Indians frequently risked their boats, their nets, and their fish. They also risked their personal safety in confrontations with game wardens. The exercise of fishing rights led to imprisonment. Over and over, Indians' efforts took them into court: a new series of even more complex cases evolved to define the nature of the treaty fishing right. In the early fishing rights cases at the beginning of the twentieth century, Indians had secured right of access to their usual and accustomed fishing grounds, but their right to fish off-reservation without restrictive state regulation remained in jeopardy. The post-World War II struggle would center on defining the nature of the treaty right, particularly the issues of fair allocation and the tribes' authority to regulate their own fishing.

During the 1960s, confrontations with the state would propel Indians onto television screens and into newspaper headlines. Just as the sit-ins in the South would increase and accelerate federal enforcement of black civil rights, so also the fish-ins would focus public attention on the Indians' appeal for federal enforcement of their full treaty right in the face of almost a century of state restriction. Treaty fishing rights would become an issue of major national concern.

CONCLUSION: ANOTHER BEGINNING

Indians do not recall this period of unrest as a thing apart, but rather see it as a continuation of what had gone before. One fishing rights leader, Hank Adams (an Assiniboin-Sioux who grew up on the Quinault reservation on the Washington coast), recalled "many beginnings,"[44] pointing back to those who had fished surreptitiously in the 1920s and 1930s; to the efforts of Sampson Tulee, the Yakima who fished without a state license; and to the fishermen of the Makah Tribe, who set their nets in the Hoko River. As the struggle to secure tribal fishing rights continued, the pattern of quiet persistence in the face of state restriction turned increasingly to open resistance. What would distinguish this period would be the increase in the pace and intensity of confrontation, along with the growth of nationwide relations among Indians asserting their rights and other groups also seeking social and legal change. Concerns specific to the Northwest would become linked with social change movements throughout the country. An account of this tumultuous era is the subject of the next chapter.

Chapter 5

Fishing for Justice

Nets in City Waters. The Puyallup River flows under bridges and on into Puget Sound through the city of Tacoma, Washington. The river is the traditional grounds for the Puyallup Indian harvest of salmon and steelhead. In 1925 the state declared the steelhead a game fish, reserved for sports fishermen, and forbade capture by net except by Indians fishing on their reservations. In 1927 the state extended the ban to Indians as well. In 1934, the state forbade setting fixed gear, including nets, in the river for salmon.[1] In the early 1950s, Puyallup tribal members living alongside the river tried to challenge these laws. Notifying state agencies of their readiness to start a test case, they cast nets in their traditional fishing places. No one arrested them.[2] Then in 1954, encouraged by the advice of tribal elders and attorneys, Puyallup tribal members Robert Satiacum and James Young fished the river repeatedly in full view of city traffic coursing over bridges above.

This time the state acted, and arrested the two. The local justice court, in the case of *State* v. *Satiacum,* convicted them on several counts of illegal fishing. Their appeal, which reached the Washington State Supreme Court, resulted in 1957 in a dismissal of the charges with four judges voting in their favor and four opposed.[3] The split decision, certainly a weak affirmation of the Puyallups' right, still carried sufficient strength to enrage sports fishermen whenever they saw Satiacum and his fellow Puyallups fishing for steelhead, as the ruling permitted. Alvin Ziontz, an attorney in Seattle whose firm has worked closely with Indians for many years, recalled how "non-Indian sports fishermen vented their anger by acts of violence; cutting the Indians' nets, pushing their boats in the river . . . and threatening physical harm to Indian fishermen."[4]

The Satiacum decision encouraged both individuals and families from other western Washington tribes to fish more openly during the late 1950s. However, the state still refused to honor their fishing rights and the arrests continued. Many Indian fishermen lost fishing gear, seized as evidence. Unable to afford replacements, many lost income as well.

Nets in the Columbia. Meanwhile, south on the Columbia River, other tribes attempted to assert their rights and began challenging Oregon's regulations for fishing the Columbia and its tributaries. Three Umatilla Indians (descendents, like the Puyallups, of signers of an Isaac Stevens' treaty) fished during a closed season in 1958. The state arrested them. H. G. Maison was Superintendent of the Oregon State Police. The tribe hired an attorney to bring a civil action against the Oregon Game Commission and state law enforcement officers, and the tribe won. When the state appealed, their case—*Maison* v. *Confederated Tribes of the Umatilla Reservation*—began its travels through the court system to the Ninth Circuit Court of Appeals.

U.S. Circuit Judge Montgomery Oliver Koelsch issued a decision on February 15, 1963, affirming the lower court's ruling in support of the Umatilla's treaty rights.[5] He also took a long look at the issue of conservation, which the state of Oregon was using as a rationale to restrict Indian fishing. Judge Koelsch agreed with rulings by judges in the earlier Tulee and Makah cases: a state could only regulate Indian fishing when necessary for conservation. First, however, that state must actually prove both the following conditions: necessity (that limits on taking fish really are needed), and indispensability (that the regulation of Indian fishing being considered is indeed "indispensable" for limiting the catch).

The state of Oregon, Judge Koelsch found, had been interpreting conservation to mean resolving the competing interests of commercial and sports fishermen—without any regard to Indian needs. He concluded that it was wrong for white economic and recreational needs to take precedence over fish preservation and Indian treaty rights. Oregon's brand of conservation met neither the criterion of necessity nor that of indispensability. Instead, the judge ruled, the state could restrict Indian rights only if restricting other fishermen had failed to conserve the fish. He added that restricting non-Indians, if done in a reasonable manner, is consistent with the requirements for due process of law guaranteed by the Fourteenth Amendment to the United States Constitution.[6]

The Conflict Intensifies. As the federal appeals court was considering Oregon's case against the Umatillas, Washington state stepped up its arrests of Nisqually and Puyallup Indian fishermen. The Indians reported that thieves, in what was presumably a demonstration of opposition to Indian fishing on the rivers, were destroying unattended Indian nets and stealing the fish.[7] By 1963, when many other Indians had joined the protests, Indian fishermen complained of being shot at.[8] Indians of other tribes came forward in support of Indian fishermen. The National Indian Youth Council, formed in 1961 by Indian college students, sent representatives to the Northwest. One of its members, Hank Adams, was to become increasingly involved. Janet McCloud, a Tulalip and a leader of another Indian organization, the Survival of American Indians Association, led a major march and demonstration on the Washington state capitol in Olympia on December 23, 1963.

The fish-ins and demonstrations came when protest marches and political activism were common throughout the country. Yet some Indians viewed the fishing rights protests as overly strident. Those protestors who marched and those who participated in the fish-ins were sometimes criticized by Indians who favored seeking change through more established channels such as initiating legal cases. The more conservative tribal members criticized the protestors as "renegades" and "militants." It is important to note, however, that the division of Indian opinion centered upon means and not upon ends. As Nisqually historian Cecelia Carpenter expressed it, "there were two camps, but within the heart they had the same goals."[9]

Search for a Scapegoat. As the raids and arrests continued, it became increasingly difficult for people in Washington state to gain a clear understanding of the issues involved in the controversy. The fish-ins of the early 1960s coincided with one of the worst "fish famines" (declines in harvest) in Northwest history.[10] As always, state officials felt severe public pressure to distribute the diminishing supply of salmon as widely as possible among an ever growing number of white commercial and sports fishermen. The sight of Indians fishing the traditional places—on the rivers, where whites were forbidden to fish commercially—appeared unjust to non-Indians. Indians, however, saw themselves having to wait at the end of the line. The treaties permitted tribal members to fish in only two areas: on the reservations and in the usual and accustomed tribal fishing sites identified in the treaty negotiations of the 1850s. Most of these sites were near the end of the salmon's return journey to the spawning grounds. Any salmon reaching them must first escape non-Indians, who fished with nets and hooks from boats powerful enough to gather many fish at the start of the salmon's migration home.

Non-Indian fishermen, frustrated by competition with each other over fewer and fewer fish, found it possible to believe that pulling Indians off the line altogether would assure enough fish for everyone else. The thought of Indians using nets on the rivers—a relatively cheap, effective and efficient method—also irritated non-Indians. The attitude of many non-Indians was one of "let Indians take their chances and fish like everybody else," which ignored both the treaty right and the large fleets of gasoline engines and sophisticated equipment which few Indians could afford.

The local media blamed first one, then another group of "others"—Japanese, Canadians, Russians, Indians—for the harvest problem. Instead of pointing to the overabundant, non-Indian commercial fleet, or to dams, or to habitat destruction as reasons for the paucity of fish, the Seattle *Times* ran an increasing number of feature stories blaming Indians for the poor catches during this period.[11] Northwesterners continually heard from state officials, non-Indian fishermen, and the media that Indians threatened the resource, yet this claim was unsubstantiated and obscured the real causes of the problems facing the fishery. As Quinault Tribal President James Jackson observed, there was little logic in this approach: "It's like telling the Plains Indians that they destroyed the buffalo."[12]

An Unpalatable Reality. While focusing attention on Indian fishing, the state and its citizens avoided confronting the region's real issue—too many boats, crowding waters that contained too few fish. When Washington state legislators commissioned a report on the problem in 1963, a team of biologists, economists, and lawyers informed them that one-third to one-half the boats then fishing were unnecessary to catch the number of available fish, and that this surplus of boats was responsible for the low level of fishermen's earnings.[13] Efforts to enact legislation to limit the sale of fishing licenses failed because of commercial and public pressures. The state-licensed fleet doubled in size between 1965 and 1974, thereby making a bad situation worse.[14]

IN CONGRESS

The Washington state legislature reacted to the Puyallup and Nisqually fish-ins by petitioning Congress to exercise its power to enact legislation on Indian matters and resolve the controversy. Warren G. Magnuson, senior senator from Washington state, and the U.S. Senate Committee on Interior and Insular Affairs responded. Two resolutions were introduced into the Senate and the House of Representatives. Senate Joint Resolution 170, while it did recognize the Indians' treaty right to fish off the reservation at usual and accustomed sites, also provided for state regulation at those sites. Senate Joint Resolution 171 would have extinguished by purchase—bought out—the tribes' right to fish off-reservation. The Senate Committee held hearings in Washington, D.C., on August 5–6, 1964.

The state of Washington supported both resolutions, while Oregon and Idaho favored buying out the tribes. Sportsmen and commercial fishermen also testified in strong support of the resolutions. Clarence Pautzke was then commissioner of the U.S. Fish and Wildlife Service, which, like the Bureau of Indian affairs, had its home in the Department of the Interior. Pautzke testified that "unregulated" Indian fishing could not be allowed to proceed.[15] Even the Interior Department itself termed Indian fishing "a serious and growing threat."[16]

No one, however, was able respond to the Senate Committee request for firm data on fish catches. The Makah tribe estimated—and no one present disputed—that Indians were catching 5 percent or less of the total catch at the very time the committee was so critically scrutinizing tribal fishing.[17]

Tribal members present at the hearing clearly felt like scapegoats, blamed for the mismanaged fishery. Wayne Williams of the Tulalip Tribe cited the 1963 University of Washington study, commissioned by the state legislature, which had concluded that "the excess fishing gear used to harvest the salmon resource of the North Puget Sound and the Strait of Juan de Fuca has endangered the conservation of the salmon runs and greatly reduced the earnings of men and vessels engaged."[18] (By "excess" gear, the report meant more boats and harvest equipment than the supply of salmon could support.)

Many Indian leaders told of the tribes' reliance upon the Columbia River for fish and of their continuing need for them. The statement of the Yakima Nation summarizes the Indian perspective:

The reason this is so important to us is that we are not just talking about dry legal rights, and only the treaty, even though it be the solemn document that we believe it to be, but we are talking about people. As was brought out in the recent conference in Washington, D.C., on Indian poverty, the Yakima Indians come from an average education level of 3.8 grades, and the dollars derived from the Indian fishery have a ratio of 7 to 1, because these fishermen have no other venue or trade to fall back on. Many of our fishermen are beyond the age of relocation, vocational training, and haven't the necessary education to learn a living in another way. Are these fishermen to be deprived of their livelihood, guaranteed to them by treaty, by non-Indian landings, and particularly by the sports landings?[19]

The two resolutions died in committee, due perhaps to lack of firm data[20] or to the high cost of purchasing the Indian right.

IN COMPANY

Assistance from the Prominent. The struggles of Northwest Indians had gained prominence in both local and international media when actor Marlon Brando and Episcopalian Canon John Yaryan of San Francisco joined Indian fisherman Robert Satiacum, by then a ten-year veteran of the fishing controversy, and staged a dramatic fish-in on the Puyallup River on March 2, 1964. The *Tacoma News Tribune* carried a front-page photo of Brando and Satiacum with the headline "Marlon Nets 2 Steelhead in the Puyallup."[21] All three were arrested and taken to county jail amid swarms of newsmen. Brando spoke strongly in support of Indian treaty rights to the crowd. Pierce County officials booked Brando and then shook hands and released him. Canon Yaryan was also booked and then released. No formal charges were filed against them. Satiacum was not booked, but was told that he had violated a court order prohibiting the Indians from net fishing in the Puyallup River, and that he would later have to appear at a court hearing.

Continuing Confrontations. Satiacum, Bill Frank, Jr., of the Nisqually Tribe, and other Indians (many of them from the small tribes such as the Muckleshoot at the south end of Puget Sound) persisted in their fish-ins during the spring of 1964. More arrests and days and nights in jail followed. Out of these fish-ins arose the first of a series of cases concerning Puyallup and Nisqually treaty rights to net salmon and steelhead. The case began to make its way through the lower courts, raising questions of whether the fishermen were truly Indian and whether the Puyallup and the Nisqually actually existed as tribes. Issues such as these were to be considered in subsequent cases growing out of the fish-ins.

At the southeast end of Puget Sound, returning salmon and steelhead enter the Nisqually River and swim past Frank's Landing. There Bill Frank, Sr., a Nisqually tribal elder, lived and fished with his children, grandchildren, and other relatives. The landing had seen trouble for many years. One longtime resident, Suzette Bridges, remembers fishing seasons when she watched state motorboats, big spotlights flashing, follow fishermen up and down the river. Parents would warn their children to stay inside. Game wardens hid in the bushes, and adults of the tribe searched for the glimmer of white t-shirts the wardens wore under their open-collar uniforms. "But we didn't expect that particular attack in October '65," she said. "We thought people would be decent."[22]

Early in October, state officers had spilled an Indian boat on the Nisqually River. Several nights later they came in force and attempted to raid Frank's Landing. The Indians resisted, and state patrol officers were called in. Then, on October 13, in a well-publicized protest at the same spot, Indians put a canoe in the water. Officers tried to arrest them for illegal fishing, setting off an emotion-charged battle of paddles, sticks, and stones.[23] Newspaperman Robert Johnson, witnessing what he termed "a pitched battle," was so distressed to see game wardens beating Indians with flashlights and leather-covered clubs that he and an attorney flew to Washington, D.C., to lodge complaints in person with Philleo Nash, the Bureau of Indian Affairs Commissioner.[24] Observers from the American Friends Service Committee arrived at the landing to find an aftermath of confusion and tension. On October 26, members of the Survival of American Indians Association gathered in Seattle and marched in protest at the federal courthouse.

Protests occurred again in the spring of 1966. Dick Gregory, nationally-known black comedian and civil rights activist, came to participate in the fish-ins. Unlike Marlon Brando and Canon Yaryan, he was arrested and convicted and later was made to serve a sentence for illegal fishing. He fasted while serving his term in jail, and petitions asking Washington's Governor Daniel Evans to pardon and release him were rejected.[25]

Fish-ins also took place in 1966 at Cook's Landing on the Columbia River near Stevenson, Washington. A group of Yakima Indians, acting independently of their tribal council, provided armed guards while tribal fishermen set their nets.[26] Local newspapers blamed the federal government for encouraging the Indians to defy state law.[27] In their dispute with both state and tribe, the Yakimas at Cook's Landing believed that any kind of regulation other than their own community-based conservation provisions should be invalid.

Widening Ripples of Support. As Indians continued to fish and to be arrested during the era of the fish-ins, they also continued to enlist support for their efforts. In 1965, the American Friends Service Committee (AFSC) sent observers to the protests. The AFSC's Western Washington Indian Committee drew together a study group to assemble information, published subsequently by the University of Washington Press as the book *Uncommon Controversy*. In 1966, the Washington Chapter of the American Civil Liberties Union entered its first fishing rights case to defend fishermen of the Muckleshoot Tribe south of Seattle. The Native American Rights Fund began to work with the Puyallup Tribe and later with other tribes as well. Indians also enlisted assistance with their cases in the 1960s from several attorneys in law schools, private practice, and foundations.

Pressures were also being brought by Indians and their supporters for federal officials to act in support of the tribes, rather than against them. Although centuries of Indian policy had been based on the concept of federal responsibility for Indian affairs, federal support had been weak. But federal Indian policy was shifting away from the 1950s termination approach, which had encouraged the dissolving of tribal governments and reservations. In place of this policy, the administrations of Presidents Lyndon Johnson and Richard Nixon advocated freedom of choice and self-determination for Indian peoples. This policy shift back toward strengthening the tribes appeared to be accompanied by an increase in tribal advocates within federal government departments. Within the Department of Justice, for example, there were also attorneys who were watching the controversy with concern for the tribes. More vigorous federal support first manifested itself as a March 1966 announcement that the Department of Justice would, in response to tribal request, defend Indians arrested for fishing off-reservation under tribal regulations.

IN COURT

The fish-ins produced many court cases. Two of these cases were especially important for the tribes. The first has come to be known as "the Puyallup Trilogy," because it went up to the U.S. Supreme Court on three separate occasions. The second is the case of the Yakima Indian, Richard Sohappy, which later became known as *United States* v. *Oregon*.

The Puyallup Case. The Washington case of the *Puyallup Tribe* v. *The Department of Game et al.* arose from the Nisqually and Puyallup river fish-ins. In this case, Washington sued these two tribes and several individual fishermen to enjoin them from fishing contrary to state regulations. The trial court ruled in favor of the state.

In May 1966, federal attorneys filed an *amicus curiae* brief in support of the Puyallup and Nisqually tribes as their case went before the Washington State Supreme Court. The state supreme court affirmed part of the trial court decision and sent back the questions to the trial court concerning the state's role in regulating Indian fishing for conservation purposes. The federal government played an even more active role when the Puyallups appealed the decision and their case first went before the U.S. Supreme Court, which issued its ruling in 1968. (This decision became known as "Puyallup I.")

In a majority opinion, Justice William O. Douglas upheld the Puyallup and Nisqually's special treaty right to fish off-reservation on the Puyallup and Nisqually rivers. But he also held that the state could regulate Indian fishing in the interest of conservation, "provided the regulation meets appropriate standards and does not discriminate against Indians."[28] Washington had argued that its regulations banning net fishing on those rivers were necessary for conservation. But were they? The High Court sent this question back to Washington state courts.

The Washington Department of Fisheries responded to the ruling by changing its regulations so as to permit Indians to set nets for salmon in the Puyallup River. The Department of Game, however, was responsible for regulating non-Indian steelhead fishing. Unlike the Department of Fisheries, it did not receive support from the state general fund, and operated from a budget primarily dependent upon license fees. The Game Department was thus extremely responsive to pressure from sports fishermen.[29] Following the 1968 Supreme Court decision in the Puyallup case, the Game Department banned *all* Indian net-fishing for steelhead trout in the name of conservation. Game officials argued that any steelhead the sportsmen failed to catch were needed for spawning. In Indian eyes, it was discriminatory to grant the entire run to fishing with rod and reel while forbidding tribes to set nets. Indians contested the ban and the case began its second long climb toward the Supreme Court.

Test Case for the Columbia—Sohappy v. *Smith.* In the summer of 1968, a delegation of Northwest Indians from the Survival of American Indians Association attended the Poor Peoples' Campaign in Washington, D.C. They took with them information about the fish-ins in western Washington and on the Columbia River. They brought home an increased consciousness of the national scope of the human rights struggle. They had also garnered national support—expressed as financial assistance from the National Office of the Rights of the Indigent (NORI) and the Ford Foundation—to pay partial costs of a court case to test the rights of the Columbia River fishermen. *Sohappy* v. *Smith* was this case. It was pursued with additional assistance from attorneys Fred Nolan, David Hood, and Ralph Johnson, who volunteered their time.

Richard Sohappy is a Yakima Indian. His family was among the dissident tribal members who took up arms in 1966 to protect their fishery at Cook's Landing. Sohappy had enlisted in the Army at age eighteen and re-enlisted twice thereafter. Wounded four times, he had received two Purple Hearts, a Silver Star, and a Bronze Star, as well as an Army medal of commendation for meritorious service. He was selected to initiate the test case because of his distinguished record as a brave and loyal American. While on furlough he joined his uncle, David Sohappy, and contrary to state regulations, fished with a gill net in the Columbia. Oregon officials promptly arrested the two. On June 28, 1968, the front page of their local newspaper, The *Skamania County Pioneer,* displayed a large photo of the Sohappys and above it the headline, "Yakima Indian War Hero, Uncle, Bailed Out After Fishing Arrest."[30]

Initially, fourteen Yakima fishermen from Cook's Landing, acting as individuals rather than as representatives of the Yakima Tribe, brought the Sohappy case against McKee A. Smith, Oregon state fish commissioner, and other fish and game officials. Shortly thereafter, the federal government demonstrated its increasing involvement in the issue by filing its own complaint against Oregon, in which the four Columbia River treaty tribes (Warm Springs, Yakima, Umatilla, and Nez Perce) intervened as plaintiffs. The two cases, *Sohappy* v. *Smith* and *U.S.* v. *Oregon,* were consolidated for trial.

Sohappy: "A Fair and Equitable Share." In his decision, U.S. District Judge Robert Clinton Belloni recognized that treaties guaranteed the fishing rights of tribes as separate and distinct from those of non-treaty fishermen. His decree in *Sohappy* v. *Smith* states that the tribes are entitled to take "a fair and equitable share of all fish which it (Oregon) permits to be taken from a given run."[31]

The judge ordered Oregon to manage the fishery in such a way that "a fair share" of the Columbia River fish reached the Indian fishing grounds. As in the Puyallup ruling on which he relied, Belloni ruled that any regulations that Oregon made must be non-discriminatory as well as reasonable and necessary for the conservation of the resource. The state must also choose the least restrictive conservation method possible without jeopardizing the survival of the fish runs. Judge Belloni was more specific than previous judges about the logistics of managing the fishery to ensure the treaty share of the total catch. He ordered preliminary hearings to evaluate proposed regulations, suggested limiting the non-Indian catch, and told the state to work closely with the tribes in developing and promulgating regulations.[32] Like the 1963 Columbia River ruling involving the Umatillas, *Sohappy* v. *Smith* recognized that what prompted the state's "conservation" measures was as much economic as biologic: regulations served as a way to distribute fish to various user groups.

This ruling also showed concern for the Indian fishery within the larger context of the Columbia River salmon's entire life cycle, from birth in the river to adult life in the ocean. Specifically, the ruling talked in biological terms about predicting sizes of salmon runs and about setting escapement goals, i.e., the number of fish that must escape to spawn. There was a different tone to this case, because it set the issue of securing the Indian right within the workings of the natural as well as the management system. Conservation, according to this decision, had to be based on the need to preserve the species.

What was least clear about Judge Belloni's decision was the meaning of the concept, "fair and equitable share." This phrase lent itself to differing interpretations by individual Indian fishermen, by the tribes, and by state agencies, which found themselves facing Judge Belloni again and again in the years after the decision. Despite the new framework within which to distribute the fish, working out the allocations continued to cause dissension, and the Columbia River tribes caught fewer fish in 1970—the year after the decision—than they had the year before.[33]

Toward U.S. v. Washington: The Puyallup Encampment. As for the Puget Sound tribes, despite their efforts they saw few if any tangible improvements in the state of Washington's attitudes toward their fishing. They expressed their frustration in continuing protests and repeatedly called for federal assistance. In the early summer of 1970, George Dysart, the Assistant Solicitor for the Department of Interior in its Northwest Regional office in Portland, Oregon, had written to headquarters in Washington, D.C., urging the government to act immediately, but initially his request went unheeded.[34] That summer, Indian protest culminated in the establishment of an encampment along the Puyallup River, which the Indians attempted to protect with their own security force. Police tried to raze the camp and in the ensuing melee a nearby railway trestle was set ablaze. Officers used tear gas and arrested many Indians.

When the controversy reached this peak, the federal government stepped in to launch a major suit to force the state of Washington to respect the treaty fishing rights of the Puget Sound tribes. The drama of the fish-ins, the encampment, and the burning railway trestle appeared to be the catalyst for a significantly higher level of federal assistance, which entailed a significantly higher cost and commitment. In the fall of 1970, Justice Department attorneys filed a complaint against the state of Washington in U.S. District Court for western Washington on behalf of seven western Washington tribes. Later, seven more tribes entered in the case. The court was being called upon to explore all of the issues in depth, including the need for new management to accommodate the needs of each stock of fish and the rights of each tribe. Judge George H. Boldt would hear the case of *U.S. v. Washington.*

. . . *and Another Tense Wait.* Three years of background preparation preceded the trial. It is important to point out that the controversy did not abate during this period. A cloud of confusion and emotionalism shrouded the issues. As *Uncommon Contro-versy* observed, "the long years of nonunderstanding of Indian life by whites has made it nearly impossible for either side to talk to each other."[35]

It was this same atmosphere that had worked so strongly against any attempts to seek lines of communication between parties to the dispute or to explore avenues for working out differences by other means than confrontation on the rivers and in the courts.

Events continued to illustrate the intensity of the issue. In January 1971, Hank Adams, who had participated in a decade of fish-ins, was shot in the stomach while watching a set net for a friend on the Puyallup River.[36] Adams said that two white men shot him, one of them saying, "You . . . Indians think you own everything." Police disputed his account. Indians continued to be arrested by state officials and convicted and put in jail by state courts.[37]

Preparations for the trial of *U.S.* v. *Washington* did not bring the pursuit of judgments being sought in other courts to a stand-still. The most important was the case of the Puyallup fishermen who had witnessed the blocking of their efforts to net steelhead after the U.S. Supreme Court first reviewed the Puyallup case in 1968. In 1973 the High Court reviewed the case again, agreed that the complete ban on Puyallup net fishing by the state of Washington indeed constituted discrimination, and struck it down. (This decision became known as "Puyallup II.")

Once again the Indians' victory was limited. The newest Supreme Court decision had affirmed tribal rights by demonstrating that even Washington's Department of Game must take steps to accommodate treaty fishing. The court stated that "rights can be controlled by the need to conserve a species . . . and the time may come when the life of a steelhead is so precarious in a particular stream that all fishing should be banned until the species gains assurance of survival. The police power of the State is adequate to prevent the steelhead from following the fate of the passenger pigeon; and the Treaty does not give the Indians the right to pursue the last living steelhead until it enters the nets."[38]

Thus the judges left the door open for continued state regulation of Indian fishing but only if the preservation of the species required it.

The Game Department accommodated this ruling by allocating 45 percent of the harvestable runs of *wild* steelhead to Indian fishermen. This raised a new question: how should the state allocate hatchery fish? The question became one more issue requiring resolution in Judge Boldt's court.

CONCLUSION:
ATTEMPTS TO FIND, AND TO FRUSTRATE, A SOLUTION

Judge Boldt, determined to thoroughly examine the issues and to deliver a decision so precise as to settle the controversy, announced his ruling on February 12, 1974. Chapter 1 described the nature of his decision. The next chapter tells how he strove to ensure that his decision was put into effect and how commercial fishermen and state officials attempted to frustrate that goal. The controversy would continue as the judge and the tribes tried to implement his resolution, and the state and non-Indian fishermen sought to overturn it. Even the federal government, having won a victory in its suit against the state of Washington, would attempt through its executive branch to soften the effects on non-Indians. Finally its judicial branch, through the U.S. Supreme Court, would be called upon to review Judge Boldt's comprehensive ruling.

Chapter 6

The Boldt Decision:
Enforce or Efface?

GETTING THE SYSTEM GOING

Judge Boldt's ruling in *United States* v. *Washington* affirmed the right of treaty tribes to fish at their usual and accustomed grounds and stations off the reservation and "in common with" the other citizens. He interpreted "in common with" to mean "sharing equally": 50-50. He authorized the tribes to manage the fisheries in their traditional fishing sites and required the state to observe strict limitations on the extent to which it restricted treaty Indians' off-reservation harvests. He envisioned a system in which tribes, managing their own fishery, would work in close consultation with the state. The new system of dividing and managing the harvest thus had important implications for state management, for Indian tribes, and for non-Indian commercial and sports fishermen. Judge Boldt retained jurisdiction in the case in order to resolve problems as they arose. The mechanisms for implementing that decision began to be put into place.

Who, Where, and When? Under the decision, treaty Indians could fish off-reservation in their traditional sites and be protected by treaty. While primarily along the rivers, these sites also were located in bays, lakes, and coastal waters. One task the decision demanded was the charting of these "usual and accustomed places." In addition, tribes had to update their tribal membership rolls so that they could certify all those legally qualified to fish in traditional places.

At about the time of Judge Boldt's decision, non-Indians operated five fishing boats for every one Indian boat, and often the boats in the non-Indian fleet were bigger and more efficient.[1] To harvest an equal share, the tribes took steps to "gear up." And because the non-Indian fleet was so much larger, non-Indians had to reduce the number of days they fished to prevent them from catching more than their share.

A Council for Treaty Managers. The tribes took steps to see that the decision was implemented. The tribes began to improve their capacity to manage their off-reservation fisheries. For some tribes, this meant hiring biologists and training enforcement officers. For others, it meant forming fisheries committees to oversee the seasons. Some tribes, such as the Quinault, already had their management system in place while others, such as the Stillaguamish, had more extensive work ahead of them.

In 1974, the nineteen tribes then involved in the area covered by the decision (later one more was included) formed five treaty councils (fig. 6.1). Each council included those tribes covered by the treaty of the same name: Medicine Creek, Neah Bay, Point Elliott, Point No Point, and Quinault. Some councils, such as Point Elliott, included many tribes; nine tribes had signed that treaty. Another—Neah Bay—represented just one tribe, the Makah. However many tribes each council represented, it could send one representative to a new coordinating body, the Northwest Indian Fisheries Commission. Decisions among the five commissioners were to be made on the basis of majority vote. The preamble of the Northwest Indian Fisheries Commission's constitution stated:

> "We, the Indians of the Pacific Northwest, recognize that our fisheries are a basic and important natural resource and of vital concern to the Indians of this state, and that the conservation of this resource is dependent upon effective and progressive management. We further believe that by unity of action we can best accomplish these things, not only for the benefit of our own people but for all of the people of the Pacific Northwest."[2]

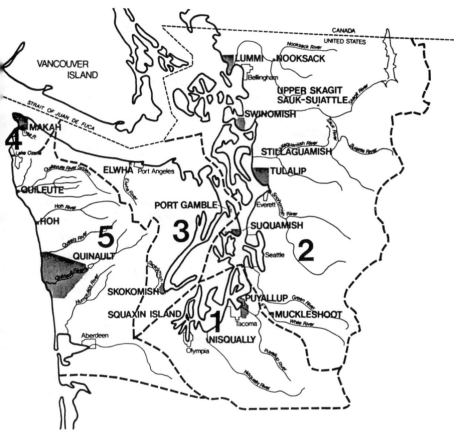

Fig. 6.1. Treaty areas in western Washington. Jamestown, the twentieth tribe, is located northwest of Port Gamble. (SOURCE: Northwest Indian Fisheries Commission)

Such concerted effort was a significant step for the tribes involved. The emerging intertribal organization had three major goals:

1. To assist in the development of programs to protect and coordinate treaty fishing rights of member tribes.

2. To provide technical advice and coordination as needed to tribal fisheries management programs.

3. To develop good will through public information and education projects, and to provide clear and accurate information on

treaties and other Indian fishing matters to the Indian and non-Indian public.[3]

Within six months, nearly $700,000 in federal money was made available to the U.S. Fish and Wildlife Service to work with the commission on implementing the decision.[4] Tribes needed this assistance to develop their regulations for off-reservation fishing, to gain expertise in enforcement and to obtain equipment. For the decision to work, the new system required this investment in generating and analyzing new data. Statistics on the Indian catch had to be collected and compared with the non-Indian catch using a new computerized system. Improved run-size predictions were needed, as were more accurate spawning ground counts. Survival and out-migration studies were necessary, as was additional work to set goals for how many salmon should be let escape to return and spawn. Thus, one of the immediate effects of the decision was an intensified scientific effort to understand the key characteristics of the fishery.

More Questions and Answers. Questions about the technical aspects of the decision arose almost immediately.[5] Judge Boldt had appointed a special master (to serve as a representative of the court) and a technical adviser, Dr. Richard Whitney, to assist him in dealing with fisheries management issues. How, for example, should two tribes divide the fish that swam in grounds traditionally shared by both? The judge, respecting tribal autonomy, left it to the tribes to divide shared property among themselves.

There was also the question whether Indians could catch Canadian fish spawned in the Fraser River, which flows through British Columbia (the Canadian province that borders Washington state on the north) and empties into the Strait of Georgia, which is the northern extension of Puget Sound. A substantial portion of sockeye and pink salmon returning to spawn in the Fraser leave the Pacific and swim inland through the Strait of Juan de Fuca and northern Puget Sound, passing the traditional fishing grounds of eight treaty tribes, including the Makah, Lower Elwha Klallam, Nooksack, and Lummi. A U.S.-Canadian commission, the International Pacific Salmon Fisheries Commission (IPSFC), governs part of the fishing on the Fraser runs. (In 1974, for example, the Fraser River sockeye run totaled 8.5 million, 5 million of which were caught in the internationally regulated waters.[6]) American fishermen harvest a portion of the runs bound for the Fraser River, just as Canadian fishermen harvest a portion of the runs bound for American rivers. Judge Boldt ruled that the tribes could harvest Fraser River salmon as the runs passed through the Indians' usual and accustomed fishing places.

On March 22, 1974, Judge Boldt ordered an interim plan to aid the transition to the court-mandated system.[7] This called for the state to begin making significant reductions in the number of fish it would permit non-Indian fishermen to catch. According to the plan, the state also had to begin closely monitoring the catch to obtain statistics on which to base future regulation. Biologists from both state and tribes had to meet to set guidelines and exchange all available data to better monitor the catch. Tribes had to file their regulations with the state and meet with the state to confer over them. In his decision the judge required that before imposing any regulation on Indian fishing, the state must demonstrate its necessity for conservation of the salmon. In short, the interim plan provided a framework for setting the new system in motion.

REACTIONS TO THE PLAN

The interim plan did not begin to work as ordered. Instead, both non-Indian fishermen and the state of Washington began to fight the decision. Far from setting the court-ordered system in motion, they set out to immobilize it. The dust generated by the post-Boldt battle should not, however, obscure an important underlying fact: the people of Washington state were not clearly divided into proponents and opponents of the decision. The situation was more complex than that and bred considerable diversity in reactions to the ruling.

Many Viewpoints. Consider the following observations by people the new system was affecting:

—An official of a local fishing club calls the decision "a bitter pill."

—Another sportsman sees the decision as "an important thing to have happened even though it affected me adversely." He feels a sense of loss so great that he would personally pay money to buy out Indian rights, but he knows that they wouldn't—and shouldn't—sell.

—A non-Indian gillnetter defies the court ruling and fishes illegally during a time when state closures are in effect and only treaty fisheries, regulated by the tribes, are open. He radios the movements of enforcement officers to other illegal fishermen so that they can evade citations and fines. He sees his actions as justifiable resistance to a decision with which he vehemently disagrees.

—Another gillnetter sees his own illegal fishing as a way to turn a quick profit.

—Still others—frequently older fishermen—do not fish illegally because they view the legal system with great respect: they will not disobey the law, whatever their personal feelings about it might be.

—Many Indians welcome the decision, seeing in it the promise of "a better future for the children coming up and the children still unborn." They see also an immediate chance for these people: "who never had anything but who now can fish."

—Some Indians see not the gain but the loss in the requirement to allot the additional 50 percent to non-Indians, whereas in earlier times the Indians owned and cared for 100 percent of the resource.

Although this diversity of opinion clearly existed, what the public heard most frequently was the outcry of the non-Indian fishermen. Just as in the past, when Indians themselves had been scapegoated as threats to the resource, now the decision that vindicated their right to fish was targeted as the source of all non-Indian fishermen's woes.

Noisy Opposition. Judge Boldt himself became a target of the non-Indian fisherman's anger. Bumper stickers, protests, and petitions were directed against him. Protests occurred frequently throughout the years following the decision. Perhaps the noisiest one took place when fishermen blowing their boats' whistles and waving anti-Boldt slogans, crowded the Seattle harbor to greet President Gerald Ford during his 1976 visit.[8]

The judge was neither deterred nor disturbed by the unpopularity of his decision. In a rare interview with reporters on the eve of his seventy-second birthday in 1975, Judge Boldt declined to discuss details of the case, but commented that he was working as hard as he ever had in his twenty-two years on the bench and that he wouldn't feel comfortable if he weren't doing the best he could. Although eligible for retirement at full pay, the judge— sometimes called the "Durable Dane"—planned to continue his judicial duties,[9] which were frequently to be dominated by the fishing rights issue in the years that followed.

THE STATE'S SOLUTION

The subsequent controversy centered on the court's attempt to enforce its decision while opponents of the decision tried to efface it. The two developed quite different means to "resolve" the issue.

Concede a Little, Balk a Lot. Washington's Department of Fisheries and its legislature did take some steps following the decision in *U.S.* v. *Washington.* A decade after commissioning the study that described the oversized fleet and its devastating effect upon fishermen's income, the legislature finally passed a bill requiring a moratorium on the sale of licenses for fishing vessels.[10] But it was too little, too late: the state's fleet had doubled (from 2,834 boats in 1965 to 5,814 in 1974) in the decade preceding the decision.[11] Now the problem of overcrowding required additional remedial action. During days when the state closed, but tribes permitted fishing, non-Indians forced to stay behind on the dock were angered by the sight of Indians out on the water. Some non-Indians fished despite the regulation.

The state enforced its regulations sporadically and generally with little effect: when the state issued citations to non-Indians, the lower state courts dismissed them. Frequently, the state's agencies set forth regulations which did not permit Indians an equal share. As a result, the Federal District Court had to inter- vene again and again to force state compliance with the Boldt decision. In response, the state attorney general repeatedly ap- pealed Judge Boldt's rulings.

Fish the Courts Again. For the state attorney general's office, Indian fishing rights became a central concern. Attorney General Slade Gorton came from a family involved in the fish industry. The family corporation, Slade Gorton and Co., Inc., was a whole- sale fish-distributing firm in Boston. In the 1975 Public Disclosure form he filed as an elected official, Gorton listed himself as a shareholder in the company, although his interest income from the company was quite small.[12] It was several years before he placed these holdings into a blind trust as he had his other assets.[13] Thus it does not seem unreasonable to consider that Gorton's views on Indian fishing rights may have stemmed from both his political philosophy and his tie to the commercial fishing industry.

Gorton began to refer to Indians as "supercitizens" because of the rights which, in his view, the courts had bestowed on them. In the years following Judge Boldt's decision, he and attorneys in his office regarded the overturning of the ruling as a key mission. Their initial appeals were unsuccessful. On June 4, 1975, the Ninth Circuit Court of Appeals affirmed Judge Boldt's decision and the propriety of his continuing involvement in the case.[14] The court made it clear that it was Washington state's failure to imple- ment the decision that required the judge to retain jurisdiction. As the judge of the circuit court stated in his concurring decision, "the record in this case, and the history set forth in the Puyallup and Antoine Cases, among others, make it crystal clear that it has been the recalcitrance of Washington State officials (and their vo- cal non-Indian commercial and sports fishing allies) which pro- duced the denial of Indian rights requiring intervention by the District Court. This responsibility should neither escape notice nor be forgotten."[15] Six months later on January 26, 1976, the U.S. Supreme Court declined to review *U.S.* v. *Washington*.[16] Its action meant that the Boldt's decision was the law of the land.

Despite the Supreme Court's refusal to review the case, the attorney general's office did not give up. Commercial fishermen's associations were suing the state, challenging its authority to allocate fish to implement the Boldt decision; these legal attacks raised hope for judicial review in the future. Assistant Attorney General James Johnson encouraged commercial fishermen to believe that their legal assault would succeed. To a rally of commercial fishermen in Bellingham, Washington, in August 1978, he said: "The Boldt decision shall be overturned. While optimistic, I think that's a realistic assessment of where we are now and where we're going and I'll tell you why in a moment. I hope it's realistic . . . I've had over 150 hearings there since this decision came out and I've seen how it's spread and gotten worse from where it started. As far as we are concerned, the tide has turned and as I say it shall be overturned."[17]

Buoyed by this attitude, it is little wonder that many non-Indian fishermen failed to respect the decision, now federal law, and that an "outlaw fishery" ensued.

THE NON-INDIAN FISHERMEN'S SOLUTION

Judge Boldt's ruling caught the non-Indian fishermen in the middle. State agencies had long led them to believe that Indians had no rights: the agencies had managed the fishery so as to exclude Indians. Now the U.S. District Court and the appeals courts were telling them that Indians had to be included—even though it meant limiting non-Indian fishing.

The Boldt decision, permitting Indians the opportunity to catch up to 50 percent of the harvest, meant that each boat in the oversized non-Indian fleet would be allotted an even smaller share of the catch. Commercial fishermen rather than sports fishermen were being required by the state to bear the major burden of the decision. A state program to reduce the non-Indian fleet as painlessly as possible, by buying boats back from the owners, could not overcome the outrage expressed by many commercial fishermen, partly because the program did too little and partly because the outrage was too great.[18]

Returning to Court. They attacked the decision in several ways. Some fishermen began a publicity campaign against Judge Boldt himself. Other associations of fishermen prepared to attack his decision in state court. Only a few months after *U.S.* v. *Washington* was decided, first the Puget Sound Gillnetters Association and then the Washington State Commercial Passenger Vessel Association and the Washington Kelpers Association (representing trollers who fish near the kelp beds) sued the Washington Department of Fisheries to keep it from enforcing its allocation order. They won favorable rulings in Thurston County Court.[19]

Judge Boldt, exercising his continuing jurisdiction in *U.S.* v. *Washington,* took action. He reminded the Department of Fisheries of its obligation to implement the decision, and he enjoined the Thurston County Court from carrying out rulings which deprived Indians of their treaty share.[20] The judge also noted that these cases pitted parties who were really allies—the state and the non-Indian fishermen—against each other. In any court case, the two opposing sides are supposed to be true adversaries with the proceedings a valid contest between them. In these cases, the evidence suggested that both sides wanted the same result—reversal of the decision in *U.S.* v. *Washington.* Judge Boldt warned that such attempts to subvert his decision would misuse the legal system: "That which was so carefully decided by this court is hastily being undone by a series of proceedings hardly resembling contested cases."[21]

Fishing "in Spite of." Provisions in Judge Boldt's interim plan of March 22, 1974, called for the Washington Department of Fisheries to make significant reductions in non-Indian fishing so that Indians could catch their share. In an action that fishermen called civil disobedience, but that others saw as opportunity for "outlaw" fishing, many non-Indian commercial fishermen simply ignored the state restrictions and fished on days when fisheries were closed to them. In 1975, a major illegal fishery occurred on the fall coho run: the state did little to prevent it. County prosecutors and judges dismissed almost all citations; only one of the 300 issued to non-treaty fishermen drew a penalty.[22]

Massive illegal fishing continued for years following the decision. The numbers indicate the magnitude of the problem: when the court ordered closure of the fishery in the fall of 1976, fisheries patrol officers saw some 247 fishermen fishing illegally.[23] In 1977, according to evidence later introduced in court, an illegal harvest of 7,036 chinook, weighing 109,204 pounds, was caught in Bellingham Bay alone, while 33,359 chum, weighing 337,623 pounds, were caught illegally in northern Hood Canal.[24]

On the water, the situation was extremely tense. After non-Indians hurled threats at Lummi fishermen, the Federal Bureau of Investigation was called in to investigate complaints. "Our people are seriously concerned for their safety," was how Bernie Gobin of the Tulalip Tribe described the atmosphere surrounding the 1976 fall fishing season.[25] Indeed, on October 25, only a few days after the FBI arrived, a violent confrontation did occur off Foulweather Bluff on the northern tip of the Kitsap Peninsula, although this incident involved non-Indians and an enforcement officer of the State Department of Fisheries. A department patrolman shot and seriously wounded a non-Indian gillnetter, William Carlson, whom he was attempting to ticket for illegal fishing.[26] State fisheries officials said the patrolman fired the shot because he thought the gillnetter was going to ram his boat. Other fishermen in the area disputed that interpretation. Carlson was fishing without a license during a closed period; he said he needed the money to pay the mortgage on his boat. Washington Governor Dan Evans called for an inquiry but said, "where you have an illegal activity, whether it is on the waters of Puget Sound or on the streets . . . those who are charged with the responsibility of upholding the law simply must carry on that task. And we intend to attempt to do that . . . the best way to avoid violence is . . . to live up to the law."[27]

Nonetheless, the protests and the illegal fishing continued.

JUDGE BOLDT RESPONDS: NEGOTIATE AND ALLOCATE

In the face of state resistance, defiance from non-Indian fishermen, and continuing legal challenges, Judge Boldt took several steps to cope with the situation. First, he established the Fisheries Advisory Board, a nonjudicial mechanism, to resolve disputes as they arose. Second, as state court decisions came into conflict with his decision, the judge found it necessary to take more and more responsibility for managing Washington's fisheries.

A Board to Mediate Disputes. The Fisheries Advisory Board was established by Judge Boldt during the uneasy fall of 1975, when he was faced with the prospect of interminable "revolving door" proceedings concerning disputes over the season's openings and closings. Shortly after his decision in *U.S.* v. *Washington,* Judge Boldt had appointed Dr. Richard Whitney as technical adviser to the Federal District Court. On October 28, 1975, he expanded Whitney's role by selecting him to be chairman of the new Fisheries Advisory Board to deal with the issues before they reached the court.

Judge Boldt originally selected Whitney as technical adviser because of his expertise and his experience in fisheries matters. A professor in the College of Fisheries at the University of Washington, he had led the Washington Cooperative Fishery Research Unit for many years, supervising projects that involved state, federal, and tribal agencies. His experience in working with all parties in the case was a key qualification for his new position. In addition, he was a federal employee in the U.S. Fish and Wildlife Service, which made the logistics of his appointment by the federal court somewhat easier.

The board was to be made up of one tribal representative and one state representative. When the two were unable to agree, Whitney would recommend a solution. His role as chairman became that of a "medium of communication," to ensure timely discussions and to encourage negotiated agreements in a setting less adversarial than the courtroom.[28]

According to Whitney, the process operated like this: whenever a disagreement arose, the state appointed its representative (e.g., an official from the Department of Fisheries or Game) and the affected tribe or tribes appointed its representative (e.g. an official from the tribe whose fishery was involved). Thus the state and tribal representatives would change, depending on the details of the issue at hand. Sometimes the representatives met in person with Whitney and sometimes a telephone conference call was sufficient to resolve an issue. Spectators—biologists, commercial fishermen, attorneys—were permitted, but were not allowed to speak unless requested to do so by a member of the board, and then only under delineated conditions.[29]

Some issues still went before the court, but others were resolved by the state representative and the tribal representative inching closer to effective exchanges of information and joint analyses of fisheries data. The three-member board considered issues ranging from setting a period of closure on the sport fishery on the Quillayute River to establishing a joint committee to develop a method for updating chum run sizes.

George Dysart was the solicitor in the Department of Interior's Portland, Oregon, office who had urged officials in Washington, D.C., to intervene immediately and prevent violence on the Puyallup River before the encampment in 1970. He saw the development of the Fisheries Advisory Board in 1976 as a positive process and he watched it with particular interest. In his analysis of summaries of the fifty-one board meetings in 1977, he saw progress: out of fifty subjects that were considered, he believed that full agreement had been reached on thirty-two occasions and partial agreement in four cases, indicating successful negotiations 72 percent of the time.[30]

On the other hand, some of the Indians involved with the board decision-making appear to have felt that Whitney tended initially to favor the data presented in support of the state positions and that the tribes needed to make extensive presentations to assert their views.[31] In the words of one tribal biologist who observed several of the meetings, the Fisheries Advisory Board "at least removed decisions from the political arena."[32] For the attorneys the board provided a way to avoid constant court proceedings. Mason Morisset, attorney for several of the tribes, estimated that one year he spent 150 out of 200 workdays in court. Since everything the FAB considered was "a potential lawsuit," the process saved considerable time and money.[33] Whitney himself can recall some midnight phone calls and tense moments, but, in general, the board appears to have realized its calming potential.

Continuing to Clarify. As the board proceeded, it requested clarification from Judge Boldt on several key issues. Whitney formulated twelve questions that needed answers from Judge Boldt so that the board could better determine how to implement the court's ruling.

One of the most critical was whether in allotting the harvest, fish of Canadian origin should be counted in with those of United States origin. This was especially important because it included the huge Fraser River sockeye and pink runs, which were harvested according to provisions in a treaty between the United States and Canada. Judge Boldt had ruled previously that the tribes were entitled to the 50 percent treaty share of the American portion of the Canadian-origin runs. Upon Whitney's request for further clarification, Boldt issued an order on April 13, 1976.[34] The Canadian stocks were to be considered as a river system separate from United States rivers. Had Judge Boldt ruled otherwise, then the Fraser River sockeye caught by the eight tribes fishing in waters covered by the U.S.-Canadian treaty could have constituted so large a portion of the tribal allocation that these and other tribes might miss out on a share of smaller runs.

A second question also had important implications for defining with precision how the fish were to be categorized and allocated. Were shares of the Indian and non-Indian allocations to be calculated stream-by-stream, river-by-river, or on a regional basis?

Judge Boldt said the shares were to be calculated on a river-by-river basis whenever possible. In areas such as Hood Canal, where the fish stocks pooled before returning to their natal streams and where information on when and where they separated was then unavailable, management of the harvest was to be on a regional basis.

The management system that was emerging stressed as close a correlation between the fish and their river homes as possible. Greater technical clarity could be achieved if biologists were not forced to look at a mixed stock and try to guess how many fish from each river were milling around in it. This problem of how to manage the mixed stocks was to loom even larger after 1976, when the federal government declared its jurisdiction over waters within the 200 nautical miles that lay beyond the three nautical miles of coastal waters that states controlled as their territory. In its Fisheries Conservation and Management Act of 1976, Congress set up a federal management system for this vast underwater nursery where the mixed stocks fed and grew. It established a series of regional councils with scientific advisers, such as the Pacific Fisheries Management Council, to develop policy, establish seasons, and limit catches. As this issue became more important in subsequent years, the implications of the precedent that Judge Boldt had established for allocating the fish on a river-by-river basis became increasingly important. In the process of clarifying the new system, Judge Boldt held that fish caught in this ocean area by non-Indian fishermen from Washington state, and by other U.S. fishermen who landed fish in Washington state, had to be counted within the non-Indian share. The number of fish caught in the federal area thus had implications for Washington state. If too many fish were caught by non-Indians at sea, others fishing closer in would have their allocations cut. If too many fish destined for Indian river-fishing sites were caught as part of mixed stock groupings at sea, not enough fish would reach Indian sites on the rivers. There was a growing need for closer state, federal, and tribal coordination to make the complex system work.

Non-Indian Gillnetters Drag the Judicial Waters. While the Fisheries Advisory Board was working quietly in the background, Judge Boldt faced a legal assault from the non-Indian commercial fishing organizations. Until the summer of 1977, Washington state agencies had reluctantly provided the regulations required by the federal court to limit non-Indian fishing. By reducing the non-treaty fishing days, the state attempted to increase the number of fish that reached the Indians' fishing grounds. The commercial fishermen's organizations had challenged these regulations. (See page 92.) In June 1977, the Washington State Supreme Court upheld the Thurston County Court decision in *Puget Sound Gillnetters Association* v. *Moos* (Donald Moos was the Director of Fisheries)[35] which had the effect of curtailing the state's allocation system.

The gillnetters association sought a court order directing the state Fisheries Department to issue regulations which would give no special recognition to Indian fishermen. The department did not object. In fact it urged a decision on the merits of the matter (i.e. upon the substantive legal issues rather than upon procedural considerations). This situation seemed like "collusive" litigation, because the Fisheries Department and the gillnetters were not really adversaries: in fact, both desired the same result—eliminating allocations to tribal fishermen. By entering into this litigation as the defendant, Fisheries was put in the position of arguing for a decision it disliked; its defense was less than aggressive.

State Court v. Federal Court. The state supreme court ignored the fact that the basic ruling of the U.S. district court had been unanimously upheld by the Ninth Circuit Court of Appeals, and that the U.S. Supreme Court had denied *certiorari* (review). Even though the district court was continuing to exercise jurisdiction over the subject matter of this dispute, the majority of the state supreme court judges in *Puget Sound Gillnetters* v. *Moos* agreed that "being cited no authority for the proposition that federal district courts have exclusive jurisdiction to construe Indian treaties—treaties which affect important interests of the state—we adhere to our own interpretation of the treaty."[36] The state supreme court then went on to deny the Indian rights so carefully considered and upheld in the Boldt decision.

The state supreme court ruled that the Department of Fisheries had authority to regulate the harvest only for conservation purposes: the department had to issue regulations that treated everyone alike. In another case heard a few months later, *Washington State Commercial Passenger Fishing Vessel Association v. Tollefson* (the new Director of Fisheries), the state court affirmed its position in the gillnetters case with a new rationale: recognizing special treaty fishing rights for Indians would violate the equal protection clause of the Fourteenth Amendment.[37]

The net result of these decisions was that the Washington State Supreme Court had overruled a federal court. This was a very precarious position for the state jurists to take, as the Supremacy Clause of the U.S. Constitution makes federal laws and treaties the supreme law of the land and binds state judges to uphold them. Furthermore, state executive and judicial officers promise in their oaths of office to support the U.S. Constitution. The rulings were especially puzzling in view of a July 1977 decision handed down by the U.S. Supreme Court in its third consideration of the Puyallup case. There the High Court upheld the state's authority to allocate 45 percent of the steelhead on the Puyallup River to the tribe.[38] The state decisions were in direct conflict with the federal decisions.

The state supreme court rulings gave the Fisheries Department reason to avoid implementing the Boldt decision. The director of Fisheries was in an uneasy position. If he allocated fish between Indians and non-Indians, he might be found in contempt of the state supreme court order. If he failed to allocate, he would be in contempt of the U.S. District Court order. Unless the district court took decisive action, Indians might have absolutely nothing to show for many years of intensive litigation from which they thought they had won a considerable victory.

Allocation: The Judge Takes Over. Judge Boldt recognized the severity of the problem. Rather than force a direct confrontation by forbidding the Fisheries Department to enforce the state supreme court order, he himself assumed responsibility for allocating fish to the Indians. He asked the Fisheries Advisory Board to develop a management plan for the 1977 season which he then adopted as a court order. A few months later, he also had to take over the allocation of fish to non-Indians. The U.S. Court of Appeals, affirming the district court's authority, later stated: "The state's extraordinary machinations in resisting the (1974) decree have forced the district court to take over a large share of the management of the state's fishery in order to enforce its decrees. Except for some desegregation cases . . . , the district court has faced the most concerted official and private efforts to frustrate a decree of a federal court witnessed in this century."[39]

The federal district court was now effectively the agency in charge of securing the treaty right to the fish. An interagency pool of federal enforcement officers from the Departments of Interior, Justice, Commerce, and Transportation was created to carry out the court's orders.

Increased Outlaw Fishing. While the federal court order was in effect, non-Indian fishing associations and individual fishermen were served notice that failure to comply would lead to charges of contempt of court. Nonetheless, non-Indian illegal fishing increased during both the 1977 and 1978 fishing seasons during which the district court's management plan was in effect. The nontreaty fishermen caught some 183,000 salmon illegally in 1977.[40] By November 1978, 177 citations had been issued to non-treaty fishermen ordering them to appear in court on charges of contempt of the federal court order.[41]

There were threats of violence and, in one incident at Point Roberts, two non-Indian boats interfered with Lummi Indians who were fishing on a day set aside for Indian fishing. An angry interchange followed, and one Indian boat was damaged before Coast Guard boats arrived and escorted the non-Indians to shore.[42] The situation became so grave that the American Friends Service Committee in cooperation with the Northwest Indian

Fisheries Commission instituted a project to observe and document the illegal fishing.[43]

In the face of the opposition to *U.S.* v. *Washington* by fishermen's organizations and state agencies, it would have been appropriate for the executive branch of the federal government, as trustee for the tribes, to play a strong role in enforcing the law as set out by the Boldt decision. Had federal officials done so, they might have prevented much of the controversy and political maneuvering that followed. As the United States Commission on Civil Rights pointed out after an intensive investigation, the explosive situation following the Boldt decision required a strong federal presence.[44] Instead, the various branches of government chose different ways to deal with the decision.

There is some evidence—mostly anecdotal—to suggest that the federal officials who were in office when *U.S.* v. *Washington* went to court did not fully anticipate the consequences of the case, especially the outcry and constituent pressure against the decision. According to one former government official, "it was an example of Uncle standing firm and then backing off." The *Bulletin* of the National Congress of American Indians reported:

> When an Interior official delivered the news of Judge Boldt's decision to then-secretary Rogers C. B. Morton, the following exchange was reliably reported to have taken place between the two:
> MORTON: "Well, appeal it, appeal it!"
> OFFICIAL: "We can't, Mr. Secretary. We won."[45]

Settlement by Committee. Instead of rallying behind Judge Boldt and the tribes, the executive branch of the federal government eventually responded to the pressures from the state of Washington's strong congressional delegation (who were themselves responding to constituent pressure). In the spring of 1977, President Jimmy Carter established a task force to study the issue and make recommendations.

The guidelines of the task force were to establish:

1. The optimum utilization of the fisheries resource, including Federal assistance for fisheries enhancement.

2. A healthy commercial and sport fishery that will provide an opportunity for all who depend upon salmon fishing for their livelihood to earn a good living.

3. A utilization of the fishery consistent with recognized treaty fishing rights reserved under the Stevens Treaties of 1854 and 1855.

4. Development of management systems that will ensure that the salmon fishery is preserved and developed so as to satisfy points 1 through 3.[46]

The task force was composed of regional representatives of the three executive departments that had an interest in the controversy: the Department of Interior, which had a traditional role in administration of Indian policy and was traditional bearer of the trust responsibility to the tribes; the Department of Justice, which had brought suit against the state on behalf of the tribes; and the Department of Commerce, which was involved in management of the ocean fisheries through the National Marine Fisheries Service.

That the task force was designed to facilitate high-level inter-departmental communication was seen as its most innovative and promising characteristic.[47] The presence of high officials from all three departments reflected the power of Washington state's congressional delegation, led by Warren Magnuson, the state's senior senator.[48]

The regional representatives performed the work of the task force. Its members apparently intended to resolve the controversy anew, despite the district court decision in force to accomplish this very task. Testifying later before the U.S. Commission on Civil Rights, the team members described themselves as seekers of a "solution" that would be a "fair and equitable settlement for each of the participants in the fishery."[49] Their objective was "to devise a new set of arrangements under which the principal concerns of each of the parties could be accommodated."[50] As John Merkel, a

Indians fishing in their traditional manner at Celilo Falls on the Columbia River (UW Libraries, Special Collections)

(*Left*) Leschi, (*right*) Isaac I. Stevens (UW Libraries, Special Collections, nos. NA1536 and 379)

Muckleshoot Indian march, May 1966 (*Seattle Times*)

Demonstrators protest the Boldt Decision, September 1976 (*Seattle Times*)

Fishing rights demonstration, September 1981 (*Seattle Times*)

Bill Frank, Jr., and his ninety-nine-year-old father Willie, on the banks of the Nisqually River (*Daily Olympian*)

Yakima Indian netting fish on the Yakima River, June 1974 (*Seattle Times*)

John Goodwin, a Quinault gillnetter (photo by Kim Steele)

U.S. Attorney on the regional team, explained: "You can't negotiate a court case after the case has been decided without somebody giving up something that he won in the court decision."[51] Modifying the arrangements established by Judge Boldt was thus implicit to the team's assignment.

The regional team met separately with representatives of tribes, user groups, and the state. Later, tribes and state arranged negotiations with each other. Participants' goals differed from those of the team. The tribes, for example, originally saw the team's mission as that of implementing the Boldt decision and making it work better. Therefore, they were concerned to see the task force including non-Indian user groups on an equal footing with the management entities of tribes and state. The Indians became increasingly wary as they watched the team negotiator, James Waldo, trying to juggle his continuing role as a federal trial attorney representing the tribes and his new role as the chief negotiator among the participants.

Tribal members recount that they felt considerable pressure to cooperate with the team. Two threats loomed: Washington's congressmen might urge cutbacks in the funding for tribal programs; and bills to abrogate the treaties, introduced in Congress in the fall of 1977 by Washington's junior U.S. Representative, Jack Cunningham, might become law. One of these bills bore the ironic title "Native American Equal Opportunity Act" and would have eliminated *all* Indian treaty rights, thereby unilaterally stripping Indians of their treaty assets and making them "equal" to all other citizens.[52] The act provided for an unspecified amount of compensation. Critics pointed out that the cost would have been monumental. The tribes unanimously asserted that their rights were not for sale.

The Task Force Way. In June 1978 the regional team of the task force unveiled its plan for settling the controversy.[53] The fisheries management system it envisioned established non-Indian and Indian management zones similar to the system on the Columbia River. The "tribal management zone" would replace the Indians' "usual and accustomed places"; a "tribal commission" (rather than individual tribes) would manage it. The state would manage the "state commercial management zone." A "fisheries review board," consisting of three state, three tribal, and one neutral member, with limited powers to settle disputes, would oversee the state and the tribal commissions. The plan proposed an extensive enhancement program, projected to increase the *number* of fish, in return for which the tribes apparently would be required to accept a smaller *percentage* of the fish. Under the plan, tribes would also have been forced to phase out their commercial fishing of steelhead. The team further recommended a gear-reduction program to bring the number of non-Indian commercial fishing licenses into line with the limited availability of fish.

Nobody liked the plan. The tribes, the fishermen's associations, and the state all rejected it. There were three major drawbacks from the state's point of view: too much federal involvement; failure to significantly alter the Indian and non-Indian sharing plan established by Judge Boldt; and failure to recognize the concurrent need for review of *U.S.* v. *Washington* by the U.S. Supreme Court.[54]

Commercial and sports fishermen felt that any acceptable settlement must: include U.S. Supreme Court review of *U.S.* v. *Washington;* base management upon equalizing the sizes of the Indian and non-Indian fleets rather than upon other methods; and phase in distribution of the harvest more gradually.[55]

The tribes rejected the plan because it took away too much and returned too little. It removed their authority to manage their share of the resource, and decreased their allocation of the harvest. Billy Frank, Jr., one of the five board members representing the tribes under the Northwest Indian Fisheries Commission and a veteran of the Nisqually River fish-ins that led to *U.S.* v. *Washington,* explained:

> One of the things in that last report of the task force . . . is that it takes away our enforcement. It takes our usual and accustomed fishing areas, and it also takes away our management.

Now, without the management, then I [might] just as well have never even started any kind of a process to have the *U.S.* v. *Washington,* and go through all these years of putting a good lawsuit against the State of Washington. . . .[56]

A U.S. Commissioner for Civil Rights, Frankie M. Freeman, pointed out another key issue raised by the task force process and its product. "A problem that troubles me . . . is the perception . . . that one can negotiate away basic . . . treaty rights . . . ," she said. "If rights will not be respected and laws will not be obeyed by the federal and state governments, we are establishing a dangerous precedent."[57]

The plan had produced still another stalemate.

Senators Call on Uncle to Stall. Members of the congressional delegation, the prime movers of the task force, were not pleased.[58] On March 1, 1978, Washington Senators Warren G. Magnuson and Henry M. Jackson sent a letter to U.S. Attorney General Griffin B. Bell, questioning federal support for Indian litigation and calling for a review of federal policy in this area. They expressed particular concerns that "federal advocacy" had increased tensions between Indians and non-Indians, stating that "both Indians and non-Indians in our own Washington state now endure the divisive effects of the infamous 1974 fishing rights decision handed down in *U.S.* v. *Washington* while the resource—and the livelihoods of all those who rely on it—is in jeopardy."[59] Then in August 1978, the senators sent a letter to the Secretary of the Interior urging him to refrain from fully enforcing the Boldt decision:

As you know, the implementation of the so-called Boldt Decision has caused four years of conflict and controversy in Washington State . . . it has become impossible to provide adequate protection of the resource with present enforcement capabilities. . . . In 1976, illegal non-Indian fishing accounted for an estimated 34 percent of the total non-Indian catch in all of Puget Sound . . . adequate escapement levels necessary for the perpetuation of the resource are in jeopardy . . . while we work together for a long-term solution, we must urge your very serious consideration of less than full implementation of the Boldt Decision for this year."[60]

The senators twice blame Judge Boldt's decision for the problems of the overcrowded fishery and for the depredations on the resource wrought by defiant fishermen fishing illegally. Magnuson and Jackson could have suggested remedying the situation by more vigorous enforcement or by more effective programs to assist the non-Indian fishermen. Instead, they recommend "less than full implementation"—that is, cutting the Indians' allocation to less than their legal share. According to the U.S. Commission on Civil Rights, "the letter, in effect, said that illegal activity should be stopped via a payoff to the lawbreakers and the amount should be assessed against the tribes."[61] To the tribes, it seemed a puzzling suggestion after so many years of struggling to have their rights affirmed.

Chapter 7

Seventh Knock
at the High Court Door

REQUESTING A HEARING

Bid Them Enter? Its task force effort a failure and the fishing rights conflict still unresolved, the federal government spent the summer of 1978 debating whether to support or oppose U.S. Supreme Court review of *U.S.* v. *Washington*. Washington state's request for review would haul Northwest fishing cases before the High Court for the seventh time (Winans in 1905, Seufert Brothers in 1919, Tulee in 1942, and the Puyallup Trilogy in 1968, 1973 and 1977). The case being considered was a consolidation of the Washington State Commercial Passenger Vessel Association and Puget Sound Gillnetters Association suits in which the non-Indian commercial fishermen had challenged the state's authority to implement Judge Boldt's decision in *U.S.* v. *Washington*. The Washington Supreme Court had ruled in favor of the fishermen and forbade the state to enforce Judge Boldt's orders allocating the catch. Both the fishermen and the state of Washington were urging Supreme Court review. Key members of Washington's congressional delegation were also known to support this effort.[1]

In considering its response, the Justice Department called upon the Department of Interior—home of the Bureau of Indian Affairs—to state its position. Leo Krulitz, the Interior Department's solicitor, wrote to Wade McCree, the Justice Department solicitor general, urging that the United States agree to the review.[2] He made his recommendation conditional to an understanding that the Department of Justice would confine its review to the treaty interpretation and no other issue (such as the enforcement orders set out by Judge Boldt), and that the full record of the district court in *U.S.* v. *Washington* be considered. He based his recommendation on three considerations: the divergent state and federal court interpretations of the treaties; the potential for direct confrontation between the federal and state courts; and the possibility that the existing conflicts could endanger the resource.

There had been vehement objections to McCree's position within the Interior Department. The Associate Solicitor for Indian Affairs, Thomas Fredericks, had advised the department to "oppose certiorari review as being neither a good legal position nor an advisable resolution to any practical or political problems."[3] The Assistant Secretary for Indian Affairs, Forrest Gerard, had expressed similar views to Solicitor Krulitz:

> As trustee, we cannot reward the chaos and lawless atmosphere created by Washington State and its citizen-fishermen by acquiescing in their petition for certiorari. The United States won the decision; the law has been clear for the past four years. I have confidence that the decision is correct as the United States must. As winning plaintiffs in the case and as trustee for these treaty Indian fishing tribes, I feel we must strongly urge the Department of Justice to oppose any grant of certiorari in this case.[4]

The U.S. Commission on Civil Rights and the Northwest tribes wrote strong letters to Krulitz opposing review.

Although it seemed possible that a strong affirmation from the High Court might finally bring the tribes and their supporters full implementation and compliance with *U.S.* v. *Washington,* the risk seemed great. Generally, parties—and their attorneys—who have won a significant victory in one court do not encourage another court to review the case, because there is always the chance of loss. It would be like asking the winning baseball team to play the World Series over again.

The Door Opens. On October 16, 1978, almost five years after Judge Boldt's decision, the U.S. Supreme Court justices agreed to review the case. Several factors contributed to the Court's decision when only two years earlier it had declined to examine it:

1. There were now the commercial fishermen's cases and the resultant clash between the state and the federal court systems— a confrontation which the U.S. Supreme Court no doubt viewed with considerable concern.

2. There was the chaotic situation created by the non-Indian commercial fishermen's defiance of the Boldt decision.

3. There was the highly unusual situation in which the United States Justice Department—which had brought *U.S.* v. *Washington* on behalf of the tribes—had acquiesced to the state's request for review.

Several delegations traveled from Washington state to Washington, D.C., to present the fishing case before the nine justices of the Supreme Court on February 28, 1979. State officials, Indians, and non-Indian fishermen went to participate and observe the proceedings. Tribal delegations included elders, council members, and fisheries managers. Attorneys appearing before the court were: Attorney General Slade Gorton, on behalf of the state of Washington; Philip Lacovara, on behalf of the commercial fishermen's associations; Mason Morisset, on behalf of the tribes; and Louis Claiborne from the Department of Justice, on behalf of the United States.

Added to written materials submitted by the parties to the case were several *amicus curiae* briefs. The Northwest Steelhead and Salmon Council of Trout Unlimited, the Pacific Seafood Processors Association, and the Pacific Legal Foundation[5] submitted briefs arguing that Indians had few or quite limited rights. They suggested that the *U.S.* v. *Washington* decision be overruled. The American Civil Liberties Union, the National Congress of American Indians, and a large body of national religious organizations coordinated by the American Friends Service Committee presented briefs supporting the tribal position. The *amicus* brief of the American Institute of Fisheries Research Biologists supported neither side but argued that a comprehensive management plan was necessary for the productivity of the resource.

On the morning of the hearing, a long line waited to be admitted to the Supreme Court. Oral presentations are the window through which the general public can view the deliberations of the court. The setting and ritual are impressive, as indeed they are meant to be. According to one observer, "the total effect is like being in church and a very high church at that."[6] The hearing began at 10:05 A.M. Each attorney was permitted fifteen minutes to present a summary of his argument; the justices interrupted frequently with questions.

What Do the Treaties Mean? Washington state's attorney general, Slade Gorton, argued that Indians were only entitled to access to their traditional fishing places. While they should have an "equal opportunity" to fish with non-Indians, this did not give them the right to a specified allocation of the harvest. Justice Potter Stewart questioned him:

> JUSTICE STEWART: The District Court in its original opinion and the Court of Appeals in its original affirmance thought that the phrase "in common with all citizens of the territory" was the key and critical phrase, but it may not be.
>
> GORTON: Exactly. The crux of our position here, Mr. Justice Stewart, is that the District Court's decision mandating a 50 percent allocation of anadromous fish to treaty Indians is without support, either in that treaty language or in the circumstances surrounding the execution of the treaties.
>
> Our view is that the treaty language secured for the Indians the right to participate in a common fishery from which they might otherwise have been excluded. In other words, the treaties guaranteed in perpetuity an equal opportunity fishery.[7]

Later, Justice Stewart asked tribal attorney Mason Morisset how he interpreted the same treaty language:

> MORISSET: . . . but I think the important thing for us to get across is that we must construe the treaty as a whole. It was designed to guarantee that the Indians would continue to make a good liveli-

hood fishing. The record is full of evidence and there are findings of fact which support that.

JUSTICE STEWART: Let's say one agreed with you. Didn't then Judge Boldt err in his first decision by thinking almost that he had no discretion, that "in common with" meant 50 percent?

MORISSET: No, I don't think he erred. I think that it is a little dangerous to try to pigeonhole this whole process that the state has, and try to say this was purely a legal decision or purely an equitable decision. I think it was a mixture and there are elements of both. I think he exercised more equity in deciding whether or not it was necessary to have an allocation at all, in which he looked at all the facts. Once he decided that, he decided more or less as a matter of law that's what it was.

JUSTICE STEWART: That "in common with" meant 50 percent, and then the Court of Appeals in affirming it said, well, it is a tenancy in common, and that means 50 percent.[8]

It was difficult for observers to discern how Justice Stewart's intense questioning would influence the final outcome. Following the presentation of arguments, speculation on the outcome of the ruling increased in the Northwest throughout the spring of 1979. Perhaps because of the press of other cases, but perhaps also because of the difficulty of reaching a conclusion in this case, the justices delayed until the day before the Court's term ended to issue their decision. On July 2, 1979, the decision came in by teletype to Seattle.

U.S. V. WASHINGTON UPHELD

In a six-to-three opinion, the Supreme Court upheld Judge Boldt's interpretation of the treaties and his actions following the decision in almost all respects.[9] All nine justices had agreed on the sections of the decision concerning the nature of the Northwest anadromous fisheries, the treaty negotiations and the principal elements of the litigation leading to the review, with the remainder of the decision having the clear majority of six concurring justices. The Supreme Court first dealt with the Washington Supreme

Court's contention that the Boldt decision went against the equal protection principles in the Constitution. The High Court said that this argument was "without merit."[10] In a brisk footnote, it stated:

> The Washington Supreme Court held that the treaties would violate equal protection principles if they provided fishing rights to Indians that were not also available to non-Indians. The simplest answer to this argument is that this Court has already held that these treaties confer enforceable special benefits on signatory Indian tribes, and has repeatedly held that the peculiar semi-sovereign and constitutionally recognized status of Indians justifies special treatment on their behalves when rationally related to the Government's "unique obligation toward the Indians." [Citations omitted.][11]

The court rejected the state's equal opportunity argument as well:

> The State characterizes its interpretation of the treaty language as assuring Indians and non-Indians an "equal opportunity" to take fish from the State's waters. This appellation is misleading. In the first place, even the State recognizes that the treaty provides Indians with certain rights—i.e., the right to fish without a license and to cross private lands—that non-Indians do not have. Whatever opportunities the treaty assures Indians with respect to fish are admittedly not "equal" to, but are to some extent greater than, those afforded other citizens. It is therefore simply erroneous to suggest that the treaty language "confers upon non-Indians precisely the same right to fish as it confers upon Indians." [Citations omitted.]
>
> Moreover, in light of the far superior numbers, capital resources, and technology of the non-Indians, the concept of the Indians' "equal opportunity" to take advantage of a scarce resource is likely in practice to mean that the Indians' "right of taking fish" will net them virtually no catch at all. For the "opportunity" is at best theoretical. Indeed, in 1974, before the District Court's injunction took effect, and while the Indians were still operating under the "equal opportunity" doctrine, their take amounted to approximately 2 percent of the total harvest of salmon and trout in the treaty area.[12]

Reaffirming the Treaty Commitment. Then the High Court considered the nature of the "right of taking fish" that was secured by the treaties. It said that the tribes had reserved the right to the fish and that this right had repeatedly been affirmed by the Supreme Court, beginning with the Winans case and continuing through the Puyallup Trilogy:

> In our view, the purpose and language of the treaties are unambiguous; they secure the Indians' right to take a share of each run of fish that passes through tribal fishing areas. But our prior decisions provide an even more persuasive reason why this interpretation is not open to question. For notwithstanding the bitterness that this litigation has engendered, the principal issue involved is virtually a "matter decided" by our previous holdings.
>
> The Court has interpreted the fishing clause in these treaties on six prior occasions. In all of these cases the Court placed a relatively broad gloss on the Indians' fishing rights and—more or less explicitly—rejected the State's "equal opportunity" approach; in the earliest and the three most recent cases, moreover, we adopted essentially the interpretation that the United States is reiterating here.[13]

The justices reviewed the High Court's earlier decisions and concluded:

> The purport of our cases is clear. Nontreaty fishermen may not rely on property law concepts, devices such as the fish wheel, license fees, or general regulations to deprive the Indians of a fair share of the relevant runs of anadromous fish in the case area. Nor may treaty fishermen rely on their exclusive right of access to the reservations to destroy the rights of other "citizens of the territory." Both sides have a right, secured by treaty, to take a fair share of the available fish. That, we think, is what the parties to the treaty intended when they secured to the Indians the right of taking fish in common with other citizens.[14]

The justices also upheld Judge Boldt's formula for allocating equal Indian and non-Indian shares. They ruled, as had Judge Boldt, that this formula also applied to the American share of those Canadian fish that passed through tribal fishing grounds on their way to the Fraser River. They also reinforced the principle that the United States government had an obligation to police the take of fish by Washington citizens in offshore waters within its 200-mile zone so that the treaty obligations could be fulfilled.

Tribal management authority was left intact. The Supreme Court did not address the issue, although it cited with approval Judge Boldt's findings that nothing in the historical record of the treaty-making indicated that government negotiators had told the Indians of any restrictions in their fishing activities or tribal control over them.

The Supreme Court did make some modifications in Judge Boldt's ruling. He had excluded ceremonial and subsistence catch from the treaty share (non-Indian fishermen also are permitted a subsistence or "take home" catch). He also had excluded the fish caught on the reservations where Indians had exclusive rights spelled out in the treaties. The Supreme Court held that these fish had to be included in the treaty share.

In addition, they viewed the 50 percent allocation to the Indians as a maximum share:

> . . . Indian treaty rights to a natural resource that once was thoroughly and exclusively exploited by the Indians secures so much as, but not more than, is necessary to provide the Indians with a livelihood—that is to say, a moderate living. Accordingly, while the maximum possible allocation to the Indians is fixed at 50 percent, the minimum is not; the latter will, upon proper submission to the District Court, be modified in response to changing circumstances. If, for example, a tribe should dwindle to just a few members, or if it should find other sources of support that lead it to abandon its fisheries, a 45 percent or 50 percent allocation of an entire run that passes through its customary fishing grounds would be manifestly inappropriate because the livelihood of the tribe under those circumstances could not reasonably require an allotment of a large number of fish.[15]

The justices did not, however, spell out the meaning of "moderate income" or how it would be determined if the Indians could support themselves with fewer fish in the future.

The three dissenting justices—Stewart, Powell, and Rehnquist—disagreed with the majority interpretation that the treaties required an apportionment of the fish.[16] Even though in 1973 the Supreme Court had supported apportionment of the steelhead catch between Indian fishermen and sportsmen in Puyallup II, the dissenting justices saw that division as "dictum," and therefore not binding as precedent.[17] This narrow reading of the treaties contrasts sharply with that of the Court's majority.

Stern Talk to the State. The Supreme Court also upheld Judge Boldt's orders for implementing his decision. The justices ruled that the state supreme court could not prohibit, as it had tried to do, the Washington Department of Fisheries from complying with what the district court had ordered: namely, to allocate the fish in accordance with the court ruling. The reason that the state supreme court's prohibition was unlawful was that it violated the Supremacy Clause of the U.S. Constitution, which, in Article Six, binds state judges to rule in accordance with treaties which are made by the United States and are the supreme law of the land.

Furthermore, the justices ruled that "the federal court unquestionably has the power to enter the various orders that state official and private parties have chosen to ignore and even to displace local enforcement of those orders if necessary to remedy the violations of federal law found by the court."[18] In short, Judge Boldt had the authority and had acted properly to step in and order and enforce the fisheries allocation system once the state officials refused to do so.

RESPONSE

The State: Reconsideration and Requests for Aid. The state's response to the U.S. Supreme Court ruling embraced plans both to resist and to cooperate.

Attorney General Gorton, by this time a contender for the Senate seat of Warren G. Magnuson, immediately filed a motion for reconsideration. He also indicated that he would be exploring the issue of "moderate living" to see if the tribes really needed the current 50 percent allocation.[19] Gorton also said he was pleased that the state could now administer the fishery once again, since the state supreme court prohibition against allocation had been overruled.[20] The Washington Supreme Court subsequently reconsidered its ban, as the U.S. Supreme Court decision required it to do, and brought its decision into line with the High Court ruling.

The immediate reaction of some members of the state's congressional delegation to the Supreme Court ruling was to speak of legislation for modifying or "renegotiating the treaties." Later they began to talk of a new program to build up the fish population and coordinate management.[21]

Commercial fishermen, understandably disappointed that their efforts to overturn the Boldt decision had failed, also looked to Congress for relief, particularly for compensation for having to reduce the fleet and money for enhancing the fishery. State Director of Fisheries Gordon Sandison spoke of requesting $200 million from the federal government to implement the ruling.[22]

The Press: Passion and Reflection. The press treated the decision as if it were "the hottest of hot potatoes in Washington State politics."[23] Editorials in major Seattle papers supported the decision. The *Seattle Post-Intelligencer* spoke of a "Fair Share for Indian Fishermen."[24] The *Seattle Times* editorial, viewing the next round in Congress, concluded that "whatever is done next, though, will have to be accomplished within the framework of those ancient treaty agreements, for the 'Boldt decision,' now more than ever, has been affirmed as the 'law' of the land."[25]

The front pages, however, seemed to encourage bitterness over the decision. One *P-I* article described the news thus: "Yesterday's high court ruling upholding the 1974 Boldt decision on Indian fishing rights hit the Fisherman's Terminal in Ballard like a slow rising tide bringing in crud to foul the gear."[26] Above this description was a huge picture of a fisherman beside his two boats, which had "For Sale" signs on them. The caption read: "With 'For Sale' signs on his boat, Dan Severson was angry at the Supreme Court decision." Two days later, in a tiny box on page seven, the *P-I* "clarified" its earlier caption by stating that "Severson since has explained that the boat's 'For Sale' signs had nothing to do with the court ruling or the Boldt decision."[27]

The press carried stories on Indian reactions to the ruling on July 3 as well. The *Post-Intelligencer* relegated its story, "Indians

Hail 'Complete Vindication,'" to page seven.[28] The *Seattle Times* similarly gave non-Indian fishermen top coverage, placing its headline story, "Fishermen Upset By High-Court Decision," across the top of a page. The story "Indians Pleased By Ruling On Boldt" was placed in two columns in the bottom corner of the page.[29]

The Judge: An Elated Farewell. One person very pleased with the decision was Judge Boldt, now seventy-five years old and in full-time retirement. In a rare television interview he recounted to KIRO reporter Ken Woo that he felt "quite elated" upon hearing of the decision—"in fact, so much so that I was quivering a little."[30] He told newspaper reporters that the Supreme Court ruling "is a victory for justice"[31] and that "it brings me, in my decision, to a conclusion. It is, for me, the end of my decision-making; I'm totally withdrawn from the court now. . . ."[32]

Indian Fishermen: An End and a Beginning. Indians who had participated in the case saw the U.S. Supreme Court ruling as both conclusion and beginning.

They looked back on the decades of fish-ins and litigation and looked forward to increasing participation in the fishery, both as fishermen and as co-managers of the salmon passing through their fishing grounds. Forrest Kinley, a Lummi tribal fisherman and councilman who had contributed lengthy testimony to the Boldt court, reflected: "It's been a long struggle, but it's certainly not over. . . . We've got to be happy, there's no two ways about it. . . . But we've now got to protect the resource and get back into managing the fishing."[33] And Bill Frank, Jr., who had persisted in the fish-ins that led to the early case on the treaty rights of the Nisqually and Puyallup tribes, stressed the need for Congress to pass legislation to implement the Boldt decision as soon as possible. "We hope that Congress will start writing to protect that contract we signed back in 1855."[34]

Chapter 8

Fishing the Columbia: Can Negotiation Replace Litigation?

As the controversy in western Washington churned on through public outcry, court orders, task force scrutinies, and U.S. Supreme Court review, events on the Columbia River to the south took a different turn. There, tribes seeking to restore their fishing rights agreed to put negotiation to the test: they promised to abide by a plan for harvest and management which pledged to deliver them their fish.

A Different Situation. The situation on the Columbia River differs in many respects from that on Puget Sound and the Washington coast. The river, once renowned for the world's largest runs of chinook and steelhead, and for abundant coho and sockeye, has become the Northwest's center for hydroelectric power production.[1] Dams within the Columbia Basin, impounding the Columbia itself, the Snake, and their tributaries, have reduced by half the habitat accessible to spawning salmon.[2] In the past the most plentiful runs were of wild chinook and steelhead that spawn upriver—that is, above today's Bonneville Dam, which lies some 150 river miles inland from the Pacific Ocean. Now these runs are the most threatened.[3] An important reason for their decrease is that federally-funded hatcheries, built largely to replace upriver

118

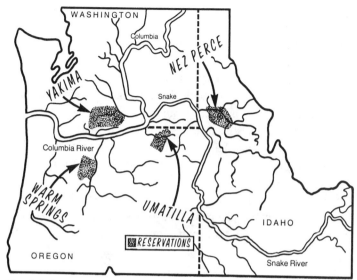

Fig. 8.1 Reservations of Columbia River treaty tribes (SOURCE: Columbia River Inter-Tribal Fish Commission)

runs diminished by dams, were placed in the lower river. The salmon that return to these hatchery sites are now harvested by non-Indian fishermen in the ocean and the lower river, while the Columbia River tribes continue to depend on those chinook, steelhead, and sockeye that were spawned upriver and that were able to get past the dams to return home. The tribes rely upon these runs for their culture and livelihood.

The Columbia fishery offers further differences:

1. There is one river system to manage, rather than the multitude of rivers in western Washington, and that system has far fewer fish to allocate.

2. Indians from four reservations share treaty-fishing rights along the river, while members of five times as many reservations exercise treaty fishing rights in western Washington. The Columbia River Indians are the Nez Perce Tribe in Idaho, both the Con-

federated Tribes of the Umatilla Reservation and the Confederated Tribes of the Warm Springs Reservation in Oregon, and the Confederated Tribes and Bands of the Yakima Indian Nation in Washington (see fig. 8.1).

3. State governments in Oregon and Idaho, which share jurisdiction over the Columbia with Washington state, have not made Indian fishing a key political issue. This is an especially significant difference. These states, while not particularly sympathetic to Indian rights, have had no political personage comparable to former Washington Attorney General Slade Gorton to champion a crusade against Indians. One tribal fisheries manager from the Columbia River likened Washington state's resistance to Indian treaty-fishing to the adamant stance of southern segregationists who literally blocked the entry of black children into white schools. The manager commented: "Washington stands in the schoolhouse door. Oregon just pats us on the heads."

Columbia River tribes, like their counterparts north on Puget Sound, had gained the ear of the courts by fishing contrary to state regulations. Five years after a 1958 fish-in by three Umatillas, a federal court affirmed the tribe's treaty right to fish. (See *Maison* v. *Confederated Tribes of the Umatilla,* pp. 68–69.) The judge also declared that Oregon could restrict Indian fishing in the name of conservation, but only if restrictions on other fishermen failed to preserve the fish. Five years later still, war hero Richard Sohappy and his uncle, David, both Yakimas, staged the fish-in that produced the 1969 ruling in *Sohappy* v. *Smith* (later consolidated into *U.S.* v. *Oregon,* and also known as the "Belloni decision.") Not only did Judge Belloni assign the tribes "a fair and equitable share" of Oregon's fish, he also called for a management system that could secure the Indian right and still accommodate the needs of the biological system. (See pp. 77–80.)

A System of Zones. Oregon's response to this ruling was to use a two-part system similar to the one established in 1957 when The Dalles Dam inundated the tribes' major usual and accustomed fishing sites at Celilo Falls. This system provided for a general

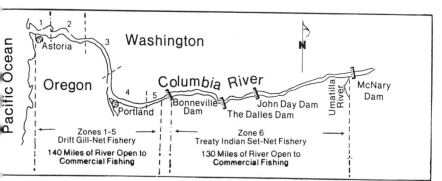

Fig. 8.2 Map of the Columbia River below McNary Dam showing areas open to commercial fishing (SOURCE: Columbia River Intertribal Fish Commission, CRITFC News, Vol. 5, No. 1, Jan./Feb./March 1982)

commercial fishery from the mouth of the Columbia River at the Pacific on upstream to the Bonneville Dam. Non-Indians could fish commercially on this 140-mile stretch of river in Zones 1 through 5 (see fig. 8.2). Above Bonneville, in a 130-mile-long stretch designated Zone 6, including the area where Celilo Falls once was, only Indians could fish commercially. Because non-Indians could catch most of the fish before they reached the Indian fishery zone, in 1970 the Indians actually caught *less*—both in terms of percentages and in actual numbers of fish—than they had caught prior to the 1969 *Sohappy* v. *Smith* decision.[4]

In May 1974, Judge Belloni adopted for the Columbia River the 50-50 harvest allocation and provision for tribal co-management of Judge Boldt's ruling in *U.S.* v. *Washington.* Years of what Judge Belloni termed a "commuter run" between Oregon state agencies and the courthouse followed this decision, as the tribes continued to seek their "fair share" and state agencies continued to resist implementation. Although there was good fishing on some runs in some years—e.g., the autumn 1976 and 1977 runs of fall chinook salmon—in most years few salmon reached the tribes. Some Oregon non-Indian fishermen and buyers defied the ensuing court orders that limited non-Indian fishing,[5] but public outcry and outlaw fishing along the Columbia never reached the massive proportions they achieved in Puget Sound.

Five-Year Trial for Joint Management. Following the years of commuter litigation, the tribes, states, and federal government negotiated a comprehensive management plan. An agreement between Oregon, Washington, and the tribes, the plan entered as a federal court order by Judge Belloni on February 28, 1977. It was binding for five years and had far-reaching provisions. Entitled "A Plan for Managing Fisheries on Stocks Originating from the Columbia River to Its Tributaries above Bonneville Dam," it became generally known as the "Five-Year Plan."

Judge Belloni saw the plan as a means to avoid the battles that had occurred repeatedly in his court and which persisted in Puget Sound. He strongly encouraged all parties to enter into it. Some Indian tribal leaders and fishermen recall that his encouragement felt like pressure: as they perceived it, "we were ordered." They believed, however, that if the fish runs maintained their level, the plan had a chance of working out.

The judge's remarks upon signing the plan into law indicate his high hopes and expectations:

> The extreme importance of this settlement and consent decree is difficult to express. Every person in the Northwest gains by it. It's the most important development involving Columbia River Indian Treaty Fishing Rights and Responsibilities since the treaties became effective in 1855. The settlement will have a meritorious effect not only upon Indian and non-Indian fishermen, but on many of our other major industries, such as tourism and fish processing, food processing.
>
> It's interesting to compare the negotiation and signing of this agreement with the negotiation and signing of the original treaties. The Indians were displaced persons, using a totally unfamiliar language, and were represented by chiefs who were appointed by the Federal Negotiators. This time, well-informed tribal members were freely chosen leaders, represented by the finest legal counsel, reached an arms-length agreement. The past few years have been traumatic ones. Fishermen have been disappointed and angry, jus-

tifiably so. The economic loss has hurt badly. The responsible state agency officials must have been—must have felt—frustrated many times. It has been equally traumatic to me. *Yet I have had to be firm and apply the law as it is. It was my Constitutional duty. Had I yielded to the strong temptation to bend a little to relieve some of the pressure, this agreement would never have been reached, and the trauma would have continued. Not only was the integrity of the law at stake, but so was the very survival of the salmon resource in the Columbia River.* [Emphasis added.]

Of course, problems will continue to plague us. All of our problems are not solved. The Court might be called upon to resolve some disputes. But now, everyone knows the rules of the road. We have a pact voluntarily reached by informed people. This is far better than having rules imposed by a Court or any other outside agency.

I have followed the negotiations from the beginning. I have had a copy of the agreement for a few weeks, and I've carefully studied it. I wholeheartedly accept it and make it a decree of this Court."⁶

Provisions and Promises. Major goals in the plan were to conserve and enhance the resource, to allocate it fairly, and to provide a mechanism for Indian involvement in management decisions so that the frequent court battles of previous years would be avoided.⁷ In its key provisions, the plan's sharing formula for the Columbia River allotted 60 percent of the fall chinook run to treaty fishermen—for ceremonial, subsistence and commercial harvest—and 40 percent to non-treaty fishermen. Washington's and Oregon's goal was that, through proper management, a harvestable run of 200,000 fall chinook would return to the river mouth. For the spring chinook run, the sharing formula was reversed: 40 percent to Indian fishermen and 60 percent to non-Indian fishermen. Both states' goal for the spring run was a minimum average run of 250,000 chinook at the rivermouth. Additional provisions were made for coho and sockeye runs, expected to be much smaller than the chinook.

In an important conciliatory move towards sports fishermen, the tribes agreed not to target steelhead as a commercial harvest. To assure the sportsmen a supply, Indians would limit their commercial catch of steelhead to those caught incidentally along with other runs.[8]

The plan included many promises among the parties:

—Tribal, state, and federal agencies agreed to work cooperatively to maintain present runs, rehabilitate declining runs, and to develop larger runs through enhancement projects. (Such efforts could include habitat maintenance as well as fish-rearing programs.)

—The managing agencies agreed to "make every effort to allocate the available harvest as prescribed by the agreement on an annual basis."[9] If their efforts failed, they would arrange for adjustments to be made within the five-year time frame, so that fishermen who caught less than their share in one year would receive compensatory allocations in a subsequent year.

—The plan also established a Technical Advisory Committee (TAC) with fisheries scientists representing Oregon, Washington, Idaho, the National Marine Fisheries Service, the U.S. Fish and Wildlife Service, and each of the four tribes. The TAC was to develop and analyze data and to make recommendations to the managing agencies, especially the Columbia River Compact, the joint Washington-Oregon agency that establishes regulations for Columbia River fishing.

The plan was a sharing agreement for the river. It did not include a sharing formula for fish caught before the runs could return to the Columbia, but it did take notice of the ocean fishermen, who were catching many immature fish native to the Columbia River (and to coastal Washington as well) as these pooled with other fish out at sea. Fish in this pool, called "mixed stocks," respect no political boundaries and range from the waters off Northern California up through Canada to Alaska. Fishermen seek them out all along the way. The mixed-stock pools contain fish from many streams, both wild fish and hatchery-bred ones. The parties to the plan agreed to "joint efforts to collect and gather data on this fishery and to reduce inefficient and wasteful harvest methods."[10] Participants would then make recommendations for better management of the ocean fishery to the Pacific Fisheries Management Council (PFMC), one of the regional federal regulatory commissions responsible for fishing within the 200-mile limit of ocean the U.S. claimed.

Columbia River Indians Establish Inter-Tribal Fish Commission. In 1977, after the plan was negotiated, the Columbia River tribes formed an intertribal body to coordinate their fisheries management policies and to provide tribal decision-makers with technical information. The preamble to their constitution and by-laws echoed those of the tribes to the north, with whom they established a formal alliance:

> We, the Indians of the Columbia River Inter-Tribal Fish Commission, recognize that our fisheries are a basic and important natural resource and of vital concern to the Indians of these states and that the conservation of this resource is dependent upon effective and progressive management. And that it is further recognized that federal court decisions have specifically established that the Tribes have treaty rights to an equitable share of the Columbia Basin fishery resource. We further believe that by unity of action we can best accomplish these things, not only for the benefit of our own people but for all of the people of the Pacific Northwest.[11]

The commission set to work helping member tribes deal with the Columbia River Five-Year Plan.

HIGH GOALS, LOW YIELDS

Paper Harvests. The plan contained impressive goals but few guarantees. Its run size and harvest goals had been based on the relatively large runs of 1975 and 1976 and optimistic views about the possibility of further increases by habitat rehabilitation and fish-rearing programs. But runs did not increase; they shrank.

Throughout the five years of the plan the runs were disappointing. Reasons for the poor returns included the 1975 and 1976 drought and the completion of dams on the Snake River. Spring chinook stocks, for example, were so depressed that after 1977 *no* commercial fishing was permitted for either Indians or non-Indians.[12] Fishing for fall chinook thus became the major source of income for Columbia River fishermen.

The fall chinook run consists of two distinct stocks of fish: "tules" (pronounced too-lees) and "brights." Tules are a lower-river stock, mostly reared and released from hatcheries. Tules are close to the spawning stage by the time they enter the Columbia. Brights, however, are predominantly wild fish, originating upriver above Bonneville Dam. They are not yet ready to spawn when they enter the river; thus the name bright, referring to the silver bright appearance they retain longer than do tules. Tribal members value brights more highly, both for food and for ceremonial purposes. Brights also bite more readily at the sportsman's hook, have firmer flesh, and bring a higher price commercially than the tules.[13]

While the treaty catch before the Five-Year Plan was 122,300 fish in 1975 and 121,500 in 1976, the harvest fell by more than half by 1981.[14] Furthermore, many of the fish caught by Indians were the less valuable tules, rather than the brights. At the end of the five years, the plan had delivered nearly the percentage of fish allocated (the deficit owed to the tribes was about 5,000 fish[15]). The problem lay not so much in the allocation formula but in the diminished numbers of fish returning to the river.

There was also concern among the tribes that the Technical Advisory Committee (TAC), on which tribal biologists served, did not give Indians a big enough role in decision-making. Instead of joint meetings to develop management recommendations, the state biologists prepared their own reports for the compact. Tribal biologists could only make responses, which appear to have been given little weight.[16] In September 1980, when the tribes objected to part of the compact's 1980 harvest plan, Federal District Court Judge Walter Craig, now the presiding judge overseeing the Five-Year Plan, ordered all members to develop a means to improve the TAC.

Thus several problems on the Columbia River—especially depressed runs, and problems in co-management—hindered the

Five-Year Plan. However, a key factor impeding the plan's effectiveness lay far beyond the Columbia River itself. That problem was the ocean troll fishery.

The Ocean Barrier to Inland Fishing. The Indians shared the problem of declining catches with the Columbia's non-Indian fishermen. All river fishermen suffered the effects of a major problem: a voracious ocean troll fishery.

The problem is not new. In 1976, a year prior to the inception of the Five-Year Plan, the Columbia Basin Salmon and Steelhead Analysis prepared for the joint state-federal Pacific Northwest Regional Commission stated:

> Due to mixing of salmon stocks in the ocean, the indiscriminate nature of the fisheries is a potentially serious threat to troubled wild runs of the upper Columbia and Snake rivers.
> The ocean fisheries intercept the vast majority of Columbia River coho and fall chinook salmon that would otherwise return to the Columbia River.[17]

The federal Fisheries Conservation and Management Act of 1976 led to increased regulation of ocean harvesters, but not enough. Indeed, one federal analysis indicated that prior to 1980, the ocean catch off Washington, Oregon, Alaska, and Canada accounted for 64 percent of the Columbia River fall chinook destined for the upper reaches of the Columbia. To permit adequate escapement for spawning, river fishermen, Indian and non-Indian, would be able to harvest less than 20 percent of the river's total production.[18]

Problems at Sea: Prediction, Allocation, and Conservation. The Five-Year Plan had included provisions to deal with ocean fishermen. Parties to the plan were to make recommendations to the PFMC, the federal commission that is responsible for the regulation of Oregon, California, and Washington coastal waters. Two parties to the Five-Year Plan—Washington state, through the Department of Fisheries, and Oregon, through the Department of Fish and Wildlife—sit on the PFMC. Both, along with representatives of other states, the federal government and the commercial and recreational fishing industry, are also members of the North Pacific Fishery Management Council (NPFMC), which manages Alaskan coastal waters (Columbia River chinook swim through the jurisdictional waters of both councils and through Canadian waters as well) (see fig. 8.3). The two councils were established by the Department of Commerce and represent primarily commercial interests.

The councils that manage the ocean fishery follow a complex process of forecasting runs and establishing seasons. By definition, the stocks of the mixed-stock ocean fishery have not separated one from another and the size of a run is hard to estimate. The councils set harvest seasons in the context of strong pressure from ocean fishermen, who argue that they need the fish to make a living.[19] To these fishermen, the fish caught at sea by the troller's hook appear ideal for the market: they have no net marks and their flesh is firm. Some say they are the perfect size for the cook's fry pan. If the PFMC, to protect a weak run from within the mixed stock, curtails fishing, it means that ocean fishermen will miss out on the harvest of the strong runs, thus "wasting" fish that could otherwise be caught.

The Columbia River tribes had the opposite perspective, believing that the seasons set by the PFMC permitted too much rather than too little ocean fishing. The Indians saw themselves bearing the burden of conserving what remnants of runs actually reached the river.[20] The tribes subsequently began challenging in court the seasons set by the PFMC and the Secretary of Commerce.

RECOURSE TO LITIGATION

A Suit for Commerce. The suits were brought against the Secretary of Commerce over the ocean regulations. One of the first judges to be presented with these cases was Robert Belloni, the author of the Sohappy decision and the hopeful proponent of the Five-Year Plan. In July 1979, two and a half years into the Five-Year Plan, the tribes that were parties to the Columbia River

United States
-
NORTH PACIFIC
FISHERY MANAGEMENT
COUNCIL waters...
3-200 miles

CANADIAN waters...
0-200 miles

Columbia
River

Cape Falcon

United States
-
PACIFIC FISHERY
MANAGEMENT
COUNCIL waters...
3-200 miles

Fig. 8.3 Ocean jurisdiction map (SOURCE: Columbia River Inter-Tribal Fish Commission)

agreement brought suit against the U.S. Secretary of Commerce, Juanita Kreps, over the off-shore regulations that the Pacific Fisheries Management Council had issued for the ocean summer season. In *Confederated Tribes* v. *Kreps*[21] the tribes charged that the ocean troll season would permit non-Indians to catch too many coho and fall chinook and would thereby prevent Indians from harvesting their share on the upper river. Judge Belloni permitted the Shoshone-Bannock Tribe of Idaho to join in the suit because it had a treaty right to a subsistence harvest of four salmon per family.

The attorney for the trollers then insisted that Judge Belloni remove himself from the case for bias in favor of the Indians. In a surprise move, Judge Belloni agreed to step down. His subsequent remarks contrasted sharply with his earlier optimism over the Columbia River agreement and depicted his growing frustration with efforts to assure the Indian right to fish. Speaking of the Shoshone, who were last in line for the fish, he said:

> I would hope to have these two questions addressed:
> 1. Does the Secretary of Commerce and those intervening on her side believe that a court of the United States does not have the power to protect these treaty rights?
> 2. Are there provisions in her plan to guarantee that the ocean catch will not take from a Shoshone family its four fish per year?[22]

Judge Belloni also agreed with the trollers' contention that he had a personal prejudice in the case that would interfere with his ability to handle the issue impartially:

> I have great empathy with the Shoshone Family and their fight to retain their four salmon per year. I will admit that it is inconceivable to me that a court of the United States is powerless to protect that family.
> I will admit an almost disbelief when I see cartoons in the newspapers where the Indian and the white fisherman are fighting over the last fish in the Columbia River. The Indian in the cartoon is the same size and has the same strength as the other fisherman. The true picture more resembles an elephant and a mouse.
> I commenced hearing the series of Indian fishing cases in 1967.

I was then certainly without a bias. If anything, I might have even believed the Indian was the greedy one because like everyone else, I read newspapers. After literally thousands of hours of study and hearing evidence, the facts come through strong and clear. The facts themselves cause one to have strong beliefs. We excuse jurors because they know too much about the facts. A judge should accept the same standards that he requires of his jurors.[23]

Several weeks after Judge Belloni stepped down, Judge William Schwarzer of the U.S. District Court of Oregon, heard the case. The federal government presented its arguments against those of the tribes.

Alliances Shift. An Indian woman observing the trial in *Confederated Tribes* v. *Kreps* wanted to know, "Where is the United States government, Justice or Interior? Where is our trustee?"[24]

The answer was that government forces had been marshaled to support the Commerce Department and its plan for the trollers. The same government which had helped see *United States* v. *Oregon* and *United States* v. *Washington* through the courts now shifted its alliance over the ocean issue. The Secretary of the Interior had written to Commerce Secretary Kreps in the spring and early summer asking her to reduce the troll season for conservation purposes and to provide a more equitable allocation between outside, ocean fishermen, and inside fishermen, including treaty Indians.[25] This she refused to do. Both the Department of Interior, backing a reduced season, and the Department of Commerce, backing the PFMC season, presented their biological assessments to the Justice Department. Officials in the Justice Department maintained that the department could only argue in support of one of these sides. The Justice Department chose to accept the Commerce Department's pro-troller position, accepting both the ocean run size that Commerce had predicted and the ocean season it had set. (This decision so angered the U.S. Attorney for Oregon, Sidney Lezak, by what he considered its poor treatment of the Indians, that he refused to participate in the government's brief defending Kreps.[26])

On July 3, 1979, the U.S. Supreme Court had issued its ruling substantially affirming *U.S.* v. *Washington.* (See Chapter 7.) Judge Schwarzer thus ordered Kreps to draft emergency regulations that would be in line with the treaty obligations as spelled out by the Supreme Court. She complied.

The tribes soon found themselves in court again, challenging PFMC ocean seasons. In the summer of 1981, the tribes brought two cases against the new Secretary of Commerce, Malcolm Baldrige: *Confederated Tribes and Bands of the Yakima Indian et al.* v. *Baldrige* and *Hoh Tribe et al.* v. *Baldrige.*[27] The rulings of Judge Walter Craig of the U.S. District Court of Western Washington had important implications for the future management of the ocean fishery. In *Confederated Tribes* v. *Baldrige,* Judge Craig did not accede to a tribal request to curtail the 1981 PFMC seasons. He did order the parties to meet with the court's technical adviser to develop a "reasonably satisfactory decision." He emphasized the importance of conservation and of treaty rights, stressing that these take precedence over economic concerns.[28] In *Hoh* v. *Baldrige,* a case brought by western Washington tribes also affected by the ocean fishery, Judge Craig considered the contention of the Hoh, Quileute, and Quinault tribes of the Washington coast that PFMC management practices had denied them their treaty-protected allocation. In particular, they argued that their allocation could not come from aggregates of different runs of fish, but that a river-by-river, run-by-run basis was required. The judge required Baldrige to reconsider his plan and agreement was reached on the principle of allocation desired by the tribes.[29] Judge Craig ordered these tribes also to work with the court's technical adviser and the other parties to develop a long-term plan.

In both cases, Judge Craig noted that the PFMC had substantially reduced ocean harvests since 1977.[30] Nonetheless, the tribes still bore the burden of conservation when forecasts were overly optimistic. The plans that he ordered the parties to negotiate were to "attempt to develop practical and flexible rules for management of the fisheries in accordance with the tribes' treaty rights and other applicable law."[31] These negotiations are still going on.

Missing Fish and a Salmon Sting. During this time, the National Marine Fisheries Service, an agency in the Department of Commerce—defendant in the lawsuits described above—began an undercover investigation of Indian fishing on the Columbia River. From April 1981 to May 1982, its agents ran a fish-buying company called "Advanced Marketing Research" in the hills behind Cook's Landing. The activities of this operation culminated in an early morning raid on Indian fishermen.[32] Among those charged were David Sohappy, uncle of war hero Richard Sohappy and an original defendant in *Sohappy* v. *Smith,* and many of his family.

The fishermen at Cook's Landing had long challenged restrictive regulations by both tribes and states. Fishing was extremely important to David Sohappy: he has frequently opposed the regulations. As he said in 1979, "We will always have a net in the water . . . when the time comes that we can no longer put a net in the water, that's the time when everything will be lost."[33]

During this same time, officials noticed that each year about 40,000 fall chinook disappeared between the time they were counted at Bonneville Dam and the date they were awaited, three dams later, at McNary Dam on the Columbia River where they were expected to spawn. (The deficit took into account expected reductions due to legal harvests and to fish diverting into tributaries.) In the publicity surrounding the salmon sting, the National Marine Fisheries Service suggested that illegal Indian fishing was responsible for the missing fish.[34]

The Columbia River Inter-Tribal Fish Commission, while not discounting the seriousness of poaching, pointed out that nearly all the confiscated fish were spring chinook, yet the 40,000 missing fish were fall chinook. The commission also noted that the alleged illegal catch, fifty-three tons or about 6,000 fish in all, was small compared with that taken by non-Indian ocean trollers. Of the fifty-three tons of fish confiscated, twenty tons were said to be upriver chinook; the ocean fishery, in contrast, caught 1,000 tons of upriver chinook.[35] Others, Indians and non-Indians alike, worried that the amount and type of publicity generated by the federal government's arrests on the Columbia—and in a similar undercover operation against poaching in Northern California—would make a fair trial for the defendants difficult.

A series of trials, involving about 100 cases in several jurisdictions, were held from 1982 to 1984. In three of these trials, thirteen defendants were convicted in April 1983 of breaking a federal law against the violation of state and tribal fishing regulations. The defendants also were accused of a conspiracy to sell the fish, but were not convicted of that charge.[36] David Sohappy, his son, David, Jr., and his nephew, Bruce Jim, received maximum sentences of five years in federal prison and five years' probation. One of their attorneys, Jack Schwartz, has expressed concern that the tribes, non-Indians, and the more established legal defense groups did not lend support to these fishermen who had spearheaded the early fishing rights struggle. The National Lawyers Guild coordinated the defense. The convicted fishermen are currently appealing their convictions. Schwartz describes these events as a concerted attack upon the Columbia River fishermen, especially those at Cook's Landing and Celilo, Oregon.[37]

Despite these convictions, the missing-fish mystery remained unsolved. Approximately the same percentage of fish continued to disappear after the sting operation. In 1982 an Enforcement Task Force, including support and participation from the tribes, escorted the fall chinook runs from their entry of the river up to McNary Dam and patrolled heavily during the season. A 50 percent increase in patrol efforts produced arrests and citations for illegal fishing, 93 percent of them non-Indian, but still about half the bright fall chinook run disappeared.[38] A National Marine Fisheries Service study, which radio-tagged fall chinook and then tracked them upstream, revealed some surprising preliminary results: the "lost fish" appeared to be spawning in such areas as the mouth of the Deschutes River, before they reached McNary Dam. According to biologists, interdam spawning, hatchery release problems, environmental problems, (which prevent the fish from navigating intermediate dams) and perhaps even the counting methods themselves seemed likely prospects for further study to resolve this mystery.[39]

The tribes have voiced considerable concern about the impact of the salmon sting and the initial placement of blame for the annual fish disappearance upon Indians. S. Timothy Wapato, executive director of the Columbia River Inter-Tribal Fish Commission, has stated that "contrary to widespread publicity concerning presumed largescale Indian poaching activities, there is no supporting evidence that it is a major conservation problem which explains the loss of some 40,000 fish between Columbia River dams. Blaming Columbia River tribes for these problems is irresponsible, and a disservice to the tribes. It discredits the abilities of all fisheries management entities and calls into question their sincerity."[40]

CONCLUSION: AFTER THE FIVE-YEAR PLAN, WHAT NEXT?

In January 1982, the Columbia River tribes' Council of Councils unanimously declared the Five-Year Plan a failure.[41] Subsequently, two tribes, the Umatilla and the Yakima, took a further step and formally notified the U.S. District Court of their withdrawal from the plan. Programs that were promised to increase stocks that spawned upriver had not been accomplished. Appropriate ocean regulations still were not in place. Negotiation had not spared the tribes from litigation. Indeed, it was recently observed that "a scorecard will soon be needed to track all the legal actions that involve Columbia River tribes."[42]

Judge Craig, successor to Judge Belloni and Schwarzer, ordered the plan's participants to negotiate further to develop a new proposal. In working out a new arrangement, the tribes are proposing an equitable distribution of fish between ocean and river fishermen and increased releases of lower river hatchery fish into upriver areas, where they will return to Indian fishermen. New programs for habitat improvement, stream-flow regulation, and improved passage facilities at dams, projected as part of the Northwest Regional Power Act of 1980, hold promise if the act's provisions can be well-implemented.[43] If successful, such programs could increase the runs and thus ease the problems caused by dwindling harvests.

Nonetheless, a comprehensive plan for Columbia River salmon and steelhead—one that views management of the fishery within the context of the entire cycle of the salmon—has not yet been completed. As of the winter of 1984–85, negotiations between the parties were still ongoing. Such a plan, forcefully implemented and consistent with Indian treaty rights, was still being awaited some fifteen years after *Sohappy* v. *Smith* and some seven years after the initiation of the Five-Year Plan.

Chapter 9

Securing the Habitat

Tribal fishing rights mean nothing unless there are fish for Indians to catch. Empty waters mean empty nets—and empty rights.

Judge Boldt recognized this issue and the difficult problems it raised when he began hearing *U.S.* v. *Washington*. He thus isolated the topic and assigned it to the Phase II portion of the case for separate consideration.

It took six years after the decision on Phase I for Phase II to come to judgment. Judge Boldt retired from the bench for health reasons—he was 76 years old—in 1979. U.S. District Court Judge William Orrick had been assigned to the case shortly before Judge Boldt retired. He began hearing arguments on April 10, 1980.

TWO QUESTIONS FOR PHASE II

Phase II dealt with two questions:

Did the Indian share of the harvest include artificially-propagated fish and fish bred in hatcheries?[1] Both are techniques to increase production, the former being any facility even a simple streamside incubation box, the latter being the more elaborate facilities with buildings, raceways, etc.

Did the treaties contain an implicit right protecting the runs from human destruction?

The two questions were intertwined. Overfishing was only one cause of declines in the natural runs. Dam builders, loggers, farmers, industrialists, and developers had failed to protect the natural habitat and so shared with fishermen the responsibility for the reduced population of wild fish. The breeding of hatchery fish was in part an effort to replace natural stocks whose environment had been violated.

Despite the connection between environmental degradation and the development of hatcheries, the two issues had come before Judge Orrick's court by separate routes.

Do Treaties Include Hatchery Fish? The question of the right of Indians to catch hatchery-bred fish arose during the second round of the case *Puyallup Tribe* v. *Department of Game*.[2] This was the case that was to make three trips to the U.S. Supreme Court. In the first round, the Supreme Court had upheld the right of Puyallup fishermen to use nets to catch both salmon (managed by the state Department of Fisheries) and steelhead (managed by the state Department of Game) in the Puyallup River. The justices had also said that in the interest of conservation, the state could regulate Indian fishing providing the rules met appropriate standards and did not discriminate against Indian fishermen. This first decision in 1968 is known as Puyallup I.[3]

When the Department of Game subsequently banned Indians from catching steelhead on the river, the Puyallups went back to the Supreme Court, claiming they were being discriminated against. The Court agreed in 1973.[4] In this second round of hearings (Puyallup II), Game Department officials held that most of the steelhead in the river were hatchery fish from a program substantially financed by license fees paid by white sports fishermen. Although the court did not rule on this issue, three justices suggested in a concurring opinion that hatchery fish subsidized by sports fishermen should not be included with fish the treaties promised to Indians.[5] The case reached the Court for the third time (Puyallup III), when the justices were asked to re-examine the subsequent 45 percent allocation of steelhead, but again the Court, in its 1977 decision, did not rule on the hatchery issue.[6]

Throughout Phase I of *U.S.* v. *Washington,* Judge Boldt had not distinguished between wild fish and hatchery fish. Whether Indians did indeed have a right to hatchery fish was the problem left for Judge Orrick to determine in Phase II of *U.S.* v. *Washington*. Judge Orrick explained that "the hatchery issue thus entered this litigation collaterally, as a spin-off from Puyallup II, and was later broadened by the parties here to the question whether all hatchery-bred fish should be excluded from the allocation."[7]

Do the Treaties Protect Fish Habitats? Following a separate route through the courts, the issue of protection for fish habitats appeared in 1970, when the Department of Justice originally filed *U.S.* v. *Washington* and the tribes raised the question. Judge Boldt set that determination aside to be considered under Phase II of the case. By asking for environmental protection for the fish in Phase II, the tribes exacerbated the federal government's long-standing ambivalence about its role as tribal advocate. Federal dollars had paid for many of the dams that made the rivers inaccessible to fish. This fact was not lost upon either federal or state officials. Federal officials feared additional lawsuits to determine who—the federal government, the state, private companies, or individuals—had done the damage in specific cases. One federal official interviewed for this book, who asked not to be named, said his colleagues had seemed to wish the case "would die a natural death."

There is evidence to suggest that the federal government reluctantly agreed to continue its role in Phase II of *U.S.* v. *Washington* only when the tribes agreed not to sue for damages suffered in previous losses of fish caused by destructive environmental policies. In return, the federal government would continue to provide the support the tribes needed to pursue Phase II.[8]

Washington state officials voiced their concerns about the impact of the case as soon as the Supreme Court ruling upholding Phase I made pursuit of a decision in Phase II seem sure to follow. Governor Dixy Lee Ray told reporters in July 1979 that "were all the claims now identified by various Indian tribes to be granted, it would totally break the bank so far as the economy of the state and the nation is concerned. . . . If taken to the extreme, Phase II would give the Indian citizens a very large amount of control over entire areas."[9]

The larger implications of the case were also perceived by environmentalists such as the Federation of Western Outdoor Clubs, which counted among its members the Sierra Club, the Admiralty Audubon Society, and the Mountaineering Club of Alaska. In 1978, the federation had sent members to hear a panel of Indians and conservationists discuss the issue. Several leaders from each group subsequently met to explore common concerns. In addition, a conference for Indians and conservationists was held at the Daybreak Star Indian Cultural Center in Seattle on September 28–30, 1979. The meeting was co-sponsored by the American Friends Service Committee, tribal groups, and environmental organizations.

One official of the Federation of Western Outdoor Clubs commented that "the closer you look at this controversy, the more you realize it isn't an Indian problem."[10] In March 1979, Hazel Wolf, a former president of the federation, wrote the federation constituency and asked for support to prepare an *amicus curiae* brief to the federal district court hearing Phase II of *U.S.* v. *Washington*. In her letter, she stated:

> It is the Federation's belief that the Second Phase, to which our brief will be addressed, is of concern not only to the Indian tribes but to non-Indian fishermen and conservationists on behalf of the general public's interest in the preservation of the environment. In the Second Phase, it is contended that the State of Washington has inadequately enforced the environmental laws such as the Shorelands Management Act, the Forest Practices Act, the Hydraulic Act and others, which is its obligation under Indian treaties.
>
> Much blame for the decline in the fishery resource has been laid to the aggressiveness of Indians, with little attention to major environmental sources of degradation such as logging, road-building, stream channelization, dams, agricultural practices, etc. Efforts by Indians to so identify the environmental causes may not get the credence they are entitled to because of the Indian's obvious economic stake in the matter. Expression of these views by an *amicus* brief filed by the Federation having no such direct economic stake

will help to focus attention on these serious questions. We also believe that our *amicus* will contribute to changing the widespread misconception of this as a racial conflict. The successful outcome of this lawsuit would provide a new source of environmental control of value to the entire community.[11]

DISTRICT COURT RULING: PHASE II, ROUND I

The U.S. Supreme Court decision, substantially affirming Judge Boldt's decision on Phase I, set the stage for a ruling on Phase II. Judge Orrick heard arguments on April 10, 1980, and handed down his decision on September 26. Judge Orrick ruled that hatchery-bred and artificially-propagated fish were "fish" within the meaning of the treaties and therefore should be included in the tribal share; and that the right to have the fishery habitat protected from man-made despoliation was implicit in the treaty fishing clause.[12]

Because the treaty itself contained no language concerning either hatcheries or environmental protection, Judge Orrick based his analysis upon the accepted judicial canons of treaty interpretation. Thus treaties must be interpreted to promote their central purpose, and in the way that the Indians at the time would have understood them. All ambiguities must be resolved in the Indians' favor; this is consistent with the general legal doctrine that whenever contracts are made between parties with unequal bargaining power, the court will interpret ambiguities against the stronger party and in favor of the weaker one.

These rules of treaty interpretation may appear to tip the scales of justice toward the Indian position. It must be remembered that the rules grow out of the process of treaty negotiation, in which the United States, as the more powerful negotiator, was seen to have a responsibility to avoid taking advantage of the tribes, which were ceding vast amounts of territory.

Hatchery Fish Can Be Treaty Fish. Judge Orrick concluded that hatchery fish had to be included as part of the rightful Indian share of the catch in order to fulfill the purpose of the treaty. Due to the

decline of the natural runs—which had by 1980 shrunk to less
than half of their pre-treaty size[13]—and the development of hatcheries to replace the wild fish lost to overfishing, pollution, and
dams, the proportion of hatchery fish in the case area was high.
The state estimated that in 1980, some 60 percent of all steelhead
were hatchery fish.[14] An expert witness for the tribes, biologist
Phil Mundy, estimated that for Puget Sound coho and chinook,
the hatchery share exceeded 60 percent.[15] These fish were primarily produced by state hatcheries, sometimes with federal assistance. Significant numbers also came from federal and tribal hatcheries. For example, projections of the period from June 1978
through June 1979 indicated that tribal programs would produce
20.4 percent of the fish released in the *U.S.* v. *Washington* case
area,[16] and these fish would be caught by both treaty and nontreaty
fishermen.

Without the hatchery fish, according to Judge Orrick, the central thrust of the treaties would be subverted. As the Supreme
Court had stated in Phase I, the treaty secured the fish to meet
Indian needs. Clearly, the Indians needed the hatchery fish in order to be assured of their fair share of the total catch that would
meet those needs. The state could not say that by "creating" new
fish in hatcheries, it therefore owned them and thus could exclude
Indians from a share of the total catch.[17]

Fish Need Protection. "The most fundamental prerequisite to
exercising the right to take fish is the existence of fish to be
taken,"[18] Judge Orrick ruled. The tribes' needs could not be met
if the state were permitted to destroy the fishery habitat. The state
could not deny the Indians' right to fish by destroying the environment, any more than it could deny that right by other means the
courts had struck down—by fish wheels, by prevention of access,
by discriminatory application of conservation rules.[19] Thus, Phase
II of the decision said that the treaties provided an implicit right
to have the fishery habitat protected, or else the explicit right to a
share of fish would be meaningless.

The court left the determination of the nature and scope of the state's duty to protect the environment for a subsequent stage of the litigation. This task would require the court to consider whether the state had violated the treaty right to environmental protection for the fish and to examine the appropriate remedies.

Judge Orrick did identify the areas within which state agencies would have to consider what direct effect their decisions would have upon the environment. Agency staff would have to consider the implications on fish habitat in approving annual logging plans and permits for hydraulic power projects, and in setting policy for grants of water rights. The state agencies, along with federal agencies and third parties, such as timber companies, would have to "refrain from degrading the fish habitat to an extent that it would deprive the tribes of their moderate living needs."[20] Both tribal government and state government shared the burden of proof in opposing or defending specific actions. Each had a different element it must demonstrate. The state must show that any degradation that it (or the third parties it authorized) proposed would not impair the tribes' ability to satisfy their needs for the fish. The tribes must demonstrate that state action would indeed cause environment degradation reducing the fish runs.

REACTION I: ASSESSING THE IMPACT

The state immediately appealed Judge Orrick's decision. Before the decision was handed down, and then as it awaited review by the Ninth Circuit Court of Appeals, the tribes were increasingly involved in responding to proposed development projects that, if completed, might harm the fish.

Denying a Dam. The Skagit is one of the major rivers in Washington. Originating in British Columbia, it flows 162 miles before emptying into Skagit Bay, between Bellingham and Seattle. The river has important wild chinook, coho, pink, sockeye, chum, and steelhead runs. As the salmon come in to spawn, bald eagles follow them and spend half the year feeding upon the spawned-out carcasses. The Skagit and three of its tributaries are federally protected under legislation to preserve "wild and scenic rivers."[21] Other parts of the Skagit system have been tamed by three major dams built by Seattle's public utility, Seattle City Light.

For a long time Seattle City Light had considered adding a fourth dam on a Skagit tributary called Copper Creek. Copper Creek Dam would have inundated eleven miles of prime spawning grounds in the Skagit River, so that the returning runs would no longer find a place to breed.

The Indians of the Skagit River—the Upper Skagit Tribe, the Sauk-Suiattle Tribe, and the Swinomish Tribal Community—depend on the returning salmon for a considerable portion of their yearly income. After the Boldt decision, the tribes had formed the Skagit System Cooperative to jointly gather and share information that would help them manage their fishing. The Skagit System Cooperative, using the environmental impact statement process, opposed the Copper Creek project. The prospect of a lengthy court battle with the tribes over the Skagit River salmon was a major factor that persuaded the Seattle City Council to drop its plans for Copper Creek in April 1981.

Protesting a Pipeline. Several tribes also decided that they did not have to accept the construction of the Northern Tier Pipeline, a plan which envisioned an oil port at Port Angeles on the Olympic Peninsula delivering Alaska crude oil to the upper Midwest through a 1,500-mile pipeline around or under Puget Sound and on to Minnesota. The Lower Elwha Klallam Indians, along with other tribes and environmental groups, took the issue to court. The Point No Point Treaty Council—representing the Skokomish Tribe and the Lower Elwha and Port Gamble Klallam Tribes—stated: "The Northern Tier Pipeline and its oil port are one of the largest proposed industrial developments in the State of Washington today. It would adversely affect a substantial portion of marine and freshwater resources in western Washington."[22] A study commissioned by the National Marine Fisheries Service (which also opposed the pipeline) warned that a spill from tankers in the Strait of Juan de Fuca on their way to the oil port would poison the sea, as salmon fry, and the shrimp larvae on which they feed, die when exposed to low concentrations of crude oil or its ingredients for short periods of time.[23] Indian opposition was one of many factors which finally caused Governor John Spellman to reject the company's plan on April 7, 1982.

Negotiating with a Corporate Committee. The 1980 Phase II decision brought the tribes the support of environmentalists as new allies. But it also brought a more powerful source of potential opposition—the large corporations. These business interests were not harvesters of salmon, but they appeared worried that the protection of Indian fishing rights might require limits on their future development projects. The Phase II ruling had said that "third parties" could not destroy the environment which salmon needed. In their actions opposing the Copper Creek dam and the Northern Tier Pipeline, the tribes had shown how closely they would monitor development projects, especially for impacts upon water quality and quantity.

Following Judge Orrick's Phase II decision, major Northwest companies (many of them timber industries which included such giants as Weyerhaeuser and Georgia-Pacific, and corporations such as International Telephone and Telegraph, Burlington Northern Railroad, Puget Sound Power and Light, and Seattle First National Bank) organized the Northwest Water Resources Committee.[24] The committee hired James Waldo to work on the issue. Waldo had been chief negotiator in the task force talks set up by President Jimmy Carter in 1977.[25] His analysis laid out the following options for the corporations: (1) concentrated judicial attack on the Phase II appeal; (2) congressional abrogation of treaty rights; (3) judicial attacks on a case-by-case basis; and (4) direct negotiations with the tribes.[26] Waldo recommended the fourth option and the corporations agreed.

During the fall of 1981, one year after the Phase II ruling, tribal representatives met with corporate executives to discuss the issues. In the initial meetings, the corporations agreed not to side (for example by filing *amicus* briefs) with the state in appealing

Phase II to a higher court. Tribal leaders considered this a sign of good faith. When asked why he was willing to talk with executives, Bill Frank, Jr., chairman of the Northwest Indian Fisheries Commission, stressed the need for cooperation in support of the court decision: "We can keep winning in court . . . but it doesn't protect the life of that salmon."

Protecting Salmon "Redds." Before the Ninth Circuit Court of Appeals could respond to the state's request for review of the federal district court's decision in Phase II, the lower court heard another case on the environmental issue. This case, *Kittitas Reclamation District, United States, et al.* v. *Sunnyside Valley Irrigation District,*[27] involved the regulation of water at the Cle Elum Irrigation Dam on the Upper Yakima River. At stake for the Yakima tribal fishery were some sixty chinook salmon "redds" (nests). When the Yakima Nation learned that a closure of the Cle Elum dam would limit the flow of water to the redds, the tribe asked the watermaster (who controlled the flow) to maintain enough water cover for the baby salmon to survive. The watermaster asked the U.S. District Court for instructions.

Judge Justin L. Quackenbush ordered the watermaster to provide enough water to keep the redds covered, even though this action made farmers uncertain there would be sufficient water left to irrigate their farms. His ruling responded to an emergency requiring quick action to save the redds, but the judge anticipated that the problem would recur. He therefore ordered a study of ways to accommodate the farmers' needs that would have less severe effects on the salmon.

The farmers appealed the ruling, but on September 16, 1982, a three-judge panel of the Ninth Circuit Court of Appeals upheld Judge Quackenbush's decision. Both the Quackenbush decision and the circuit court's affirmation were based on Judge Orrick's ruling in Phase II. According to the circuit court, "The parties to a treaty bear a duty to refrain from actions interfering with either the Indian's access to fishing grounds or the amount of fish present there."[28] The irrigation project had been built by the U.S. government, which was subject to the terms of the treaty. The U.S. therefore had a duty not to deplete the fish runs.

CIRCUIT COURT RULES: PHASE II, ROUND II

Two months later, on November 3, 1982, three other judges from the federal circuit court reviewed the Orrick decision in Phase II and came to quite different conclusions. The circuit court did uphold Judge Orrick's ruling that hatchery-bred and artificially-propagated fish were to be counted along with wild fish allocated to Indians under the treaty provisions. However, the judges did not agree with his interpretation of the environmental issue.

The Price of Development Is Fish. Speaking for the circuit court, Judge Sneed concluded that there is no duty on the part of the state to protect the fish from destruction. According to Judge Sneed, as Indians were entitled to a share of the available fish, they also would have to share 50-50 "the losses arising out of reasonable development."[29] Such development, he felt, would benefit Indians and non-Indians alike. He interpreted Judge Orrick's principle as one of "comprehensive environmental servitude"[30] that "guaranteed" fish to the Indians. It had too many unforeseen consequences, and could deter development. He propounded another principle instead: "The state and the tribes must each take reasonable steps commensurate with the resources and abilities of each to preserve and enhance the fishery."[31] By taking a series of "reasonable steps" toward protection, the tribes and the state would be practicing a system he called "cooperative stewardship."[32] He did not define what such reasonable steps might be.

The judges of the circuit court had indicated in their opinion that they believed several avenues of protection for Indian fishing rights already existed: state protection of the fishery because of Indian and non-Indian political pressure; state support of hatcheries to benefit Indians and non-Indians alike; and state development project guidelines that said the state could not discriminate against Indians by permitting development that would adversely affect treaty runs but leave non-treaty runs intact.

The circuit court also pointed to several state and federal statutes that had been enacted to protect the fish. Judge Sneed did not rule out, however, contingencies that might render the Indian right valueless.[33] It was possible, for example, that a state-authorized dam might wipe out the entire fish production on the Nisqually River. In that case, all that would be required is that "reasonable steps" be taken to maintain historic fishing levels.

A Puzzling Lack of Protection. The circuit court decision puzzled many who had been involved in years of fishing rights litigation. Their experience had led them to believe, for example, that while a proposal for a large development like the Northern Tier Pipeline might bring together a force of opponents strong enough to defeat the project, the fishermen by themselves would be no match politically for the applications the corporations made for small projects that threatened individual fish runs. Experience had also shown that the state could select hatchery sites that produced more fish for nontreaty than for treaty fishermen. Budget cuts could cause the state to reduce the hatchery program. Furthermore, past development projects generally failed to alleviate the widespread poverty and unemployment of reservation Indians.[34] Perhaps most puzzling was the example the judge gave of a state-authorized dam on the Nisqually River that might destroy all its runs. This suggested that a state could extinguish a treaty right. The tribal attorneys called such a suggestion "unprecedented."[35] Only the federal government has such power, which it exercised when it destroyed the Indians' ancient fishing site on the Columbia River at Celilo Falls in 1957 by building The Dalles Dam.

REACTION II: TRIBAL APPEAL

This time it was the tribe's turn to request a rehearing of a court's interpretation of *U.S.* v. *Washington*, Phase II. They asked that the entire complement of the judges on the Ninth Circuit

Court (*en banc*) hear the case in order to resolve the apparent conflict between the three judges who had decided the Kittitas case and three who had reviewed Phase II.

In asking for a new hearing, the tribes argued that the treaties did secure the right to enough fish to meet their needs for a moderate living. This right did not promise a guaranteed number of fish: after all, floods, volcanoes, or other natural disasters might deplete the runs. The security of this right, the tribes argued, meant that the state could not by its own action authorize a depleting of the runs. The tribes insisted that the decision by the three judges who had reinterpreted Judge Orrick's Phase II ruling, if it were left standing, would undermine the Indians' right to exercise their treaty rights.[36]

On April 27, 1983, the Ninth Circuit Court of Appeals agreed to withdraw the Sneed decision and to rehear *U.S.* v. *Washington*, Phase II, *en banc*. The path that this review would take was unclear. It did seem certain that Phase II would probably spend many more years in court before its fate ultimately was decided.

ENVIRONMENTAL SAFETY: VISIBLE AND INVISIBLE THREATS

Before the Ninth Circuit Court of Appeals review, Judge Orrick's decision in Phase II had seemed to herald new possibilities for protecting the longstanding partnership between fish and tribes. Now, while legal concepts concerning the implications of treaty rights for environmental protection undergo review and modification, threats to the environment which affect fish—and thereby the tribes—continue to exist.

Some threats are clearly visible. Many streams in the Northwest need to be reclaimed from the effects of logging before they can safely serve the salmon once again. Hydroelectric dams are another all-too-visible danger. Many remain as a legacy of past, often irreparable, disregard for the fish. Future hydroelectric development may be less detrimental if provisions for fishery protection included in the recent Pacific Northwest Electric Power Planning and Conservation Act are fully implemented. The act calls for a system-wide approach to protecting and restoring the fish and wildlife resources of the Columbia River Basin.[37] The effectiveness of this new legislation will not be known for several years.

Chemical Contaminants in the Water. Other threats are less visible. In some cases they cannot be seen at all. Even the measurement of their presence and calculation of their impact may be costly and time-consuming. Contamination of the waters of western Washington by highly toxic chemicals from industry constitutes one such threat. Scientists disagree about how serious the contamination is and how it affects salmon. "Five different fish biologists may give you five different answers,"[38] according to Howard Harris, Project Manager at the U.S. government's Marine Pollution Assessment Office in Seattle. On the contrary, Joe Miyamoto, fish biologist for the Puyallup Tribe, says "the day has already come" to worry about contamination of Puget Sound.[39]

Miyamoto's concern is supported in two recent reports commissioned by the federal Office of Marine Pollution Assessment. The first, entitled, "Chemical Contaminants and Abnormalities in Fish and Invertebrates from Puget Sound," reported in 1982 that "the findings indicate that hundreds of potentially toxic chemicals are present in Puget Sound sediments from as far north as Bellingham Bay to as far south as Budd Inlet. Many of the chemicals are also found in a variety of benthic and pelagic organisms. The question of the threat that they pose to these organisms or the consumer is not known at present and can only be determined through further research."[40]

The second study ranks the seriousness of the biological effects of contaminants in Puget Sound. It placed Elliott Bay, Seattle's harbor at the mouth of the Duwamish River, and Commencement Bay, Tacoma's harbor at the mouth of the Puyallup River, at the top of the list.[41] The U.S. Environmental Protection Agency similarly singled out Commencement Bay when it included it on its list of the "ten worst" toxic waste sites in the nation.[42]

The Puyallup Tribe is especially concerned about impact of contamination in Commencement Bay because the fish upon which the tribe depends—chinook, coho, chum, pink salmon, and steelhead—use the bay's estuary as a nursery and migration pathway to and from the Puyallup River. The tribe's biologists are worried that the pollution will kill the small invertebrates that salmon eat and that it may put stress on the salmon themselves and make them more susceptible to disease. Some of the chemicals, such as aromatic hydrocarbons (which can originate from accidental spills, smelters, creosote on bridge structures, or other sources), may even affect the salmon's ability to "imprint" on their natal waters and thus inhibit their ability to find the way home to spawn.[43]

The Muckleshoot Tribe is equally concerned about the salmon in the Duwamish River. "Duwamish" means "many colors" in Salish. The Duwamish waterway is formed by the White and Green rivers and flows about twenty-five miles north until it enters Elliott Bay on the shore of downtown Seattle. Major commercial and industrial facilities are located near the waterway, which receives discharges from a wastewater treatment plant, overflows from sewers, runoffs from storm waters, and effluents from industry. Between 1975 and 1980, the river system produced 235,000 salmon and steelhead each year.[44] A variety of contaminants have been found in the Duwamish; many of their sources have still to be identified.[45] The contaminants may reduce the waterway's production of fish and make the fish unsafe for humans to eat.

In 1974, a spill of PCBs (polychlorinated biphenyls) in the waterway made several fishermen ill and ruined their nets.[46] Tribal fishermen stopped eating bottomfish (such as English sole, starry flounder, or Pacific staghorn sculpin) when it became publicized that these fish contained high levels of PCBs. No similar publicity implicated the salmon, and the Muckleshoot continued to eat them. The state of Washington gave the tribe surplus salmon from its Soos Creek hatchery on the Duwamish to distribute to the elders or to can and sell. It has been estimated that each Muckleshoot Indian in the community probably ate between five and twenty salmon from the waters of the Green and the Duwamish rivers and inner Elliott Bay during the last several years.[47]

A new study has reported that salmon may also accumulate PCBs in their tissues to roughly the same extent as bottomfish. The evidence for this bioaccumulation is very limited. It comes only from the analysis of ten returning coho in 1975 and a sample of hatchery eggs.[48] Harper-Owes, a consultant firm hired by the Municipality of Metropolitan Seattle (Metro), which studied the Duwamish and summarized the PCB findings in a 1982 report, concluded that the residues "may presently be sufficiently elevated to result in an increased incidence of cancer to those who consume them."[49] The consultants recommended that additional research and monitoring of the toxic residues in salmon tissues be conducted in 1983.

Chemical threats to the salmon may assume greater importance in the future. It is not yet clear how the tribal-state allocation system will deal with a run of fish that may be unfit to eat. Nor is it clear how tribes might seek to be compensated for economic losses due to contaminated fish.

Air Pollution and Acid Rain. Although it is generally not considered a problem in the West at the present time, it is possible that in the future the salmon may have to face another invisible threat to its habitat called "acid precipitation" or "acid rain." Termed "the single most important environmental threat to the United States and Canada,"[50] acid rain occurs when fumes of sulfur dioxide and nitrogen oxides from the burning of fossil fuels, (e.g. from coal-fired power plants and car exhausts), and to a much lesser degree, from natural sources, are carried aloft into the atmosphere. There they are transformed into sulfuric acid and nitric acid. When these acids fall to earth as rain or snow, they increase the acidity of lakes and streams, with disastrous effects upon fish and other aquatic life. Wind patterns that blow the acids away and the capacity of a region to "buffer" their effects (for example, by neutralizing agents such as limestone in rocks and soil, and by alkalinity of water) may lessen the impact of acid rain on animals, trees, rocks, and soil.[51]

At present, acid rain has hit the eastern part of the continent the hardest. Few studies have been done on possible problems in the

Northwest. However, the Northwest contains many lakes that are considered sensitive to acid rain. One study of Douglas fir needles in a remote area of foothills of the Cascade Mountains, which lie downwind from urban pollution sources, showed damage to the tiny communities of algae, fungi, bacteria, and microlichens that process nitrogen for the vegetation and keep it healthy.[52] Some slight acidification of Seattle's ever-present rain has also been found, and a recent study of two Seattle city reservoirs and two rural points indicated that the area was "at the threshold of damage."[53]

Salmon are extremely sensitive to changes in the acid-alkaline balance of their streams. Many streams in the Northeast have seen salmon runs in acidified waters decline markedly.[54] Acid rain may be a future threat to the Northwest salmon, especially if emissions from fossil fuel power plants and smelters in Northwest cities are not reduced.

CONCLUSION: AN INSECURE FUTURE

The salmon have been exposed to many threats caused by burgeoning settlement of the Northwest. Their waterways have been dammed, diverted, and polluted. Threats to the salmon—and thereby to the tribes who depend upon them—have not abated. Tribes have responded to these threats by arguing forcefully in court for the protection of fish habitats, by working with other environmentalists, and by monitoring developments that could damage the resource. The possibility remains that Indians in the future may put their nets in the water and bring them up empty. And in some parts of the region, the possibility now exists that Indians may put their nets in the water and bring them up filled with fish that are dead or unfit to eat. There is cause for serious concern about the security of the environment upon which the fish and the tribes depend.

Chapter 10

Western Washington Tribes
and the Salmon Today

INDIANS NET THEIR SHARE

In the years since Judge Boldt's 1974 decision in *U.S.* v. *Washington,* the treaty tribes of western Washington have made significant gains. They also have had to face many difficult problems. This chapter focuses on the tribes' efforts to develop their fishing economies under the terms of *U.S.* v. *Washington.* It also presents issues that have yet to be resolved.[1]

After the U.S. Supreme Court upheld the Boldt decision in 1979, Washington's senior senator, Warren G. Magnuson, sponsored the bill that Congress made the $129 million Salmon and Steelhead Conservation and Enhancement Act of 1980. The act established an advisory commission to draft a plan for improving coordination among the many managers of the fishery—tribal, state, and federal. The commission would also guide enhancement efforts for the region. This may significantly increase the fish runs in the future. While it is far too early to evaluate the act's impact, it is important that Congress has indeed, as Bill Frank, Jr., urged, written a law that respects treaty rights and holds promise for conserving the resource for all fishermen.

The state also responded to the Supreme Court review. In 1979, the Washington state legislature passed stiff new penalties for illegal fishing, penalties that included loss of commercial fishing

TABLE 10.1. Treaty and Non-Treaty Catch
in U.S. v. Washington Case Area, 1970–1983

Year	Treaty		Non-Treaty	
	Catch	%	Catch	%
1970–73[a]	328,888	5.0	6,231,044	95.0
1974	788,582	11.9	5,845,482	88.1
1975	827,356	12.1	5,987,374	87.9
1976	896,153	13.8	5,600,131	86.2
1977	1,360,399	16.9	6,691,223	83.1
1978	1,391,890	27.2	3,727,355	72.8
1979	1,938,388	22.4	6,742,089	77.7
1980	1,526,571	42.9	2,030,845	57.1
1981	2,782,576	34.4	5,303,978	65.6
1982	3,026,070	42.8	4,048,212	57.2
1983	2,145,373	43.8	2,757,777	56.2

[a]Figures for 1970–73 are averages for the four years.
SOURCE: U.S. Fish and Wildlife Service and Northwest Indian Fisheries Commission.

licenses. State courts began enforcing the new regulations, making it clear that outlaw fishing would no longer be tolerated. The decision could finally be implemented and its system of allocation and management could function as designed. The result was that by 1983 the tribes were catching more fish, managing their own fisheries, and participating in the development of regional management plans. Many tribes are now catching close to their share of the salmon. Table 10.1 shows the increase in the tribes' salmon catch between 1970, when they caught about 5 percent, and 1983, when they caught 43.8 percent of the harvest. The *number* of salmon caught by Indians has risen also, from less than one million in 1974 to three million in 1982. Table 10.2 shows that the tribes' harvest of steelhead has also improved significantly.

TABLE 10.2. Treaty and Sport Harvest of Steelhead in
the U.S. v. Washington Case Area, 1961–62 through 1983–84

Year	Sport Harvest[a]	Treaty Harvest[b]	Total
1961–62	79,100	18,000	97,100
1962–63	85,900	21,700	107,600
1963–64	113,200	21,600	134,800
1964–65	80,400	18,000	98,400
1965–66	108,700	18,000	126,700
1966–67	100,100	18,000	118,100
1967–68	103,700	18,000	121,700
1968–69	86,600	18,000	104,600
1969–70	49,300	18,000	67,300
1970–71	77,100	17,300	94,400
1971–72	94,600	27,500	122,100
1972–73	56,400	25,000	81,400
1973–74	58,900	35,600	94,500
1974–75	60,200	61,400	121,600
1975–76	29,900	57,000	86,900
1976–77	32,200	42,500	74,700
1977–78	69,100	49,700	118,800
1978–79	57,100	47,000	104,100
1979–80	70,900	48,800	119,700
1980–81	55,100	40,700	95,800
1981–82	46,600	60,500	107,100
1982–83	42,400	55,400	97,800
1983–84	52,100	64,000	116,100

[a]Sport harvest data provided by Washington Department of Game.

[b]Data prior to 1974 are incomplete due to lack of an accurate catch
reporting system. No data were collected between 1964 and 1970; the
numbers presented are estimates developed by WDG. The data from
1974–75 through 1977–78 were compiled by the U.S. Fish and Wildlife
Service. Data after 1978 were jointly compiled by WDG and the treaty
tribes.

In the past decade there have been year-to-year fluctuations in the percentage and the number of salmon caught, variations based in part on the life-cycle of the pink salmon, which return to spawn in huge runs only in odd-numbered years.[2] Purse seiners (the costliest boats and gear), used primarily by non-Indian fishermen, catch most of the pinks. In 1981, for example, Indians caught only 28 percent of the pinks, lowering their overall percentage of the salmon catch. Even so, that same year Indian fishermen caught over 800,000 fish more than in 1979, the previous odd-numbered year.

Even the tribes' portion of the international salmon catch—the Fraser River pinks and sockeye that cross through both United States and Canadian waters and are managed by the International Pacific Salmon Fisheries Commission (IPSFC)—has improved. In 1974 and 1975, Indians caught only 2.5 percent of the U.S. harvest, in 1976 a mere 6 percent. In 1977 and 1978, the Indian share of the sockeye was 19 and 18 percent respectively. By 1980, the tribes caught 43 percent of the United States share of a poor sockeye run. In 1981 they caught 27 percent of a huge pink run and 43 percent of the sockeye. In 1982, the tribes harvested 1.4 million sockeye—48 percent of the United States share of the catch under IPSFC jurisdiction.[3] Thus, the improvement in the tribal catch has been both steady and significant.

The region covered by *U.S.* v. *Washington* includes Puget Sound and the Washington coast north of and including Grays Harbor. Over the years, the number of salmon caught in this region has fit a relatively consistent pattern. In several recent odd-numbered years, when the pinks return, about eight million salmon were caught. In even-numbered years, the fluctuation is greater. There is no indication of an overall decline in salmon.[4] Nonetheless long-term trends must be watched. Some individual runs on some streams are quite weak at present, and the fishery is vulnerable to climatic disturbances such as El Niño, the Pacific weather phenomenon causing higher ocean temperatures that adversely affected the 1983 fishery. Steelhead har-

vests have shown considerable fluctuation, but current levels
indicate that the runs of fighting fish are holding their own,
with approximately the same harvests in 1983–84 as in 1974–75.
(See table 10.2.)

New Prospects in the Fishery. Gaining an equal share of the
salmon has brought important benefits to the treaty fishermen. As
one veteran Skokomish Indian fisherman, Harmon Sparr stated,
"There are people who have never had anything, who now can
fish." They may start off fishing with a relative. Sparr's five nephews fished with him because they didn't have their own gear and
needed experience. After a few years they were able to start out
on their own.[5]

Young people recognize the opportunities that fishing presents.
Like Sparr's nephews, they may start off as apprentices on a fishing boat. Or, according to Tulalip fisherman Carl Jones, they may
start by beach seining or by river-fishing where they use hand-
operated gear and have little investment. They may work their
way toward what they perceive as better economic prospects by
purchasing more expensive gear to fish traditional sites in marine
waters.[6] Others, like Walter Pacheco, Jr., a Muckleshoot Indian
who works as an assistant biologist with the Muckleshoot Fisheries Department, find that "it is good to go to school in fisheries
biology because there are jobs for Indians in that."[7] In the depressed economy of the early 1980s, income from fisheries assumed even greater importance.

Fishing opportunities have presented a new problem as well:
young people may interrupt their education to begin fishing
sooner. To combat the dropout dilemma, several school districts
have initiated programs for Indian students that integrate their
fishing experience and knowledge into subjects such as biology.

Increased Indian fishing is reflected in the growth of the Indian
fleet. Even though the non-Indian fleet still significantly outnum-
bers the treaty fleet, table 10.3 shows how Indians have "geared-
up" since 1977. The rapid growth of the Indian fleet is evident on
both rivers and marine waters.

SPREADING THE BENEFITS

Tribal Fish Taxes. Income generated by Indian fishing benefits not only individual fishermen but also the tribes as a body. Such tribes as the Skokomish and the Port Gamble Klallam have enacted a fish tax. Tribes differ in their tax procedures, but among the Skokomish the tax works like this: when the fisherman sells his fish to a commercial buyer, the buyer subtracts the tax and sends it to the tribe. The tribe then uses the funds for tribal needs, including projects related to fishing. The Skokomish tax paid for most of a new steelhead-rearing project that began in the summer 1981—a cooperative effort between the Skokomish Tribe and the Washington Department of Game. In practice, a tribe can't force the buyers to collect the tax nor the fishermen to pay it. But the tribe can refuse to issue the nonpaying fisherman a license the following year. Fishermen who flout the tax rule may also encounter the censure of others. Considering the importance of the tax to the tribe, one Indian fisherman observed: "Those that don't pay it hurt themselves."

The Port Gamble Klallam Tribe have a similar system. In 1979 they set a 4 percent tax. Their fish tax funds go back into the fishery for such projects as enhancement projects. According to Ron Charles, chairman of the Port Gamble Klallam, then a commissioner on the Northwest Indian Fisheries Commission, and a fisherman himself, the reinvestment of the tax into the resource demonstrates how fishermen are taking steps to help themselves by playing an integral role in ensuring the continuity of the resource.[8]

Tribal Enterprises and Their Impact. Some tribes have used tribal funds to purchase boats on which tribal members may fish. The profit from the catch is distributed among the skipper, the crew, and the tribe. Individuals who want to fish but have no money to buy their own gear can also benefit from such arrangements. The number of tribes involved in fish processing has increased, up from two prior to the 1974 Boldt decision to six in 1981. A few tribes have ventured into other fields, not always

TABLE 10.3. Treaty and Non-Treaty Fleet Sizes in the U.S. v. Washington Case Area, 1977–82

	Troll	Power Reel Marine Gillnet	Purse Seines	Handpull Gillnet Marine Skiffs	River Fishermen	Beach Seine	Reef Net	Other	Totals[a]
Treaty									
1977	39	245	10	313	508	6	—	—	1,121
1978	56	296	10	390	620	8	2	—	1,380
1979	75	351	14	422	968	30	—	287	2,149
1980	69	356	36	270	1,026	35	—	152	1,944
1981	81	443	38	420	859	62	—	9	1,642
1982	110	448	35	450	1,057	56	—	7	2,163
									Commercial-Only Total
Non-Treaty									
1977	3,049	1,795	398				78	—	5,320
1978	3,085	1,814	399				74	517,418	5,372
1979	2,841	1,794	389				68	459,967	5,092
1980	2,803	1,752	398				66	436,413	5,019
1981	2,456	2,109	396				62	420,677	5,023
1982	2,357	2,027	385				50	—	4,819

Non-Treaty "Other" Includes:

	Salmon Charter Boats	Salmon Sports Fishermen[b]
1977	569	—
1978	535	516,883
1979	516	459,451
1980	510	435,903
1981	478	424,122
1982	414	403,210

[a]Actual treaty fleet may vary. Totals for the various categories of fishermen are not additive in that an individual fisherman may fish more than one gear type at various times of the year, and would, therefore, be counted in more than one column. Salmon license tab requirement first went into effect in 1978.

[b]Figure may include duplication of obtaining one-day salmon stamps.

SOURCES: Northwest Indian Fisheries Commission Annual Report, 1982, p. 32; and Washington Department of Fisheries Statistical Report, 1982, pp. 14, 17.

successfully. The Upper Skagit, for example, attempted to develop and distribute a line of smoked salmon products for specialty food shops. The effort encountered financial problems forcing its discontinuation, but the developers felt that they had learned some important although tough lessons in products merchandizing and business management that might be useful in the future.

It is clear that the economic potential of the fishing right is very important to the tribes. Gary Peterson, Skokomish Tribal Chairman and former fish commissioner representing the Point No Point Treaty Council, emphasizes both the economic and social importance of fish harvesting, management, and processing. He notes that fishing creates jobs, not just for fishermen, but also for biologists, managers, technicians, and processors. Indians who are employed in these jobs spread the benefits to the communities in which they live. They do not draw on government public assistance monies or unemployment compensation funds. They deposit their earnings in local banks, buy groceries at local stores, and purchase clothing, cars, gas, and appliances from local merchants. For example, Russel Barsh of the University of Washington School of Business has estimated that the fishing activities of the Quinault tribal village of Queets on the coast of Washington had an economic impact of at least $265,000 on the region in 1978–79.[9] In this way, the funds generated by Indian fishing have an economic impact beyond the tribe.

The Problem of Unequal Returns. The gains realized in recent years have been significant. It is important to note, however, that not all tribes, or individuals, have reaped equal benefits. As Barsh demonstrated in his study at Queets, some Indian fishermen's incomes may be quite low. In the 1977–79 season, households with income from fishing had a yearly mean income of $11,024, compared with $9,256 for nonfishing households.[10] Nonfishing households were more dependent on government programs. Fishing did not provide a high income for most families. The median family income in Washington state as a whole, a somewhat different yet illustrative measure, in that period was $21,635.[11] Still, fishing did provide fishing households with greater economic independence and about 20 percent more income than nonfishing households had. If ocean trollers did not intercept so many fish, the fishermen at Queets would probably be able to do much better.[12]

All Indians in the Pacific Northwest are not "fish-rich", any more than all Indians in Oklahoma are oil-rich. Small tribes on the Olympic Peninsula, like the Hoh and Quileute, and on the southern part of Puget Sound, like the Nisqually and Puyallup, have found that the fish destined for their usual and accustomed harvest sites are still being intercepted by other fishermen. Their catches have not increased at the extremely rapid rate experienced by tribes of northern Puget Sound, especially those that can fish the lucrative Fraser River runs. Precise statistics on income of fishermen from different tribes are not available,[13] but it does seem clear that the many tribes may be "catching up" at different rates in the years to come.

INCREASING RESPONSIBILITY FOR CO-MANAGEMENT

Judge Boldt's 1974 ruling has also encouraged tribes to further develop their management capabilities. His concept of tribes as self-regulating managers provided an impetus for Indians to strengthen their organizations. The ruling led tribes to define their qualifications for membership carefully, to select qualified technical staff to guide tribal decision-making, and to improve their communication with outside agencies. Some have called this a "resurgence" in tribal government—a development that has especially affected the smaller tribes, which now have a fisheries resource to manage. Indians and non-Indians have noticed that along with the power and responsibility for making management decisions has come an increase in tribal pride.

Tribal management capabilities expanded considerably after the 1974 decision. Today all affected tribes have their own or participate in cooperative management programs employing harvest managers, enforcement personnel, fisheries biologists, and technicians, largely funded through the tribal governments' contracts with the Bureau of Indian Affairs. All the tribes license their own fishermen, most impose a tax on the tribal catch, and a few maintain a tribally-owned fishing fleet. License fees, harvest taxes, and tribally-owned vessels provide revenues to the tribe, which are used to supplement the fisheries management budgets and other tribal programs.

Community-Based Harvest Management. Tribal officials now make rulings to regulate fishing at usual and accustomed tribal fishing places, rulings that formerly came from the state agencies. A tribal fisheries management committee usually is responsible for saying when people can fish. Lorraine Loomis, chairperson of the Swinomish Tribal Community, describes in the Skagit System Cooperative *Annual Report* (1981) how her tribe's committee works:

> The procedure used at the Swinomish Tribal Community for making regulations is first brought to the Fisheries Management Committee. The decision is made at these various meetings when to open or close. . . . The committee itself has learned a tremendous amount about fisheries management and continuously decisions are based on not only today, but four years from now. This has proven to be successful many times, as our runs continue to grow.
>
> All fisheries management meetings are open and we allow anyone to comment before final vote. We will have anywhere from two to 20 people attending these meetings.
>
> At our annual Fisherpersons meetings in June we had an attendance of about 50 people. We at this time made annual reports and gave what we perceived to be the salmon predictions for 1981 and the problems that we might come up against during the season. We went over all the projects that we have been working on and some of the funding problems in 1982.[14]

In Indian communities, the people making decisions may also be the people who fish, or they may be close friends, relatives, or associates of those who fish. This dual role gives the managers an intimate understanding of the fishery and provides firsthand insight into its operation. Overlapping interests may also decrease the time those involved can devote to management and may make objectivity more difficult. Some of the contributions that Indian

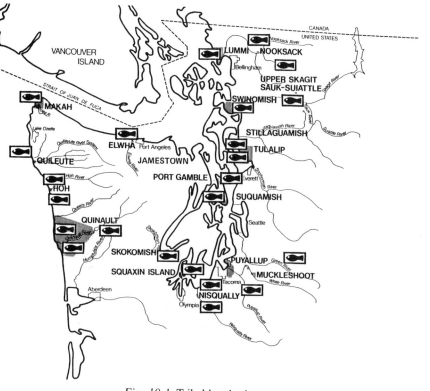

Fig. 10.1 Tribal hatcheries

fishery managers can make, and the problems they face, are discussed in the following pages.

Protecting the Runs. Tribal fisheries management has placed considerable emphasis on the restoration of weak runs by habitat rehabilitation to improve breeding areas, and upon augmentation of natural runs with a variety of fish-propagation projects, including hatcheries. Tribes are now operating important enhancement projects to increase the fish runs in Puget Sound and on the Olympic Peninsula. In March 1982, it was estimated that one out of every five hatchery-reared fish in Washington state got its start in a tribal facility.[15] Figure 10.1 shows the location of tribal hatcheries and tables 10.4 and 10.5 show the number of young fish released between 1976 and 1984, releases which in almost all

TABLE 10.4. 1984 Tribal Hatchery Releases

Tribe	Fall Chinook	Spring Chinook	Coho	Chum	Pink	Steelhead	Total Fish	Total Pounds
Lummi	3,930,370	13,695	1,664,500	1,795,700		31,224	7,435,489	135,752
Nooksack		96,410		675,000	737,000		1,508,410	1,350
Stillaguamish				95,000			95,000	1,188
Tulalip	560,000		738,500	1,853,000			3,151,500	52,345
Muckleshoot	385,000		188,000	251,000		15,900	839,900	7,965
Puyallup	483,532		321,750	234,188		51,104	1,090,574	18,187
Nisqually	753,275			30,000	19,580		802,855	9,450
Squaxin + Coop*	221,227		2,488,900	3,671,898		42,836	6,424,861	232,384
Port Gamble + Coop*			394,000	28,548			422,548	39,488
Suquamish + Coop*	1,284,000		722,297	1,290,000		44,190	3,340,487	47,127
Skokomish	561,887			942,593		30,835	1,535,315	8,414
Lower Elwha	100,850		1,228,310	99,200		69,670	1,498,030	59,525
Hoh	25,459	660				50,684	76,803	8,719
Makah	71,250		259,000			10,000	340,250	1,249
Quileute			53,000			19,300	72,300	4,072
Quinault	341,981		2,052,610	186,825		1,366,567	3,947,983	194,554
Total	8,718,831	110,765	10,110,867	11,152,952	756,580	1,732,310	32,582,305	821,769

*All or part of these projects cooperative with Washington Department of Fisheries.
SOURCE: Northwest Indian Fisheries Commission.

TABLE 10.5. Salmon and Steelhead Releases from Treaty Indian Hatcheries, 1976–1983

Year	Pink	Coho	Chinook	Chum	Sockeye	Steelhead	Total Salmon
1976	409,000	4,244,200	1,992,500	1,705,000	1,236,600	341,400	9,587,300
1977		5,319,000	1,848,000	11,504,000	186,000	288,000	18,857,000
1978	220,000	4,072,000	6,151,000	17,103,000	368,000	197,000	27,914,000
1979		4,067,000	4,998,000	18,478,000	483,000	470,000	28,026,000
1980	287,000	5,068,000	6,083,000	11,899,000	328,000	389,000	23,665,000
1981		6,959,000	5,577,000	12,647,000	297,000	1,162,000	25,480,000
1982	143,000	8,167,000	10,843,000	13,368,000	469,000	1,399,000	32,990,000
1983		9,581,000	9,987,000	12,878,000	476,000	1,127,000	32,922,000

SOURCE: Northwest Indian Fisheries Commission.

cases show dramatic increases. When these fish return to Washington waters, they will be caught by both Indian and non-Indian fishermen.

Tribal locations on the watersheds permit Indian managers to make still another contribution to regional management. The tribes form a decentralized system, providing information on important local conditions. Tribal biologists can obtain firsthand data and a feel for the resource that are difficult for the more centralized state system of management to obtain. The tribes, as co-managers, can thus serve as a balance to the state and can contribute to the overall improvement of fish resource management in western Washington.

Co-ops and Councils among the Tribes. While individual tribes conduct most of their own fisheries activities, notable examples of intertribal cooperation have emerged during recent years. Several tribes have formed cooperatives where they pool some of their resources for such joint programs as data collection, fisheries patrols, courts, and environmental monitoring. For example, the Swinomish Tribal Community and the Upper Skagit and Sauk-Suiattle Tribes, which fish the Skagit River and its tributaries, formed the Skagit System Cooperative in 1976.

Another level of intertribal coordination is the treaty council. Figure 6.1 shows the treaty areas coordinated by each council. As the name implies, a treaty council is comprised of representatives from tribes that were signatories to a particular treaty. Some of the councils now have cooperative projects, such as working directly with the state Department of Fisheries and hammering out complex plans for managing fish runs within their particular treaty areas. An example is the joint Point No Point Treaty Council–Washington Department of Fisheries plan for the Hood Canal. In addition, each treaty council sends a commissioner to serve on the Northwest Indian Fisheries Commission, which was established following the Boldt decision in 1974.

The role of the Northwest Indian Fisheries Commission, as compared with the tribes or treaty councils, is to serve as a coordinating body for the entire region under jurisdiction of *U.S.* v.

Washington. The commission represents the tribes in meetings with the various fisheries management agencies, including the International Pacific Salmon Fisheries Commission, and the Pacific Fisheries Management Council. It works with member tribes in discussions of management, fisheries enhancement, and regulation enforcement with the Washington and Oregon departments of Fisheries and Game, and with federal agencies. The commissioners and staff coordinate information-sharing with member tribes, provide information to fishermen, and serve as liaisons between the tribes, Congress, and the federal executive branch. The commission also provides public relations services for the region.

The Northwest Indian Fisheries Commission has the difficult task of coordinating and providing services to twenty political units—the tribes. It is a type of agency quite new to the tribes. Because it was organized by one vote per treaty area, and because some treaty areas represent only one or a few tribes, while others represent several, the question arose whether some tribes carry more influence than others. This issue has generated a move to provide more equal representation in 1984. The fact that the commission must deal with the common needs of all member tribes, within the context of specific and not always complementary needs of individual tribes, also makes it an agency of periodic controversy. It has, nonetheless, weathered rough waters for almost a decade.

Tribal Voices in Regional and International Management. Recent appointments of tribal officials and staff to influential policy-making boards have recognized the emerging tribal role in fish management. Guy McMinds, Quinault treaty area commissioner, was appointed to serve as a voting member of the Pacific Fisheries Management Council in 1979. In 1980, the Assistant Director of the Northwest Indian Fisheries Commission, Michael Grayum, was appointed to a position on the Pacific Fisheries Management Council's Scientific and Statistical Committee. A year later, Gary Morishima, biologist for the Quinault Nation, was appointed to the PFMC's influential Salmon Management Development Team. All these appointments mean that tribal perspectives will be represented at important stages of data analysis and policy planning. The tribes also gained a voice in the issue of how to share fish runs that pass through both U.S. and Canadian waters when Charles Peterson, a Makah fisherman with decades of experience in the fishery, was appointed to the Advisory Committee of the International Pacific Salmon Fisheries Commission in 1982. In addition, the tribes are actively involved as recognized fisheries managers in the negotiations for a new treaty between the U.S. and Canada.

Tribes and State: Working It Out. Another change wrought by the Boldt decision is the increase in communications between Washington tribes and the state Department of Fisheries. One example of such cooperation is the tribal-state Nisqually Plan, which sets a framework for federally-funded buildup of the Nisqually River runs. Another example is the Hood Canal Plan, agreed upon by the Department of Fisheries and the Point No Point Treaty Council. This council represents the Port Gamble, Jamestown, and Lower Elwha Klallams and the Skokomish Tribe. The council credits this plan with reducing management conflicts between the state and the tribes over fishing for chum salmon. In contrast with previous years, in 1980 the Point No Point tribes and the state did not have any conflict at all requiring the mediating services of the Fisheries Advisory Board (the panel established by Judge Boldt for negotiating conflicts).[16] However, state-tribal interchanges have not all been so harmonious. Disputes still occur and the Fisheries Advisory Board is still in operation. But in general, there has been improved cooperation.[17]

THREE MANAGEMENT CHALLENGES: ACCESS, ALLOCATION, AND REGULATION

Along with increased participation in the fishery have come new challenges for the tribes. Three of the major issues that appear to be facing the tribes today are:

1. The possibility that the Indian sector of the fishing industry may become overcrowded.

2. The problem of coordinating management so that the catch can be shared equitably among the tribes.

3. The difficult task of delineating and enforcing tribal fishing regulations.

It is not surprising that these particular issues face the tribes. Tribes now play a significant managerial role, and these problems—access, allocation, and regulation—face all fisheries managers, especially all salmon managers. Tribal governments, like state and federal governments, are not immune to political and economic pressure from those who use the resource. As an official of the Pacific Fisheries Management Commission once observed, "With salmon, you're always up against the wall."

The Access Issue. The problem of access to the fish has accompanied the tribal effort to "gear-up." As table 10.3 indicates, non-Indians still have far greater capacity to harvest the fish: they have twice as many boats, and their boats tend to be larger and better equipped. The Indian fleet, however, has grown dramatically. In 1977 there were 508 Indian river fishermen; in 1982 there were more than one thousand. In 1982 there were 110 Indian trollers; in 1977 there were only 39. The number of Indian purse seiners has more than tripled (from 10 to 35) in the same period.

The tribes need a strong fleet or they will be incapable of catching their share. The fish are seen as being owned collectively with all tribal members being entitled to fish if they want to. But they must seek a balance between the capacity to harvest their share and the overcrowding of their waters. Yet Indians are mindful of how overcrowding harmed the fishery when too many non-Indian competitors went after the fish and had to either settle for a smaller share or seek better chances further out in the water—with the added expense of chasing after fish that would otherwise have returned home on their own. Tribes do not want to see similar damage done to the newly-emerging Indian fishing industry. Bill Frank, Jr., whose perspective on Indian fishing spans several decades, has observed that the time has already come for many of the tribes to consider a system of gear limitation.

The Allocation Dilemma. The issue, that of equitable allocation of the fish, derives from the fact that a usual and accustomed fishing area may be shared by several tribes, and that fish may pass through more than one tribe's usual and accustomed site. Judge Boldt allocated 50 percent of the fish swimming through these areas to the tribes, but he did not allocate among the tribes. He left that difficult task to the tribes themselves. A specific example of the allocation problem is that some salmon, headed for the waiting nets of Nisqually and Squaxin fishermen at the southern end of Puget Sound, furthest from the ocean, pass first through waters at the sound's north end, where other tribes fish. Another example is the Makah, located at the most westerly point of the Olympic Peninsula, where the fish leave the ocean for the sound. The Makah have recently asserted their traditional right to fish the ocean and their trolling has intercepted fish bound for the traditional fishing sites of other tribes. Tribes sharing runs are required to file their proposed fishing seasons and then negotiate over-all plans with each other. Working out seasons to ensure fair allocation of fish to each tribe is not easy. Several lawsuits have resulted, some of which have been settled out of court. Like all solutions to the problem of allocation among fishing groups, this one will take time to negotiate.

The Regulation Problem. Regulating the fishery—setting the seasons and enforcing them—is also a challenging task. Handling pressure from fishermen, who may be relatives, neighbors, or influential members of the tribe, may be difficult. Linda Jones, former fisheries manager for the Tulalip Tribe, recalls rushed series of meetings with tribal councilmen, biologists who wanted to close a season to protect the fish needed for spawning, and fishermen, sometimes angry, who wanted to fish. She describes an Indian fisheries manager as someone who is caught in the middle, "who walks a fine line between what is legally defensible, what is biologically sound, and what is politically real."[18]

Once regulations have been decided, enforcing them is difficult. There are miles and miles of water to patrol and few patrol officers to watch over them. In 1981 on the Skagit River, for example, Skagit System Cooperative officers logged over 60,000 miles by land, boat, and aircraft.[19] Rod Marrom, who worked as the chief of fishery patrol for the Point No Point Treaty Council, said inadequate funding and insufficient equipment made his job difficult: "It drives you nuts."[20] Recently, a newly organized tribal-state fishery enforcement task force has set to work to improve tribal enforcement capacities. The project has already produced new training programs and better radio communication systems for enforcement officers.

Devising Solutions: Traditional Values, New Arena. Today's requirements for fish management—the need to deal with more fishermen with new gear and to coordinate and enforce more complex seasons and policies—differ significantly from the traditional systems of rules that have governed Indian fishing cultures in the past. Tribal managers express hope that, along with their evolving management structures, the guiding philosophy that formerly kept Indians close to the rivers and the fish will help them to deal with current issues. Fish are integral to tribal life, interwoven with ceremony and belief. It is difficult to conceive that the tribes would abandon this relationship for short-term, economically centered values which focus only on catching more fish.

Most tribes fish the terminal areas, where fish enter fresh water to spawn, and they must carefully manage both the harvest and escape of those fish which have succeeded in eluding all the prior harvesters fishing the oceans and other marine waters. Being last in line, tribal fishermen know that if *they* do not conserve, the runs may be lost forever. Finally, the tribes are limited to fishing in their own usual and accustomed fishing grounds: tribal fishermen remain relatively stationary compared to non-Indian fishermen who can roam up and down Puget Sound, into the Strait of Juan de Fuca, into other states' waters, and out into the Pacific Ocean. The traditional site is their legacy. If they overfish it, they cannot take their treaty rights elsewhere in search of better fishing. Thus the incentive to conserve for future generations is great.

Despite the challenges of cooperation the tribes confront, there appears to be a deep awareness that unity is in their best interest. The ability of the tribes to achieve such unity over the years has been demonstrated in their consistent stand against relinquishing their right to fish for steelhead commercially. They have held firm on this issue even though not all of the tribes gain significantly from the steelhead harvest, and despite the intense political pressure on the tribes, the legislature, and on Congress, from sportsmen who want the steelhead classified exclusively as a game fish, and who believe Indians should give up all steelhead fishing, either for increased allocations of salmon or for financial compensation.

BEYOND THE TRIBES: INDUSTRY-WIDE ISSUES PERSIST

Achieving 50-50: The Impact on Non-Indian Fishermen. In the years following Judge Boldt's ruling in *U.S.* v. *Washington,* the impact of the increased percentage of fish allocated to Indians has been felt by non-Indian commercial fishermen. As table 10.1 indicates, the non-Indian catch has decreased (with the exception of 1977 and 1979) from its average during the years preceding *U.S.* v. *Washington.* The non-Indian fleet has been reduced by Washington's buy-back program, but how effective such reductions have been in mitigating the impact of the decision is not clear.[21] (Table 10.3 shows these changes in the non-Indian fleet.) More recently sports fishermen and charter boat operators have been increasingly affected. When limitations on commercial fishing alone could not balance the Indian and non-Indian shares, the number of fish available for sportsmen also had to be reduced. For example, during the spring of 1982, a confrontation between sport fishermen and Indian fishermen seemed inevitable. It had become clear by 1980 that tribes were not catching their share of Puget Sound chinook. The tribes, failing to reach agreement with the state on how to resolve the issue, took the matter to federal district court. At one point, it appeared that the court might ban all sport fishing on the Sound for six to nine months per year. Subsequently, however, the tribes agreed to a more gradual phase-in of their share in return for the state's concession to some shorter closed seasons, fewer gear restrictions, and increased efforts to enforce regulations. The sport-fishing spokesmen and boathouse operators, relieved that a total ban had been averted, said that "they could live with" the new restrictions—a compromise made possible by the conciliatory attitude of the tribes.[22] Further restrictions on sports fishermen are possible in the future. While the impact on non-Indians will probably continue so long as the fishery remains overcrowded, the Salmon and Steelhead Conservation and Enhancement Act of 1980, described earlier, may in the long term provide some relief. If it does succeed in producing increased runs, then more fish will be available for non-Indians as well as Indians in the future.

Steelhead: Political Pressure Continues. Perhaps the most persistent opponents of Indian treaty fishing are the steelheaders, sports fishermen who love to battle that heroic fighter, the anadromous trout. In 1974, Judge Boldt estimated that there were some 145,000 sport steelhead fishermen licensed by the state Department of Game.[23] (Only Indians can fish commercially for steelhead.) When Slade Gorton, former Washington state attorney general, became a U.S. senator in 1981, one of his first official acts was to introduce a bill to decommercialize steelhead. Washington Congressman Don Bonker introduced the bill in the House. Called the Steelhead Trout Protection Bill, the proposed legislation would have seriously affected the tribal treaty right to take steelhead by ending the sale of steelhead by tribes and by recognizing steelhead as a national game fish. For their loss of these treaty-protected fish, tribes would have had to ask the Federal Court of Claims for compensation—a costly process that might have gone on for many years.

The tribes vigorously fought the bill, holding that they would not sell their treaty rights at any time at any price. Congressional hearings were held in Seattle in June 1981. Oregon Indians dramatized their opposition in a 300-mile walk from Celilo Falls (where their bountiful fishing site had been inundated by waters behind The Dalles Dam in 1957), to the hearings. The room in the Federal Courthouse was packed. Senator Gorton had trouble quieting the crowd, and some speakers could not be heard above the noisy exchanges between steelheaders and Indians. One non-Indian sportsfisherman spoke in behalf of Indian efforts to preserve the steelhead. He was loudly jeered by non-Indians. Indian poet Ed Edmo, speaking of the tribes' need for steelhead, stated: "The white man thinks the river is for sport, but it's not; the river is for life."[24]

The hearings were angry, and the scene resembled a rerun two decades later of the hearings on the abrogation bills of 1964. (See Chapter 5.) Local sports fishermen gave the bill their vocal support, but the National Wildlife Federation, a politically vigorous, national sportsmen's organization, and the Reagan administration opposed it. The Steelhead Trout Protection Bill died in committee, but the steelhead issue has not died, and can be expected to persist for years to come.

Ocean Fishing: National and International Quandary. The ocean fishery is another issue which presents an obstacle to Indians' full exercise of their treaty fishing rights. Recent court decisions on this issue (described in Chapter Eight) have had particular impact on the coastal and Columbia River tribes. These rulings have generally favored the tribal position.

The federal government's management of its 200-mile, offshore fishing zone affects allocations and protection of various salmon species. Setting seasons that permit off-shore trollers—almost entirely non-Indian—to catch too many fish cuts into harvests by both Indians and non-Indians fishing closer to shore. Seasons favoring trollers also permit harvests of "mixed stocks," since the fishing occurs before the fish divide up to return to their natal streams. This makes it difficult to manage and protect individual runs. Indians have frequently differed with non-Indians on the management of these areas. According to Mason Morisset, attorney for several tribes, "The Indians are more protective of smaller runs, whereas non-Indians would prefer to wipe them out so that they don't have to be bothered with them anymore."[25] (Non-Indians could then fish more heavily on the stronger stocks.)

Managing the fishing within the 200-mile zone is an issue complicated by its international implications for Canadian and United

States harvests. Since salmon do not respect international boundaries, many salmon spawned in the United States are caught passing through Canadian waters on their way home. Similarly, U.S. fishermen harvest Canadian-spawned fish. It has been estimated that Canadians catch more than half of the Puget Sound stocks of coho and chinook, stocks which are vitally important to the tribes. Some tribes, in turn, benefit from huge Canadian runs of sockeye and pink salmon headed for the Fraser River. The International Pacific Salmon Fisheries Commission was formed in 1937 to deal with these runs. New reciprocal agreements were required when both the U.S. and Canada began extending their national fisheries jurisdictions further seaward. The two countries reached a series of short-term agreements during the 1960s and early 1970s, but since 1977, when they established the 200-mile unit of jurisdiction, they have encountered more difficulties in negotiating an agreement between them.

The difficulties are hardly simple ones. The movements of the fish are not always predictable, and even the task of estimating how many of one country's fish are being "intercepted" by the other has been extremely complex.[26] The two countries operate under vastly different management systems: the U.S. supports a relatively decentralized system with many local, regional, and now tribal managers, while Canada has much stronger federal control. In 1982, after many years of negotiation, the U.S. and Canada agreed upon a draft resolution, but it has not yet been approved (as of January 1985). The tribes continue to be involved in the negotiations and to follow the progress of this draft with interest and concern.

CONCLUSION:
GUARDED HOPES, FEELINGS OF FREEDOM AND PEACE

While problems persist—there is the threat to take steelhead away from the tribes, the uncertain outcome of international negotiations, and the unsettled environmental issue—the decade since Judge Boldt's ruling in *U.S.* v. *Washington* has witnessed a renewed partnership between the Indian people and the fish. In the spring of 1983, Bill Frank, Jr., chairman of the Northwest Indian Fisheries Commission, observed in his message to the tribes: "Each year since the 1974 ruling by Federal Judge George Boldt affirming the Tribes' right to manage the resource and to catch half the harvestable amount of salmon and steelhead, the Commission has seen the Tribes receive increased recognition as fisheries resource managers. This is a good feeling for all Indian people in western Washington, this is a proud feeling."[27]

Indians have begun to feel hope, however guarded, now that gains have been made. Linda Jones, a Tulalip woman, put it this way: "My reasons for optimism are in the people coming in with their fish and their new boats. It is more than making a living—it is a way of life. There is a sense of pride. People feel like they are being their own bosses, despite their obligations. It is their established way of life. When I see my father fishing, I feel that he is free and at peace."[28]

Chapter 11

What Shall Endure?

This book has explored the controversy arising out of the Indians' struggle to secure the fish—a struggle that has persisted for more than a century, reaching a culmination with Judge Boldt's attempt at resolution in *U.S.* v. *Washington* in 1974. The events chronicled in the preceding chapters have been extremely important for Northwest Indian tribes and for salmon. The implications for American society and for the environment we share are equally important. The significance of the effort to secure the fish is the focus of this chapter.

SURVIVAL: THE INDIANS AND THE SALMON

The efforts of the tribes to preserve their right to fish from the time of the treaties unto the present attests to remarkable perseverance against great odds. Indian people fought to secure the fish on the streams and in the courts, over many years and at great personal risk. Both traditional culture and contemporary economic self-sufficiency have been at stake. Reflecting upon the Indian fishing rights struggle, attorney Harrison Sasche, formerly with the U.S. Department of Justice, said that "the real impact is that it shows the lengths that the Indians will go to to preserve their culture. It is the opposite of the myths regarding Indians— that they are lazy and don't want to work. That the Indians would keep on fishing despite adversity, despite having their nets cut and their gear confiscated, is very important."[1]

Indian perseverance has been evident in the convictions and actions of many tribal members with diverse viewpoints, who were, as Indian historian Cecelia Carpenter described it, united with one heart.[2] They were assisted in their efforts by attorneys committed to defending Indian treaty rights and by non-Indian individuals and organizations active in supporting those rights. Their tenacity was rewarded by the decision in *U.S.* v. *Washington*, issued by Judge Boldt and then affirmed by the Supreme Court. As a result, the Indians of western Washington have been able to link their deeply-held traditions and their means of support. Fishing has finally been re-established as an enterprise of major importance whereby individuals can make a living and tribes can develop and exercise their managerial authority. The Columbia River tribes, facing diminished runs, persist in their struggle to catch enough fish to meet their needs.

Indians continue to persevere, not only as fishermen but also as managers working with tribal committees, state agencies, and the federal councils where fisheries policies and programs are developed and implemented. There is no doubt that events in coming years will continue to test Indian tenacity. The tribes are faced with new management challenges from within and with continuing pressures from outside, especially regarding steelhead. The tribes will have to make their own decisions about managing their fisheries in coordination with their members, with other tribes, and with state agencies. Their problems are not over. "The answer," said Bill Frank, Jr., chairman of the Northwest Indian Fisheries Commission, "is down the path."[3]

The salmon, like the tribes, have been engaged in a century of struggle. From the bountiful runs witnessed by Lewis and Clark in 1804, the salmon have decreased to a fraction of their historic abundance. Yet the fish, like the tribes, have survived. Even after the volcanic eruption of Mount St. Helens in 1980 destroyed salmon spawning beds on the Toutle River, the fish established a route back to nearby streams within a few years. Even with over-fishing, pollution, and obstruction from dams, there are still salmon in the Northwest. Salmon with a catch value of approximately $52 million, a processed value of $108 million, and a retail value of $151 million were harvested in 1982 (a year when no pinks were harvested).[4] The salmon, too, are persistent.

Dire predictions that the recognition of Indian treaty-fishing rights would ruin the Northwest fishery have not been borne out in the decade following the *U.S.* v. *Washington* ruling. The short time that has elapsed has not given signs of a precipitous decline. Some runs are threatened and in need of protection, but causes other than Indian fishing are responsible. A relatively constant pattern seems to be emerging, and, in general, the catch in western Washington appears to be holding steady. *Seattle P-I* reporter Don Hannula observed that Judge Boldt "didn't destroy the resource. He reapportioned the harvest. He painfully shifted an economic base. Now, after a decade of bitterness, there are signs of new cooperation among Indians, government officials, and non-Indian fishermen."[5]

Indeed, since Judge Boldt's ruling, procedures have been put into place that can be expected to contribute to the long-term well-being of the salmon. These include increased monitoring of fish and fishermen and better systems of data collection and analysis. Federal legislation (the Northwest Power Act and the Salmon and Steelhead Conservation and Enhancement Act) has been enacted and holds promise for the future. Concern has at last been focused on the impact that fishing far out to sea has upon the cycle of the salmon, a problem that particularly affects the coastal and Columbia River tribes. The *U.S.* v. *Washington* decision has also directed public attention to the quality of the environment and to the river systems themselves, the waters so critical to salmon survival. It is here that Indian managers, with their intimate knowledge of and dependence upon the rivers, can make an especially important contribution to salmon management.

This book's account of two populations—the Indian tribes and the salmon—suggests several parallels. Both Indians and salmon have been the victims of the expansion of the American nation with its increasing urbanization and industrialization. Both Indians and salmon depend upon the rivers for their way of life. Just as the salmon have struggled to renew themselves, so have the tribes had to battle the political currents flowing against them. Both have persisted; both have endured.

The decision in *U.S.* v. *Washington* brought to national attention society's legal obligation to honor its commitments to Indian tribes. Despite the decision's strong affirmation of this obligation, the events following the ruling showed how difficult it is to uphold the treaties.

The process was impeded first of all by the treaty guarantor: the federal government. When it comes to upholding Indian treaty rights, the federal government, especially its executive branch, has been a most ambivalent ally. The U.S. offered support to the tribes by filing and preparing the suit against Washington state. It did so, however, only after years of tribal requests for assistance and only when the threat of violence was imminent. Once it won the case, the government provided funds to the tribes and to the Northwest Indian Fisheries Commission for implementation of the decision. But then federal officials established a task force to find a new "solution," one more satisfactory to non-Indians, to replace the federal victory. When that failed, the U.S. agreed to further review of its victory by the Supreme Court. In the face of widespread defiance, the U.S. was slow in providing the kind of enforcement assistance that would have been appropriate once the first request for Supreme Court review was denied. Once the Supreme Court ruled, Congress passed legislation to benefit the resource, yet federal support for Phase II has been less than complete. Within the government, the federal judicial system has been the most consistent guardian of Indian fishing rights, affirming them on seven separate occasions.

The federal government seems to provide assistance with one hand and remove it with the other. As one former federal official has said, Uncle "stands firm and then backs off." The basis for this apparent pattern may be inherent in the structure of the federal government itself and the Indians' special relationship to it. As many observers have pointed out, various governmental departments and even agencies within them face severe conflicts of interest over Indian rights.[6] On the one hand, historical precedents and the federal courts clearly state that the United States' obligations to the tribes are "of the highest responsibility and trust."[7] On the other hand, the government faces the demands of competing interests that may compromise the performance of its responsibilities to the Indians.

Conflicts between the Department of Interior, where the protection of Indian rights is vested in the Bureau of Indian Affairs, and the Department of Commerce, where protecting commercial fishing interests is of primary concern, have occurred over fishing policy within the 200-mile zone. Other conflicts within the Department of the Interior have occurred as well, for example, between Bureau of Reclamation irrigation projects and the protection of Indian water resources. Several solutions, such as establishing an Office of Trust Rights within a Department of Indian Affairs that is separate from Interior, have been advanced in recent years as mechanisms for overcoming this dilemma.[8] It is unlikely, however, that such corrections to the system will happen soon.

And yet the situation grows increasingly critical. The federal government's fulfillment of its obligations to the tribes seems particularly precarious in this era of concern over diminishing natural resources. Indian fishing rights have been an important issue in several areas of the country outside of western Washington, including Michigan and California. Contention over Indian water rights, which began at the turn of the century, is likely to be prominent in the future. Indians own a substantial percentage of the nation's uranium, coal, oil-shale, geothermal, natural gas, and petroleum reserves.[9] States and private companies probably will come into more frequent conflict with the tribes over the use of these resources.[10]

The states in particular can be powerful, persistent adversaries, as the experience in *U.S.* v. *Washington* has shown. In the role of owners of what others want, the Indian tribes historically have been extremely vulnerable. Their position today is equally insecure. The tribes require the support of the federal government to protect their resources. As a small and relatively powerless portion of the population, they cannot hope to exert the kind of political pressure that larger, wealthier groups can command. For this reason, public support for Indian treaty rights is particularly important.

Enlisting public support for honoring treaty commitments is a difficult task. Many people do not understand that treaties are contracts between the Indian tribes and the United States government, and that treaties are constitutionally the supreme law of the land. Such people are unaware of the historical and legal precedents underlying these solemn commitments. In the past, many people were drawn into the controversy surrounding Judge Boldt's ruling without enough knowledge to understand the reasons for the decision. Indeed, attitudes towards the decision as measured by two public opinion polls were quite negative.[11] Many people saw the decision as "unfair." According to a third poll, once the Supreme Court substantially affirmed Judge Boldt, more people, but still not a majority, considered him fair.[12] The Supreme Court conveyed to the public the legal validity of Judge Boldt's ruling; by August 1979, most people polled agreed that the time had come to abide by the decision.[13]

A segment of the population still refuses to recognize the Indian treaty fishing right. They continue to see *U.S.* v. *Washington* as a ruling based on racial bias rather than the affirmation of a legal contract. In the fall of 1983, a coalition of several sports-fishing groups, calling themselves Steelhead-Salmon Protection Action for Washington Now (S/SPAWN), circulated a petition for citizen Initiative 84 to prohibit the state from complying with federal court orders relating to natural resources unless the state legislature authorized the necessary expenditures. Further, Initiative 84 declared that no citizen can be denied access to or use of natural resources for reasons based on race, sex, origin, or cultural heritage.[14] In effect the initiative would have given the state legislature the right to veto Department of Fisheries and Game appropriations budgeted for fisheries management in accordance with the *U.S.* v. *Washington* decision. This action would have jeopardized the state's eligibility for federal matching funds.

The coordinator for the initiative, State Senator Jack Metcalf, a former commercial fisherman, framed the issue in terms of the principle of equal rights for all citizens—an argument that the Supreme Court affirmation of *U.S.* v. *Washington* stated had no merit in this situation. As a columnist for the *Seattle Post-Intelligencer* newspaper, John DeYonge, wrote: "The initiative's central doctrine that a state can override the federal mandate has been found unconstitutional many times. From a practical standpoint, the Civil War settled the issue forever."[15]

The petition, although it gathered 135,000 signatures, fell short of the 138,472 names required to put the initiative on the ballot.[16] Then, early in 1984, S/SPAWN introduced a modified version, Initiative 456. This version claimed the state's salmon and steelhead resources to be imperiled, sought national game fish status for steelhead, declared that only the state is responsible for natural resource management (and then only for conservation, enhancement, and proper utilization) and held that, as Indians are citizens, their treaty rights are unconstitutional.[17] Thus in 1984 the tribes faced still another challenge to their treaty guaranteed fishing rights. They received support from a major sports-fishing organization, the Northwest Steelhead and Salmon Council of Trout Unlimited, whose members had tired of fighting and believed their energies were better directed toward working with the tribes to enhance the fish runs. Environmental, religious, and civic organizations also opposed the initiative. Together, these groups formed a unique alliance, the Coalition for Cooperative Fisheries Management, with the purpose of keeping Initiative 456 off the ballot.

Nonetheless S/SPAWN collected the required signatures, and Initiative 456 was placed on the November 6, 1984, ballot with the wording: "Shall Congress be petitioned to decommercialize steelhead, and state policies respecting Indian rights and management of natural resources be enacted?"

The tribes received widespread support in their efforts to defeat the initiative. A Committee to Nix 456 was formed. The list of individuals and organizations condemning Initiative 456 was long and impressive. It included the League of Women Voters of Washington, the Washington Environmental Council, Trout Unlimited, the Washington Labor Council (AFL-CIO), the Washington Forest Protection Association, and the Washington State Charter Boat Association. Both Republican and Democratic candidates for governor, most of the Washington delegation to the U.S. Congress, church leaders, and major daily newpapers opposed it as well.[18]

Despite the array of civic leaders advising the public to vote down Initiative 456, a majority of Washington voters approved it by a narrow margin.[19] The effects of its passage are not yet clear. However, one lesson of Initiative 456 is obvious: the struggle is not over.

SURVIVAL: NATIONAL HONOR AND PEACEFUL COEXISTENCE

The battle over Indian fishing rights has been long and costly. A great deal has been at stake—a set of promises, a cultural system, and a natural system. But the implications go beyond the specific details of this particular controversy. The nation's honor has also been at stake. The tribes kept their promises and asked the nation to keep its word as well. When the state ignored the Indians' rights and the federal government hesitated to protect them, the tribes' desperate struggle called into question the nation's willingness to uphold its solemn commitments, and in so doing, its willingness to abide by its own system of justice.

For some it may seem that Indian treaties exist at the extremities of the system of justice. The treaties signed so long ago may appear expendable in today's society. For example, the Interstate Congress for Equal Rights and Responsibilities (a national organization sometimes called the "white backlash" for its opposition to Indian treaty rights) has argued that the constitutional rights of all Americans must supersede treaty rights of some Americans.[20] Similarly, in a survey of Washington state citizens conducted in 1978, half of those interviewed felt that it was "more important to meet the needs of local communities today than it is to maintain Indian rights guaranteed over 100 years ago."[21] Indeed some of the people who voted for Initiative 456 may see things this way. What this viewpoint fails to consider, however, is that a system of justice that sheds its past commitments may overlook its present and future ones as well. No system can retain the respect of its citizens for long under such circumstances. Even those areas that may appear to exist at the extremities of the law in time or place may have an effect upon the law at its center.

It has often been suggested that disregard for the rights of any minority portends the loss of rights for all citizens.[22] In this sense, the late legal scholar Felix Cohen drew an analogy between the Indian people with their special relationship to the federal government and the canary that miners placed in the mine to test for the presence of sufficient air to breathe: "Like the miner's canary, the Indian marks the shift from fresh air to poison air in our political atmosphere . . . our treatment of Indians, even more than other minorities, reflects the rise and fall of our democratic faith."[23]

Fair treatment of Indians helps to ensure fair treatment of all citizens in this country. It also speaks well for the nation in the eyes of the world community. The struggle of American Indians, with its own distinct history, is linked in spirit to the struggle of indigenous peoples in many other countries as well. If the U.S. government can honor its commitments to its own indigenous people, perhaps other governments will be encouraged to treat their indigenous people with fairness and respect.

CONCLUSION

On March 18, 1984, Judge George H. Boldt died. Mourning his death, the Columbia River Inter-Tribal Fish Commission stated: "It was his 1974 decision, upheld by the United States Supreme Court, that gave new hope to Northwest Indian tribes after long years of injustice. He reaffirmed our treaty rights to the salmon resource that is the center of our culture, livelihood and religion. We are grateful for his time on earth. We will not forget him."[24]

Judge Boldt had hoped that his ruling in *United States* v. *Washington* would resolve the Indian fishing rights controversy. In the decade following the decision, much has been resolved but the controversy has not fully abated.

However, even when the recent initiative passed by a narrow margin, the tribes of Washington state took heart from the new alliances they had developed in the campaign to defeat it. They prepared a salmon dinner at Daybreak Star Indian Center in Seattle overlooking Elliott Bay to honor and thank these supporters. Addressing about 300 guests, Bill Frank, Jr., stated: "You see people working together, you get energy. You start to trust each other. If the salmon were watching, he could see that energy move. In the next ten years, we're going to continue sitting down and talking with one another. The mountains are watching us here. They are our power. We've got to use that power and talk about it, try to keep the energy going. We've got a lot of work ahead of us."[25]

Notes

PREFACE

1. Record of the council proceedings wherein the Treaty of Point No Point was negotiated and executed, January 26, 1855, Exh. PL–15, Joint Appendix to *U.S.* v. *Washington,* p. 331.

2. American Friends Service Committee, *Uncommon Controversy: Fishing Rights of the Muckleshoot, Puyallup, and Nisqually Indians* (Seattle: University of Washington Press, 1970), p. 198.

3. Robert Steven Grumet, *Native Americans of the Northwest Coast: A Critical Bibliography* (Bloomington: Indiana University Press, 1979).

4. Elizabeth Rosenthal, review of *Uncommon Controversy, American Anthropologist* 73 (1971): 956–57.

Chapter 1
THE BOLDT DECISION: DESECRATION OR AFFIRMATION?

1. Vine Deloria, Jr., *Indians of the Pacific Northwest* (New York: Doubleday, 1977), p. 171.

2. Fred Brack, "The Salmon, the Indians, and the Boldt Decision," *Seattle Post–Intelligencer,* Living Textbook Supplement, March 20, 1978, p. A.

3. Walter Evans, "Battle for Indian Fishing Rights Joined," *Seattle Post–Intelligencer,* August 28, 1973. p. A4.

4. *United States* v. *Washington,* 384 F. Supp. 312 (1974), p. 330.

5. *United States* v. *Winans,* 198 U.S. 371 (1905), p. 381.

6. Ezra Meeker, *Pioneer Reminiscences of Puget Sound: The Tragedy of Leschi* (Seattle: Lowman and Hanford, 1905), p. 309.

7. Treaty of Point No Point. 12 Stat. 933.

8. *U.S.* v. *Washington,* 506 F. Supp. 187 (Phase II) (1980), p. 190.

9. Washington Department of Fisheries, United States Fish and Wildlife Service, and Washington Department of Game, *Joint Statement Regarding the Biology, Status, Management, and Harvest of the Salmon and Steelhead Resources of the Puget Sound and Olympic Peninsular Drainage Areas of Western Washington,* Exh. Jx–2a of *U.S.* v. *Washington* (1973).

10. *U.S.* v. *Washington,* 384 F. Supp. 312 (1974), pp. 393–94. After the Supreme Court ruled in Puyallup II in 1973, the Game Department had to modify its position.

11. Don Hannula, "For Whom Is State Saving Fish? Indians Ask at Trial," *Seattle Times,* September 5, 1973, p. B7.

12. Garrison Morrison, testimony, trial transcript, *U.S.* v. *Washington,* p. 4009.

13. *Sohappy* v. *Smith,* 302 F. Supp. 899 (1969), p. 19.

14. Post-trial Brief of Fisheries. (Docket No. 399): p. 36. ID, p. R. 1375 (cited in Brief of the Respondent Indian Tribes, *State of Washington* v. *Washington State Commercial Passenger Fishing Vessel Association and Washington Kelpers Association,* U.S. Supreme Court, October Term 1978, p. 53, n. 184.)

15. Forrest Kinley, testimony, trial transcript, *U.S.* v. *Washington,* pp. 3021–22.

16. Ralph W. Johnson, "The States versus Indian Off-Reservation Fishing: A United States Supreme Court Error," *Washington Law Review* 47 (1972): 207.

17. Alvin J. Ziontz, "Tribal Report to the Presidential Task Force on Treaty Fishing Rights in the Northwest: History of Treaty Fishing Rights in the Pacific Northwest," 1, part 2 (October 28, 1977): 33.

18. Bill Frank, Jr., testimony, trial transcript, *U.S.* v. *Washington,* p. 4237.

19. Judge George Boldt, comments in court, trial transcript, *U.S.* v. *Washington,* p. 4237.

20. Don Hannula, "Indian Tribes Win Fishing-Rights Case," *Seattle Times,* February 12, 1974, p. 14, columns 1–8.

21. Five other tribes which did not have federal recognition as Indian tribes at the time of the case, sought to be included (Snohomish, Snoqualmie, Samish, Steilacoom, and Duwamish). They were later excluded and currently are seeking to gain federal recognition.

22. *U.S.* v. *Washington,* 384 F. Supp. 312, p. 343.

23. Ibid., p. 401.

24. Ibid., pp. 407–8.

25. Ibid., pp. 340–42.

26. Ibid., p. 338, n. 26.

27. Ibid., pp. 343–44.

28. Ibid., p. 413.

29. Ibid., p. 329.

30. Interview with Ralph Johnson, professor of law, University of Washington, May 1984.

31. Chet Skreen, "There Goes De Judge," *Seattle Times Magazine*, December 25, 1977, p. 9.

32. Ross Anderson, "Shortened Seasons Force Them to Risk Lives, Say Fishermen," *Seattle Times*, November 13, 1981, p. B2.

Chapter 2
BEFORE THE TREATIES

1. Margot Astrov, ed., *American Indian Prose and Poetry: An Anthology* (New York: Capricorn, 1946), p. 279.

2. It is possible that even in this land of plenty there may have been periodic shortages. This possibility, and the potential of potlatching in redistributing scarce resources, has been debated. See Robert Steven Grumet, *Native Americans of the Northwest Coast: A Critical Bibliography* (Bloomington: Indiana University Press, 1979), pp. 25–28, for a review of this issue and further references.

3. The Makah are an exception because they had specific and consistent summer villages also. See Barbara Lane, "Makah Economy circa 1855 and the Makah Treaty: A Cultural Analysis," in *U.S.* v. *Washington*, USA-Exh. 21, at p. 5. For background information on traditional economic and social life of Northwest tribes, see Hermann Haeberlin and Erna Gunther, *The Indians of Puget Sound* (Seattle: University of Washington Press, 1930, reprinted 1973), the tribal descriptions prepared by Barbara Lane as U.S. Exhibits in *U.S.* v. *Washington*, and the United States Indian Claims Commission volumes in the American Indian Ethnohistory series published on Northwest tribes by Garland Press (New York); also Grumet *Native Americans of the Northwest Coast*.

4. *United States* v. *Winans* 198 U.S. 371 (1905), p. 381.

5. Edward G. Swidell, Jr., *Report on Source, Nature, and Extent of the Fishing, Hunting, and Misc. Related Rights of Certain Indian Tribes* (Office of Indian Affairs, U.S. Department of the Interior, Los Angeles, 1942) p. 368.

6. Marian W. Smith, *The Puyallup-Nisqually*, Columbia University Contributions to Anthropology 32 (New York: Columbia University Press, 1940), p. 2.

7. Ibid., p. 6.

8. *U.S.* v. *Washington*, 384 F. Supp. 312, p. 353.

9. Barbara Lane, Summary Anthropological Report in *U.S.* v. *Washington*, USA-Exh. 20, p. 19.

10. Sally Snyder, "Aboriginal Salt Water Fisheries: Swinomish, Lower Skagit, Kikiallus, and Samish Tribes of Indians," pp. 33–34, included as Appendix 1 of Barbara Lane, "Anthropological Report on the Swinomish Indian Tribal Community," in *U.S.* v. *Washington*, USA-Exh. 74.

11. Hilary Stewart, *Indian Fishing: Early Methods on the Northwest Coast* (Seattle: University of Washington Press, 1977); W. W. Elmendorf, *Structure of Twana Culture*, Washington State University Research Studies 28 (Pullman, Wash.: 1960).

12. AFSC, *Uncommon Controversy*, p. 5.

13. Frachtenberg manuscript quoted in Barbara Lane, "Anthropological Report on the Identity, Treaty Status, and Fisheries of the Quileute and Hoh Indians," in *U.S.* v. *Washington*, USA-Exh. 22, pp. 13–14.

14. George Gibbs, "Notebook II, 1854–1855, Cascade Road–Indian Notes," National Archives, Record Group E–198. Cited and discussed in Barbara Lane, "Anthropological Report on the Identity, Treaty Status and Fisheries of the Nisqually Tribe of Indians," in *U.S.* v. *Washington*, USA-Exh. 25, p. 279. (Joint Appendix 356–57.)

15. Elmendorf, *Structure of Twana Culture*, p. 531.

16. Edward Sapir, *Wishram Texts* 2 (Washington, D.C.: American Ethnological Society, 1909): 7.

17. Erna Gunther, *A Further Analysis of the First Salmon Ceremony*, University of Washington Publications in Anthropology 2 (Seattle: 1925), p. 146.

18. Frank Wright, Testimony before the U.S. Congress, Senate Committee on Interior and Insular Affairs, Subcommittee on Indian Affairs, published in *Indian Fishing Rights: Hearings on S.J.R. 170 and S.J.R. 171*, 88th Cong., 2d sess., Aug. 5–6, 1964, p. 105.

19. Elmendorf, *Structure of Twana Culture*, p. 62.

20. Ibid., pp. 65–66. See also Russel L. Barsh, *The Washington Fishing Rights Controversy: An Economic Critique* (2d ed., rev.; Seattle: University of Washington, Graduate School of Business Administration, 1979), p. 24.

21. Useful descriptions of Pacific salmon and steelhead are found in Wash. Dept. of Fisheries et al., *Joint Statement* (see chap. 1, note 9, above, for complete reference); R. J. Childerhose and Marj Trim, *Pacific Salmon and Steelhead Trout* (Seattle: University of Washington Press, 1979); and Richard S. Wydoski and R. R. Whitney, *Inland Fishes of Washington* (Seattle: University of Washington Press, 1979).

22. There are thus both genetic and ecologic requirements to this definition; see V. A. MacLean and D. O. Evans, "The Stock Concept, Discreteness of Fish Stocks and Fisheries Management," *Canadian Journal of Fisheries and Aquatic Sciences,* special issue (Stock Concept Symposium), 38 (1981): 1890. Also see P. A. Larkin, "The Stock Concept and Management of Pacific Salmon," pp. 11–15 in R. C. Simon and P. A. Larkin, eds., *The Stock Concept in Pacific Salmon,* H. R. MacMillan Lectures in Fisheries (Vancouver: University of British Columbia, 1972).

23. Wash. Dept. of Fisheries et al., *Joint Statement,* p. xx.

24. Peter Larkin, *Pacific Salmon: Scenarios for the Future* (Seattle: Washington Sea Grant, 1980), p. 9.

25. Childerhose and Trim, *Pacific Salmon,* p. 32.

26. Anthony Netboy, *The Salmon: Their Fight for Survival* (Boston: Houghton Mifflin, 1973), p. 531.

27. Childerhose and Trim, *Pacific Salmon,* pp. 31–44.

28. Wash. Dept. of Fisheries et al., *Joint Statement,* p. 5.

29. Childerhose and Trim, *Pacific Salmon,* p. 42.

30. Wash. Dept. of Fisheries et al., *Joint Statement,* pp. 4–8.

31. Ibid., pp. 17–20.

32. Olin D. Wheeler, *The Trail of Lewis & Clark 1804–1904* (new ed.; New York: G. P. Putnam and Sons, 1926), 2:139.

33. Gordon W. Hewes, "Aboriginal Use of Fishery Resources in Northwestern North America" (Ph.D. diss., University of California, Berkeley, 1947), pp. 214–28; Deward E. Walker, Jr., *Mutual Cross-Utilization of Economic Resources in the Plateau: An Example from Aboriginal Nez Perce Fishing Practices,* Washington State University Laboratory of Anthropology, Report of Investigations 41 (Pullman, Wash.: 1967).

34. Ezra Meeker, *Pioneer Reminiscences of Puget Sound: The Tragedy of Leschi* (Seattle: Lowman and Hanford, 1905).

Chapter 3
CLASH

1. Essentially the same language is present in the Treaty of Point Elliott (1855), Treaty of Medicine Creek (1854), Treaty with the Quinault et al. (1855 and 1856), Treaty with the Yakimas (1855), and Treaty with the Makah (1855). One difference is that the phrasing in the Makah treaty adds the right of whaling and sealing in the same sentence. Another is that several treaties refer to "all citizens of the Territory" rather than "all citizens of the United States." (This difference became a matter

194 *Notes*

of contention in the mid-1980s in relation to the determination of who should be included in the non-Indian allocation.)

2. Francisco de Vitoria, *De Indis et De Jure Belli Reflectiones* (1557), trans. John Pawley Bate, ed. Ernest Nys, sec. 2 titles 6,7 (Washington, D.C.: Carnegie Institution, 1917).

3. Felix S. Cohen, *Handbook of Federal Indian Law* (1942) (Albuquerque: University of New Mexico Press, 1958), pp. 46–47.

4. United States Constitution, Article I, Section 8.

5. Ibid., Article VI.

6. *United States* v. *Winans,* 198 U.S. 371 (1905), p. 381.

7. Quoted by Andy Fernando in the introduction to this book.

8. 1 Stat. 51 (1787).

9. *Cherokee Nation* v. *Georgia,* 30 U.S. (5 Pet.) 1 (1831).

10. *Worcester* v. *Georgia,* 31 U.S. (6 Pet.) 515 (1832).

11. E.g., *United States* v. *Kagama,* 118 U.S. 375 (1886).

12. For more information on the "trust relationship" see Reid Peyton Chambers, "Discharge of the Federal Trust Responsibility to Enforce Claims of Indian Tribes: Case Studies of Bureaucratic Conflict of Interest," in U.S. Senate, *A Study of Administrative Conflicts of Interest in the Protection of Indian Natural Resources* (Washington, D.C., Government Printing Office, 1971). For a more recent discussion, see United States Commission on Civil Rights, *Indian Tribes: A Continuing Quest for Survival* (Washington, D.C.: U.S. Government Printing Office, 1981), pp. 23–25.

13. See "Comment: The Indian Battle for Self-Determination," 58 *California Law Review* 445 (1970), for a discussion of plenary power, and Charles F. Wilkerson and John M. Volkman, "Judicial Review of Indian Treaty Abrogation: 'As Long As Water Flows, or Grass Grows Upon the Earth'—How Long a Time Is That?," 63 *California Law Review* 601 (1975), for a discussion of abrogation of treaties by the federal government.

14. Francis Paul Prucha, *American Indian Policy in the Formative Years: The Indian Trade and Intercourse Acts* (Cambridge: Harvard University Press, 1962).

15. Henry E. Fritz, *The Movement for Indian Assimilation, 1860–1890.* (Philadelphia: University of Pennsylvania Press, 1963).

16. Report of the Indian Agent, S. D. Howe, Puget Sound District Executive Documents 1864–65, (Washington, D.C.: 1865), p. 73.

17. Quoted in Francis Paul Prucha, ed., *Americanizing the American Indians: Writings By the "Friends of the Indian 1880–1900"* (Lincoln: University of Nebraska Press, 1978), p. 1.

18. Federal Statutes 9:323, August 14, 1848.

19. American Friends Service Committee, *Uncommon Controversy: Fishing Rights of the Muckleshoot, Puyallup, and Nisqually Indians* (Seattle: University of Washington Press, 1970), p. 16.

20. C. F. Coan, "The Adoption of the Reservation Policy in the Pacific Northwest 1853–55," *Oregon Historical Quarterly* 13 (1962): 2.

21. Ibid., pp. 4–5.

22. Ibid., p. 21.

23. Ibid., pp. 9–10.

24. Murray Morgan, *Puget's Sound: A Narrative of Early Tacoma and the Southern Sound* (Seattle: University of Washington Press, 1979), p. 85.

25. Alvin Josephy, *The Nez Perce Indians and the Opening of the Northwest* (New Haven: Yale University Press, 1965), p. 293.

26. George Gibbs to Captain McClelland, March 4, 1854, Executive Document No. 91, House of Representatives, 33rd Cong., 2d sess. Exh. PL–9, Joint Appendix in *U.S.* v. *Washington,* p. 326.

27. Treaty of Point No Point Council proceedings, Joint Appendix in *U.S.* v. *Washington,* p. 331.

28. Treaty of Point No Point, 12 Stat. 933.

29. Isaac Stevens to Commissioner of Indian Affairs, December 30, 1854, transmitting Treaty of Medicine Creek and proceedings of Treaty Commissioners between December 7–26, 1854; tracings of Nisqually, Puyallup, and Squaxin Reservations, Exhibit PL–11, Joint Appendix in *U.S.* v. *Washington,* p, 329.

30. Herbert Hunt and Floyd Kaylor, *Washington, West of the Cascades* (Chicago: S.F., Clark, 1917), 1: 143.

31. See also, Cecelia Svinth Carpenter, *They Walked Before: The Indians of Washington State* (Tacoma: Washington State Bicentennial Commission, 1977), pp. 26–30.

32. Barbara Lane, "Anthropological Report on the Swinomish Indian Tribal Community," prepared for *U.S.* v. *Washington,* USA-Exh. 74.

33. H. C. Hale, Annual Reports of Indian Agents–Washington Territory, September 1, 1863. *Annual Reports–Commissioner of Indian Affairs,* 1863, p. 440.

34. Morgan, *Puget's Sound,* pp. 118–20, and Carpenter, *They Walked Before,* pp. 31–34. These sources and Carpenter's "Leschi: Last Chief of the Nisquallies," *Pacific Northwest Forum* 1, (1976): 4–11, also provide additional information on the treaty-making period.

35. Barbara Lane, Summary Anthropological Report, in *U.S.* v. *Washington,* USA-Exh. 20, Joint Appendix 393; and Courtland Smith, *Salmon Fishers of the Columbia* (Corvallis: Oregon State University Press, 1979), p. 5.

36. AFSC, *Uncommon Controversy*, p. 154.

37. Smith, *Salmon Fishers*, p. 15.

38. Ibid.

39. Anthony Netboy, *The Salmon: Their Fight for Survival* (Boston: Houghton Mifflin, 1973), p. 276.

40. Ibid., p. 350.

41. Smith, *Salmon Fishers*, p. 13.

42. Russel L. Barsh, *The Washington Fishing Rights Controversy: An Economic Critique* (2d ed., rev.; Seattle: University of Washington, Graduate School of Business Administration, 1979), pp. 23–24.

43. Smith, *Salmon Fishers*, p. 27, describes the immigrant fishermen.

44. Howard Droker, *Puget Sound Fishermen*, This City, Seattle, Program (1979).

45. Barsh, *Washington Fishing Rights Controversy*, p. 24.

46. See ibid. for further discussion of controversy over traps and an overview of the economics of the fishery in Washington.

47. Smith, *Salmon Fishers*, pp. 91–100.

48. State of Washington, 9 Report 25, 1878.

49. State of Oregon, *First and Second Annual Reports of the Game and Fish Protector, 1894*, p. 7. Michael C. Blumm, in "Hydropower vs. Salmon: The Struggle of the Northwest's Anadromous Fish Resources for a Peaceful Coexistence with the Federal Columbia River Power System," *Environmental Law* 11 (1981): 215, n. 10, states that overfishing led to a decline in the commercial catch from 43 million pounds in 1883 to 18 million pounds in 1935.

50. Smith, *Salmon Fishers*, p. 83.

51. Brief of Respondent Indian Tribes, *State of Washington* v. *Washington State Commercial Passenger Fishing Vessel Association and Washington Kelpers Association*, U.S. Supreme Court, October Term, 1978, p. 29, citing Exh. Jx–2a, table 25.

52. Wash. Sess. Laws, chap. 31, sec. 72 (1915). For a chronology of Puget Sound salmon fishing regulations, see Wash. Dept. of Fisheries et al., *Joint Statement*, table 25 (see chap. 1, note 9, above, for complete reference).

53. James A. Crutchfield and Giulio Pontecorvo, *The Pacific Salmon Fisheries: A Study of Irrational Conservation* (Baltimore: Johns Hopkins Press, 1969), pp. 131–32.

54. Russel L. Barsh, "The Economics of a Traditional Coastal Indian Salmon Fishery," *Human Organization* 41 (1982): 171.

55. Barsh, *Washington Fishing Rights Controversy*, p. 27.

56. Smith, *Salmon Fishers*, p. 96.

57. Barsh, *Washington Fishing Rights Controversy*, pp. 33–34.

58. Smith, *Salmon Fishers*, p. 96.

59. Ralph W. Johnson, "Regulation of Commercial Salmon Fishermen: A Case of Confused Objectives," *Pacific Northwest Quarterly* 55 (October 1964): 141.

60. Hugh Smith, "Notes on a Reconnaissance of the Fisheries of the Pacific Coast of the United States in 1894," *Bulletin of the Fish Commission* 14 (1895): 244, cited in Smith, *Salmon Fishers*, p. 76.

61. Netboy, *The Salmon*, p. 285.

62. Smith, *Salmon Fishers*, p. 80, provides these calculations and gives numerous citations on p. 76, n. 19. See also Netboy, *The Salmon*.

63. Smith, *Salmon Fishers*, p. 78.

64. Ibid., citing Chaney & Perry. Also see Blumm, "Hydropower vs. Salmon," pp. 218–21, for a discussion of the impact that seasonal flow manipulations to maximize hydropower production have upon salmon.

65. Oral Bullard and Don Lowe, *Short Trips and Trails: The Columbia Gorge* (Beaverton, Oreg.: Touchstone Press, 1974), p. 79.

66. Smith, *Salmon Fishers*, p. 102.

67. Netboy, *The Salmon*, p. 355.

68. See ibid., p. 356, for more recent period.

69. AFSC, *Uncommon Controversy*, p. 161, quoting *Pollution Caused Fish Kills*, U.S. Public Health Service, Bulletin 847 (Washington, D.C.: U.S. Government Printing Office, 1964), p. iii.

70. Wash. Dept. of Fisheries et al., *Joint Statement*, pp. 22–23.

71. Washington Fish Commission, *Annual Report*, 1890.

72. Howard Droker, "History of Hatcheries in Western Washington" (unpublished MS, Seattle, 1980).

73. Netboy, *The Salmon*, pp. 335–36.

74. Droker, "History of Hatcheries." Problems with disease in hatchery-bred fish continue to the present. For example, Washington Department of Fisheries' Soleduck hatchery on the Olympic Peninsula experienced repeated outbreaks of bacterial kidney disease (BCD) in the 1970s (see Bruce Brown, *Mountain in the Clouds: A Search for the Wild Salmon* [New York: Simon and Schuster, 1982], pp. 116–18); and the Dworshak National Fish Hatchery on the Columbia suffered severe losses to its steelhead eggs and fry from IHN (a waterborne virus) in the early 1980s (see *Northwest Energy News* 4, no. 2 [March/April 1985]: 20).

75. Droker, "History of Hatcheries."

76. Smith, *Salmon Fishers*, p. 79.

77. Biologist Phil Mundy, cited in 1980 in the "Memorandum of Plaintiff Tribes in Support of Motion for Summary Judgment on the

Issue of Treaty Inclusion of Hatchery Fish," *U.S.* v. *Washington*, Civil No. 9218, Phase II, p. 35, states the following: 61.9 percent of chinook and 62 percent of coho in Puget Sound are hatchery bred; over 50 percent of available chum in Hood Canal are hatchery fish. In 1978, Sam Wright, Director of Harvest Management for Washington Department of Fisheries, testified that statewide 50–60 percent of harvested coho and chinook were hatchery produced ("Memorandum," p. 34). Also see transcript of April 6, 1978, hearing concerning 1978 Enforcement Order, pp. 263–64.

78. Crutchfield and Pontecorvo, *Pacific Salmon Fisheries*, pp. 135–36.

79. Hersherger Affidavit on Phase II, pp. 12–15; interview notes with biologists. For additional discussion of this issue, see Brown, *Mountain in the Clouds.*

Chapter 4
FISHING "IN COMMON"?

1. U.S. Congress, Senate Committee on Interior and Insular Affairs, Subcommittee on Indian Affairs, *Indian Fishing Rights: Hearings on S.J.R. 170 and S.J.R. 171*, 88th Cong., 2d sess. August 5–6, 1964, p. 12.

2. For discussion of internal self-government see Felix S. Cohen, *Handbook of Federal Indian Law* (1942) (Albuquerque: University of New Mexico Press, 1942), p. 46. For readings on the development and ramifications of the policy of assimilation see Francis Paul Prucha, ed., *Americanizing the American Indians: Writings by the "Friends of the Indian 1880–1900"* (Lincoln, University of Nebraska Press, 1978).

3. Wilcomb E. Washburn, *The Assault on Indian Tribalism: The General Allotment Law (Dawes Act) of 1887* (Philadelphia: J.P. Lippincott, 1975).

4. Ibid.

5. Kirke Kickingbird and Karen Duchenaux, in *One Hundred Million Acres* (New York: Macmillan Co., 1973) describe the land loss process including allotment; also see Wilcolmb E. Washburn, *Red Man's Land—White Man's Law,* (New York: Scribners, 1971), p. 75.

6. Roscoe Pound, "A Theory of Social Interests," Publications of the American Sociological Society, 15 (1920): 44.

7. *United States* v. *Taylor*, 3 Washington Territory 88 (1887).

8. *United States* v. *Winans*, 198 U.S. 371 (1905). The other six cases are *Seufert Brothers* v. *United States*, 249 U.S. 194 (1919); *Tulee* v. *Washington*, 315 U.S. 681 (1942); *Puyallup Tribe* v. *Department of*

Game, 391 U.S. 392 (1968); *Puyallup Tribe* v. *Department of Game,* 414 U.S. 44 (1973); *Puyallup Tribe* v. *Department of Game,* 433 U.S. 165 (1977); *Washington et al.* v. *Washington State Commercial Passenger Vessel Association et al.,* 443 U.S. 658 (1979).

9. *United States* v. *Winans,* pp. 380–81.

10. Ibid.

11. Ibid., p. 384.

12. *Seufert Brothers* v. *United States.*

13. Ralph Johnson, "The States vs. Indian Off-Reservation Fishing: A U.S. Supreme Court Error," *Washington Law Review* 47 (1972): 207.

14. *State* v. *Towessnute,* 89 Wash 478 (1916).

15. *State* vs. *Alexis,* 89 Wash 492 (1916).

16. *State* v. *Towessnute,* pp. 484–85. *Tulee* v. *Washington* overruled the decisions in Towessnute and Alexis.

17. *State* v. *Towessnute,* pp. 481–82.

18. Ziontz, "Tribal Report," p. 22 (see chap. 1, note 17, above, for complete reference).

19. *Kennedy* v. *Becker* 241 U.S. 556 (1916).

20. Ziontz, "Tribal Report."

21. Ibid.

22. Malcolm McDowell, "Report to the Board of Indian Commissioners" (Washington, D.C., 1921) pp. 85–86.

23. Cecelia Carpenter, Interview, June 1980.

24. Testimony of Hattie Cross, Joint Appendix to Briefs in the Supreme Court of the U.S., October Term, 1967, no. 247, *Puyallup Tribe* v. *Department of Game of the State of Washington and the Department of Fisheries of the State of Washington,* pp. 189–90.

25. Monroe Price, *Law and the American Indian: Readings, Notes and Cases* (Indianapolis: Bobbs-Merrill, 1973), study cited on p. 225, "Administration of the Indian Office," Bureau of Municipal Research 65 (1915), p. 17.

26. Institute for Government Research, *The Problem of Indian Administration* (Baltimore: Johns Hopkins Press, 1928).

27. Ibid., p. 3.

28. Ibid., p. 15.

29. Ibid., p. 88.

30. D'Arcy McNickle, *Native American Tribalism* (London: Oxford University Press, 1973), pp. 94–96.

31. U.S. Congress, Senate, *Hearings on S.J.R. 170 and S.J.R. 171,* pp. 141–44.

32. Ibid., pp. 67, 155–58, 184.

33. Ratified in 1859.

34. *Tulee* v. *Washington,* 315 U.S. 681 (1942), p. 685.

35. *Makah* v. *Schoettler* 192 F. 2d 224, 9th circuit (1951).

36. For a useful discussion of the termination policy see Washburn, *Red Man's Land—White Man's Law,* pp. 80–97.

37. See Nancy O. Lurie, "Menominee Termination: From Reservation to Colony," *Human Organization* 31 (Fall 1972): 257–70. It is important to note that subsequent court decisions held that termination did not affect treaty hunting and fishing rights. See *Menominee* v. *United States,* 391 U.S. 404 (1968). In 1976, after a long struggle on their part, the Menominee were restored to tribal status.

38. *United States* v. *Kagama,* 118 U.S. 375 (1886), p. 384.

39. Hazel Hertzberg, *The Search for an American Indian Identity* (Syracuse, N.Y.: Syracuse University Press, 1971), p. 291.

40. *Washington Post,* April 12, 1954, cited in S. Lyman Tyler, *A History of Indian Policy* (Washington, D.C.: U.S. Dept. of the Interior, 1973), pp. 174–75.

41. Tyler, *A History of Indian Policy,* p. 174.

42. Vine Deloria, Jr., *Indians of the Pacific Northwest* (New York: Doubleday, 1977), p. 258.

43. Alvin M. Josephy, *Red Power: The American Indian's Fight for Power* (New York: McGraw-Hill, 1971), p. 80.

44. Interview with Hank Adams, May 1979.

Chapter 5
FISHING FOR JUSTICE

1. Washington Sess. Laws, chap. 178, sec. 4 (1925); chap. 258, sec. 1 (1927); chap. 1, sec. 4–11 (1935). (Initiative passed November 6, 1934, enacted into law 1935.)

2. Interview with Frank Wright, Puyallup tribal councilman, July 1980.

3. *State* v. *Satiacum* 314. P2d (1957).

4. Ziontz, "Tribal Report," p. 26 (see chap. 1, note 17, above, for complete reference). Quoted with permission of the author.

5. *Maison* v. *Confederated Tribes of the Umatilla Indian Reservation,* 312 F2d 169 (9th cir.) (1963) Cert. denied 375 U.S. 829 (1963).

6. Ibid., pp. 172–74.

7. "Net Rippers Plague Indian Fishermen," *Daily Olympian,* March 28, 1962.

8. "Skagits on Warpath? Shots, Violence Reported in Indian Fishing Dispute," *Seattle Times,* January 8, 1963, p. 19, "Fishing by Muckleshoots Still Enjoined," *Seattle Times,* November 8, 1963, p. 12. In the

former case, state officials claimed that Indians were threatening them. In the latter, the county enjoined fifteen Muckleshoots from fishing for salmon in the Green River and its tributaries.

9. Interview with Cecelia Carpenter, June 1980.

10. Russel L. Barsh, *The Washington Fishing Rights Controversy: An Economic Critique* (2d ed., rev.; Seattle, University of Washington, Graduate School of Business Administration, 1979), p. 28.

11. Ibid., p. 30.

12. Stan Patty, "New Group Tackles Indian Fishing Issue," *Seattle Times*, December 3, 1967, p. 39.

13. W. Royce et al., *Salmon Gear Limitation in Northern Washington Waters*, University of Washington Publications in Fisheries n.s. 2, no. 1, 1963.

14. J. Carl Mundt. *Report of the Regional Task Force of the Presidential Task Force on Northwest Fisheries Problems Concerning Catch, Licensing, Gear Reduction, and Allowable Fishing Time History for Washington Salmon Fisheries 1965–1975* (December 3, 1977), p. 5 and Exhibits 13 and 14.

15. U.S. Congress, Senate Committee on Interior and Insular Affairs, Subcommittee on Indian Affairs, *Indian Fishing Rights: Hearings on S.J.R. 170 and S.J.R. 171,* 88th Cong., 2d sess., Aug. 5–6, 1964, p. 23.

16. Ibid., p. 7.

17. Ibid., p. 80.

18. Ibid., p. 147, citing Royce et al., *Salmon Gear Limitations,* p. 1.

19. U.S. Congress, Senate, *Hearings on S.J.R. 170 and S.J.R. 171,* p. 52.

20. Barsh, *Washington Fishing Rights Controversy,* p. 83.

21. Don Hannula, "Marlon Nets 2 Steelhead in Puyallup," *Tacoma News Tribune*, March 2, 1964, p. 1.

22. Interview with Suzette Bridges, June 1980.

23. American Friends Service Committee, *Uncommon Controversy: Fishing Rights of the Muckleshoot, Puyallup, and Nisqually Indians* (Seattle: University of Washington Press, 1970), p. 16.

24. Interview with Robert Johnson, Public Information Officer at Small Tribes of Western Washington (STOWW), July 1980.

25. Robert Cummings, "Tanner Asks Pardon for Dick Gregory," *Tacoma News Tribune*, June 18, 1968, pp. 1–2.

26. "Indians Fish under Guard," *Portland Oregonian*, April 28, 1966, p. 19.

27. "Armed Indians Intolerable," *Daily Astorian*, April 26, 1966, p. 4.

28. *Puyallup Tribe* v. *Department of Game et al.*, 391 U.S. 392 (1968), p. 398. See Ralph W. Johnson, "The States versus Indian Off-Reservation Fishing: A United States Supreme Court Error," *Washington Law Review* 47 (1972): 207–36, for a discussion of the first Puyallup case, and particularly of the role of the federal brief, which, he argues, acted to the detriment of the tribes when it conceded that state regulation was proper when necessary for conservation (page 225). For an alternate view on "error" in Puyallup decisions, see "Comments, State Regulation of Indian Treaty Fishing Rights: Putting Puyallup III into Perspective," *Gonzaga Law Review* 13 (1977): 140–89.

29. Barsh, *Washington Fishing Rights Controversy*, pp. 61–62, points out that although the Game Department does receive substantial funds from sportsmen's fees and fines, it also receives support from the federal government, e.g., for its steelhead hatchery program.

30. "Yakima Indian War Hero, Uncle, Bailed Out after Fishing Arrest," *Skamania County Pioneer*, June 21, 1968, p. 1.

31. AFSC, *Uncommon Controversy*, p. 201, n. 1. Cited in the *Decree* as *Sohappy* v. *Smith*, USDC D. Oregon, No. 68–409, and *U.S.* v. *Oregon*, USDC D. Oregon No. 68–513 (1969). The decision itself speaks of "fair share."

32. *Sohappy* v. *Smith*, 302 F. Supp. 899 (1969), p. 912.

33. John C. Gartland, "*Sohappy* v. *Smith*: Eight Years of Litigation over Indian Fishing Rights," *University of Oregon Law Review* 56 (1977): 680–701.

34. George Dysart, Interview, September 1979. His action was reported in William Greider, "U.S. Had Warning of Indian Wrath on Fishing Rights," *Washington Post*, September 25, 1970, p. A3.

35. AFSC, *Uncommon Controversy*, p. 107.

36. Hal Hogan, "Hank Adams Shot While Tending Net," *Daily Olympian*, January 19, 1971, p. 1; "Indian Leader Hedges, Police Cancel Lie Test," *Seattle Times*, April 7, 1971, p. E12.

37. Don Hannula, "State Stalks Indians Stalking Salmon," *Seattle Times*, July 20, 1972, p. A5.

38. *Puyallup Tribe* v. *Department of Game*, 414 U.S. 44 (1973), p. 49.

Chapter 6
THE BOLDT DECISION: ENFORCE OR EFFACE?

1. This statement applies to 1977 and 1978, the earliest years for which treaty fleet size figures are available. In 1977, the nontreaty fleet was 5,320, while the treaty fleet numbered 1,121. In 1978, the nontreaty

fleet was 1,380 and the treaty fleet was 5,372. These figures, which do not include licenses issued for Willapa Bay and the Columbia River, are based on Washington Department of Fisheries licenses issued during 1977 and 1978, cited in Northwest Indian Fisheries Commission, *Annual Report* (1978), p. 14.

2. Northwest Indian Fisheries Commission, *Annual Report* (1978), p. 1.

3. Ibid.

4. Memorandum from the regional director of the Bureau of Sports Fisheries and Wildlife, Portland, Oreg., from the deputy director, re: Judge Boldt Decision Funding, July 2, 1974. There was a dispute over these funds when Washington state tried to negotiate a subcontract to do the studies—and found significant support among the federal government. The tribes and BIA protested and the case was dropped.

5. *U.S.* v. *Washington,* 384 F. Supp. 408–412. These questions were raised by the Washington Department of Fisheries in a Motion for Reconsideration.

6. *U.S.* v. *Washington,* 459 F. Supp. 1020 (1978), p. 1051.

7. *U.S.* v. *Washington,* 384 F. Supp. 312 (1974), p. 420. Self-regulating tribes were not bound by the interim plan.

8. "Angry Fishermen Protest during Ford's Visit," *Seattle Times,* October 25, 1976, p. A1.

9. Jonathan Nesvig, "He's 72 Today: Boldt Still Going Strong," *Tacoma News Tribune,* December 28, 1975, p. A3.

10. *Revised Code of Washington* 75.30.065.

11. Mundt, *Report of the Regional Task Force* (see chap. 5, note 14, above, for complete reference).

12. Slade Gorton, Public Disclosure Commission Filing Form F1, January 20, 1976, and F1-A, July 16, 1976, with attached copy of 1975 income tax report.

13. When Gorton became a U.S. Senator in 1981, he placed these holdings in a blind trust so that he no longer received annual profits. In 1984, the holdings reportedly had an assessed value of more than $250,000. "State's Congressmen Show'n Tell Wealth," *Seattle Post-Intelligencer,* May 19, 1984, p. A1; "Correction: Gorton Isn't Getting Profits on His Stock," *Seattle Post-Intelligencer,* May 23, 1984, p. A3.

14. *U.S.* v. *Washington,* 590 F. 2D 676 (1975).

15. Ibid., p. 693.

16. *U.S.* v. *Washington,* 423 U.S. 1086 (1976).

17. James Johnson, presentation to commercial fishermen, broadcast on "Cabbages and Kings," KUOW-FM, Seattle, August 28, 1978.

18. The state buy-back program began in 1975. An initial evaluation

prepared by William S. Jenson and Douglas Egan ("Washington Gear Reduction Program: Profile and Analysis," October 1978), based upon 90 responses from 264 participants indicated that only 48 left the commercial salmon fishery; 42 (47%) still fished for salmon using different vessels and licenses. This study is marred by sampling problems but it suggests that the program was doing little to reduce the number of people engaged in salmon fishing. Scott Maier describes state mismanagement of the program in "State Fisheries' Buy Back Program: On the Rocks," *Argus* 85, no. 48 (December 1, 1978): 1, 4.

19. *Puget Sound Gillnetters Association* v. *Moos*, 88 Wn. 2d 677, 565 P. 2d 1151 (1977), *Washington State Commercial Passenger Vessel* v. *Tollefson*, 89 Wn. 2d 276, 571 P. 2d 1373 (1977).

20. *U.S.* v. *Washington*, 459 F. Supp. 1028 (1974), p. 1034.

21. Ibid., p. 1030, n. 3.

22. Brief of Respondent Indian Tribes, *State of Washington* v. *Washington State Commercial Passenger Fishing Vessel Association and Washington Kelpers Association*, U.S. Supreme Court, October Term 1978, p. 65, nn. 231, 232.

23. Ibid., p. 66.

24. Exh. PL-M-4(a) entered into Supreme Court record.

25. "Fishing War: FBI Steps In," *Seattle Post-Intelligencer*, October 22, 1976, p. 1.

26. "Gillnetter Skipper Shot," *Seattle Post-Intelligencer*, Oct. 25, 1976, p. 1.

27. Kirk Smith, "State Will Probe Gillnetter Shooting," *Seattle Post-Intelligencer*, October 27, 1976, p. A6. Carlson subsequently sued the state and later won a sizable out of court settlement; see "Injured Gillnetter's Suit Settled for $250,000," *Seattle Times*, October 10, 1978, p. D8.

28. Richard A. Whitney, Memo to Honorable Walter E. Craig, "Status Report," September 24, 1979.

29. Interview with Dr. Richard Whitney, July 21, 1980.

30. George Dysart, personal communication, May 13, 1980.

31. Some have suggested that this perception may have been based on the fact that tribal fisheries agencies had a less voluminous and established data base than the state, which had been gathering data for a much longer time.

32. Interview with Bruce Doble, fisheries biologist, Muckleshoot tribe, July 24, 1980.

33. Interview with Mason Morisset, July 22, 1982.

34. *U.S.* v. *Washington*, 459 F. Supp. 1020 (1978), p. 1069.

35. 88 Wn. 2d 677 P. 2d 1151 (1977).

36. Ibid., p. 691.

37. *Washington State Commercial Passenger Fishing Vessel Association* v. *Tollefson*, 89 Wn. 2d 276, 571 P 2d 1373 (1977). For a full discussion of the error in the equal protection argument in this case, see Ralph W. Johnson and E. Susan Crystal, "Indians and Equal Protection," *Washington Law Review* 54 (1979): 613, especially n. 151. Johnson and Crystal emphasize that an Indian treaty cannot violate the Fourteenth Amendment to the federal Constitution, because the amendment applies only to state action and the treaty is a federal action. Also, with regard to state law and administration, the federal law has supremacy over state law.

38. *Puyallup Tribe* v. *Department of Game* (Puyallup III), 433 U.S. 165 (1977).

39. *Puget Sound Gillnetters Association* v. *United States District Court*, 573 F 2d 1123 (1978), p. 1126 (9th Cir.), cert. granted, 99 S. Ct. 277.

40. Tribal Brief (see note 22, above), p. 70.

41. Ibid., pp. 71–72.

42. Ruth Pumphrey, "Point Roberts Incident Indian Fishing Vessels Damaged," *Seattle Post-Intelligencer,* August 28, 1978, p. A1.

43. A training session was held for participants. There was difficulty in obtaining permission to observe on government boats; AFSC worked closely with the tribes.

44. U.S. Commission on Civil Rights, *Indian Tribes: A Continuing Quest for Survival* (Washington, D.C.: U.S. Government Printing Office, 1981), p. 75.

45. National Congress of American Indians, *Bulletin,* Spring 1976, p. 8.

46. Regional Team of the Federal Task Force on Washington State Fisheries, "Settlement Plan for Washington State Salmon and Steelhead Fisheries," June 1978. p. 11.

47. Interview with White House staff member who asked that his name not be used, December 13, 1979.

48. The national team consisted of Anne Wexler, former deputy under-secretary for Regional Affairs, Department of Commerce; Leo Krulitz, solicitor, Department of Interior; James Moorman, assistant attorney general, Land and Natural Resources Division, Department of Justice; Forrest Gerard, assistant secretary for Indian Affairs, Department of the Interior; and Richard Frank, administrator, National Oceanic and Atmospheric Administration, Department of Commerce. The regional team members were John Merkle, United States attorney, chairman of the team; Dr. Dayton L. Alverson, director of the Northwest and

Alaska Fisheries Center, National Marine Fisheries Service; and John Hough, director of the Western Field Office, Department of Interior.

49. John Merkel, Dayton L. Alverson, and John Hough, written testimony before U.S. Commission on Civil Rights, hearing on American Indian Fishing Rights in the State of Washington (Seattle, August 25, 1978), vol. 3, exhibit 2, p. 157. The report that was prepared following the hearings, *Indian Tribes: A Continuing Quest for Survival,* provides an excellent reference for readers wishing more detailed information on the Task Force.

50. Merkel et al., written testimony before U.S. Commission on Civil Rights, vol. 3, p. 145.

51. Ibid., pp. 40–41.

52. H.R. 9054, 95th Cong., 1st sess., 1977.

53. Regional Team, "Settlement Plan" (see note 46, above).

54. State of Washington, "Comments on Settlement Plan for Washington State Salmon and Steelhead Fisheries and Alternative Fishery Management Plan," presented to the Federal Task Force on Washington State Fisheries, August 22, 1978, pp. 2–6.

55. Commercial-Recreational Fisheries Delegation, "Settlement Plan for Washington State Salmon and Steelhead Fisheries," August 1978.

56. Billy Frank, Jr., testimony before the U.S. Commission on Civil Rights (see note 49, above), vol. 3, p. 124.

57. Frankie M. Freeman, ibid., vol. 3, p. 40.

58. Only one member of the delegation, Representative Mike Lowry, was a strong and consistent supporter of Indian treaty rights.

59. Henry M. Jackson and Warren G. Magnuson to Griffin Bell, March 1, 1978, cited in testimony before U.S. Commission on Civil Rights (see note 49, above), vol. 4, exhibit 4, pp. 4–5.

60. Jackson and Magnuson to Cecil Andrus, August 4, 1978, cited in ibid., pp. 6–7.

61. U.S. Commission on Civil Rights, *Indian Tribes,* p. 72.

Chapter 7
SEVENTH KNOCK AT THE HIGH COURT DOOR

1. Observers in the departments of both Interior and Justice have suggested privately that the decision to agree to review had an important political component. Senators Jackson and Magnuson had expressed disapproval of the Boldt decision on several occasions and they held powerful positions in the Senate that directly affected appropriations to the departments.

2. Leo Krulitz to Wade H. McCree, Jr., August 18, 1978.

3. Memorandum from the associate solicitor, Indian Affairs, to solicitor, U.S. Department of Interior, Subject: Certiorari in *U.S.* v. *Washington*, August 17, 1978.

4. Memorandum from assistant secretary, Indian Affairs, to solicitor, U.S. Department of Interior, Subject: Supreme Court Review of *U.S.* v. *Washington*, no date.

5. The Pacific Legal Foundation is a California-based nonprofit organization that argued that courts were "granting" special privileges to Indians. Their position is based on an interpretation of "equal rights, responsibilities, and opportunities" similar to the abrogation bill described in chapter 6 (p. 103). See Motion for Leave to File Brief *Amicus Curiae* of Pacific Legal Foundation (U.S. Supreme Court, 1978).

6. Ed Nakawatase, national coordinator of American Friends Service Committee Indian Programs, memo to Barbara Moffett regarding the Supreme Court Hearing on Northwest Fishing Cases, March 26, 1979.

7. Transcript of Hearing before U.S. Supreme Court, *State of Washington* v. *Washington State Commercial Passenger Fishing Vessel Association and Washington Kelpers Association; State of Washington et al.* v. *United States et al.;* and *Puget Sound Gillnetters et al.* v. *United States District Court for the Western District of Washington*, 443 U.S. 658 (1979), p. 5.

8. Ibid., pp. 45–56.

9. Ibid.

10. Ibid., p. 673.

11. Ibid., p. 673, n. 20. George Dysart has suggested that the relegation of the refutation of this argument to a footnote in the section concurred to by nine justices and the citation (along with Supreme Court opinions) of the judge who had dissented in the Washington Supreme Court case was the judges' way of emphasizing their disdain for the Washington Supreme Court opinion. See Dysart, "Northwest Indian Fishing Rights: A Supreme Court Affirmation" (unpublished ms., 1979), p. 9.

12. *Washington* v. *Washington State Commercial Passenger Fishing Vessel Association et al.*, 443 U.S. 658 (1979), pp. 676–77, n. 22.

13. Ibid., p. 679.

14. Ibid., pp. 684–85.

15. Ibid., pp. 686–87.

16. Ibid., p. 705. The dissenting judges viewed the treaties as securing only: (1) the right to access over private land to reach traditional fishing sites; (2) the exclusive right to fish on reservation; (3) the guarantee of enough fish to meet their subsistence and ceremonial needs; (4)

exemption from state regulation, including the payment of license fees, except as necessary for conservation and only then if it does not discriminate against Indians (p. 707–9). Thus these judges seemed to favor the position argued by Washington Attorney General Slade Gorton.

17. Ibid., p. 704.

18. Ibid., pp. 695–96.

19. In arguing for Supreme Court review, Attorney General Gorton had asserted that the state would abide by the high court ruling. After the Supreme Court decision, the Washington Attorney General's office not only filed for reconsideration but also asked the district court judge to determine the meaning of "moderate income" and asked the tribes for information concerning income and property. The tribe refused to answer the questions and objected to the state's request. On September 16, 1980, Judge Walter E. Craig agreed with the tribes and ordered the state to make a more specific request if it wished to pursue the matter. The state did not pursue the issue at that time. Phil Katzen, Evergreen Legal Services Native American Project, personal communication, May 1984.

20. Susan Gilmore, "Gorton Sees Partial Victory in Ruling," *Seattle Times,* July 2, 1979, p. A17.

21. Dean Katz, "Magnuson for Legislative Changes in Indian Treaties," *Seattle Times,* July 2, 1979, p. A1, and "Court Fails to Take Congressmen off Fishing Rights Hook," *Seattle Times,* July 8, 1979, p. A22.

22. Paul Andrews, "Indians Pleased by Ruling on Boldt," *Seattle Times,* July 2, 1979, p. A15.

23. Katz, "Court Fails to Take Congressmen off Fishing Rights Hook."

24. "Fair Share: For Indian Fishermen," *Seattle Post-Intelligencer,* July 5, 1979, p. B2.

25. "Treaty Rights Are Law of the Land," *Seattle Times,* July 3, 1979, p. A12.

26. Jon Hahn, "Fishermen Expected Better Deal," *Seattle Post-Intelligencer,* July 2, 1979, p. A1.

27. "Fishing Story Clarified," *Seattle Post-Intelligencer,* July 5, 1979, p. A7.

28. Bruce Sherman, "Indians Hail Complete Vindication," *Seattle Post-Intelligencer,* July 3, 1974, p. A7.

29. Susan Gilmore and Warren King, "Fishermen Upset by High Court Decision," *Seattle Times,* July 2, 1979, p. A15; Andrews, "Indians Pleased by Ruling on Boldt."

30. Eyewitness News, KIRO-TV, 6 P.M., July 3, 1979, Interview by Ken Woo with U.S. District Judge (retired) George Boldt.

31. Paul Andrews, "Judge Boldt Calls High-Court Ruling on Fishing Rights' 'Victory for Justice,'" *Seattle Times,* July 2, 1979, p. A1.
32. "Boldt Elated by the Ruling," *Seattle Post-Intelligencer,* July 3, 1979, p. A6.
33. Sherman, "Indians Hail Complete Vindication."
34. KING-TV News, Interview with Bill Frank, Jr., 6 P.M., July 3, 1979.

Chapter 8
FISHING THE COLUMBIA: CAN NEGOTIATION REPLACE LITIGATION?

1. Ed Chaney, *A Question of Balance: Energy/Water—Salmon and Steelhead Production in the Upper Columbia River Basin* (Pacific Northwest Regional Commission, 1978), p. 1.
2. Ibid., p. 4. Also see p. 12 for a discussion of the technologies, such as passageways, used to deal with the problem of fish mortality at the dams and reservoirs.
3. Ibid., p. 2.
4. John C. Gartland, "*Sohappy* v. *Smith:* Eight Years of Litigation over Indian Fishing Rights," *Oregon Law Review* 56 (1977): 694.
5. "Court Order Cites Trollers," *Oregonian,* June 28, 1976, p. 1A.
6. *U.S.* v. *Oregon,* Civil 68–513, February 28, 1977, pp. 4–5.
7. Order, "A Plan for Managing Fisheries on Stocks Originating from the Columbia River and Its Tributaries Above Bonneville Dam," February 28, 1977 (C.R. 296). *U.S.* v. *Oregon,* Civ. No. 68–513 (D.Or.), pp. 1–6. For further description of these tasks and discussion of the Five-Year Plan, see L. Heinemann and K. Rosenbaum, "Securing a Fair Share: Indian Treaty Rights and the 'Comprehensive Plan,'" *Anadromous Fish Law Memo,* Natural Resources Law Institute, Lewis & Clark Law School, Portland, Oregon, Issue 21, March 1983.
8. "Plan for Managing Fisheries," p. 9.
9. Ibid., p. 2.
10. Ibid., p. 1.
11. Columbia River Inter-Tribal Fish Commission, *Information Booklet,* n.d., p. 1.
12. For Columbia River spring chinook landings 1971–82, see table II–41, p. 63–11, in Pacific Fishery Management Council, "Proposed Plan for Managing the 1983 Salmon Fisheries off the Coasts of California, Oregon, and Washington," Portland, May 1983. Their figures do not agree exactly with CRITC figures on fall chinook, because PFMC includes jacks.
13. Kay Brown, "Why Do the Indians Get All the Fish?" *Oregon*

Wildlife, December 1982. It has been reported that fish buyers will pay about three times as much for brights as for tules; see Laura Berg, "Salmon Surprises: Fall Fishing '83," *CRITFC News* (Columbia River Inter-Tribal Fish Commission), July-September 1983, p. 3.

14. Figures for 1975 and 1976 provided in memorandum from Timothy Wapato, executive director, Columbia River Inter-Tribal Fish Commission, May 27, 1982. (The figures exclude ceremonial and subsistence catches.) Figures for the period during the Five-Year Plan are from Laura Berg and Elizabeth Smith, Columbia River Inter-Tribal Fish Commission, "Five Years of the Five Year Plan," *CRITFC News,* January-March 1982, p. 6.

15. Tribal Proposal before the Columbia River Compact, August 13, 1981 (table 1, p. 13): "In the Matter of the Adoption of Rules Relating to the Management of the Columbia River Commercial Fishery under the Columbia River Compact; Reply to Proposed Rules and Recommendations, and Proposals for Management of Columbia River Commercial Fishery." According to Jean Edwards, the tribal proposal was adopted with minor revisions by the court.

16. Heinemann and Rosenbaum, "Securing a Fair Share," p. 9.

17. Ed Chaney and L. Edward Perry, *Columbia Basin Salmon and Steelhead Analysis,* Summary Report, September 1, 1976, Pacific Northwest Regional Commission.

18. Laura Berg and Elizabeth Smith, "The Ocean Connection—Crisis for Chinook," *CRITFC News,* April–June 1981, p. 4.

19. Notes from meeting of the PFMC Salmon Advisory Committee, Summer 1979.

20. Interview with Jean Edwards, biologist, Columbia River Inter-Tribal Fish Commission, September 1979.

21. *Confederated Tribes* v. *Kreps,* Civ. No. 68–541 (D. Ore. September 10, 1979).

22. Remarks made by Judge Robert C. Belloni, Portland, Ore., June 28, 1979.

23. Ibid.

24. Observation of AFSC researcher and television journalist Sandra Osawa, July 1979.

25. Cecil Andrus to Juanita M. Kreps, March 23, 1973; June 25, 1979. Also see memo from acting director, United States Fish and Wildlife Service, to secretary, Department of the Interior, Subject: Impact of Proposed Ocean Fishing Regulations on Conservation and Inside Indian and Non-Indian Fisheries, March 23, 1979. In this case, it is interesting to note that the states of Washington and Oregon, each eager to see fish

return to its own waters, lent their support to the tribal position and argued for a shorter ocean season.

26. Interview with Sidney Lezak, September 21, 1979.

27. *Confederated Tribes* v. *Baldrige*, C–80–342 (W. D. Wash.). *Hoh Tribe et al.* v. *Baldrige*, 522 F. Supp 683 (1981).

28. Cited in Heinemann and Rosenbaum, "Securing a Fair Share," p. 8.

29. *Hoh* v. *Baldrige*, p. 690.

30. Ibid., p. 687. The catches cited for Washington offshore troll were:

	Chinook	*Coho*
1977	443,000	1,206,000
1979	224,000	956,000
1980	187,000	748,000

For further information on ocean catches under PFMC regulation, see PFMC, "Proposed Plan for 1983 Fisheries," table III–40, page 58–III, and other tables.

31. *Hoh* v. *Baldrige*, p. 689. At several points, Judge Craig stresses the principle of flexibility in managing this complex fishery.

32. For further analysis of the salmon sting and the differing viewpoints it generated, see Robin Cody, "If Salmon Were Truth," *Northwest Magazine, The Sunday Oregonian,* April 29, 1984, pp. 7–16. He describes a discussion of the issue among local sportsmen and citizens in which participants could foresee a dead river, with its dams, industry, and off-shore harvests; they would later "think back on 1984, on how the mighty Columbia was lying there with a heart condition and a hangnail. And how the government went after the hangnail—its Indian fishermen—with a sledgehammer" (p. 16).

33. Interview with David Sohappy, September 20, 1979.

34. *United States Department of Commerce News,* Western Regional Center, Seattle, June 17, 1982 (NOAA-SEA-82-12).

35. "Statement of Columbia River Treaty Tribes on Allegations of Illegal Indian Fishing," adopted by Council of Councils, July 9, 1982, p.1.

36. "16 Indians Guilty of Violating Fish Laws," *Seattle Post-Intelligencer,* April 29, 1983, p. C15.

37. Interview with Jack Schwartz, March 1984.

38. Laura Berg, "Missing Fish," *CRITFC News,* July-December 1982, p. 3.

39. News release, Columbia River Inter-Tribal Fish Commission, April 14, 1983.

40. S. Timothy Wapato to Herman McDevitt, chairman, Pacific Fisheries Management Council, November 16, 1982, in PFMC, "Proposed Plan for 1983 Fisheries," p. C–11.

41. Berg and Smith, "Five Years of the Five Year Plan," p. 6.

42. Laura Berg, "In Court," *CRITFC News,* January-February 1984.

43. Interview with Laura Berg, public information officer, Columbia Inter-Tribal Fish Commission, April 16, 1984.

Chapter 9
SECURING THE HABITAT

1. For a recent collection of articles on artificial fish production and fish ranching, see John E. Thorpe, ed., *Salmon Ranching* (New York: Academic Press, 1980).

2. It arose before the state supreme court and in oral arguments before the U.S. Supreme Court, and perhaps at some point earlier in the proceedings.

3. *Puyallup Tribe* v. *Department of Game,* 391 U.S. 392 (1968) ("Puyallup I"), p. 398.

4. *Puyallup Tribe* v. *Department of Game,* 414 U.S. 44 (1973) ("Puyallup II").

5. Ibid., pp. 49–50.

6. Judge Orrick discusses this chronology and gives citations in *U.S.* v. *Washington,* Phase II, 506 F. Supp. 187 (1980), p. 196.

7. Ibid., p. 193, n. 19.

8. Information from several individuals wishing to remain anonymous.

9. Paul Andrews, "Environmental Impacts: Larger Dispute on Fish-Run Impacts Ahead as Phase II of Boldt Ruling," *Seattle Times,* July 4, 1979, p. A14.

10. Charles Ehlers, speaking at the Indian-Conservationist Conference in Seattle, September 28, 1979.

11. Hazel A. Wolf, Letter to "Friends" of the Federation of Western Outdoor Clubs, March 1, 1979. The amicus was prepared and filed in the case.

12. *U.S.* v. *Washington,* Phase II, 506 F. Supp. 187 (1980), pp. 197, 202.

13. *U.S.* v. *Washington,* Civil No. 9213, Phase II, Reply Brief (Plaintiff's), p. 4, based on Deposition of Donald Chapman and Affidavit of

Peter Larkin. Because there were no statistics gathered on the size of the fish runs during treaty times, it is not possible to quantify the decline precisely.

14. *U.S.* v. *Washington,* Phase II, 506 F. Supp. 187 (1980), p. 198, citing a disputed state stipulation, n. 43.

15. Testimony of Phil Mundy, cited in Memorandum of Plaintiff Tribes in Support of Motion for Summary Judgment on the Issue of Treaty Inclusion of Hatchery Fish, January 20, 1980, p. 14.

16. Fay G. Cohen to Senator Warren G. Magnuson, August 31, 1979, cited in U.S. Congress, Senate Committee on Commerce, Science, and Transportation, *Hearings on Northwest Salmon and Steelhead,* 96th Cong. (Washington, D.C.: U.S. Government Printing Office, 1979), p. 145. Proportion based upon statistics projected by Chuck Dunn, Washington State Department of Fisheries.

17. In oral arguments before Judge Orrick, Edward Mackey, assistant attorney general for the state of Washington, argued that the state had "created" and thus owned the fish.

18. *U.S.* v. *Washington,* Phase II, 506 F. Supp. 187 (1980), p. 203.

19. Ibid., p. 204.

20. Ibid., p. 208.

21. Andy Fernando, "The Skagit, Both Tribe and River," *Wild and Scenic Rivers Conference Newsletter,* 1980, p. 1. The Skagit Wild and Scenic River Act was passed in 1974 with additional legislation in 1978.

22. Point No Point Treaty Council Fiscal Year 1980 *Annual Report,* p. 15.

23. Laboratory tests indicated that 100 percent of chinook salmon tested died when exposed to Alaska North Slope crude oil in concentrations of 1.86 parts per million for fifteen hours. Shrimp larvae died off completely when exposed to napthalene, an ingredient of crude oil, at concentrations of 10 to 12 parts per billion for less than thirty-six hours. See "Giant Oil Spill Scenario Angers Northern Tier," *Daily Olympian,* October 13, 1981, p. A8.

24. There is the possibility that a few of the companies were interested in ocean ranching, which is permitted in Oregon but not in Washington.

25. Two other Task Force participants, John Hough and Lee Alverson, became consultants to the corporate council.

26. Peter C. Monson, "*U.S.* v. *Washington,* Phase II: The Indian Fishing Conflict Moves Upstream," *Environmental Law* (1982): 503. "Summit of Indians, Executives Praised," *Seattle Times,* November 25, 1981.

27. 187 (W.D. Wash. 1980), Ninth Circuit Court of Appeals, nos. 80–3505, 81–3002, 81–3068 and 81–3069, District Court Civil no. 21, filed September 1982.

28. Ibid. (Circuit Court) p. 5 of *slip opinion*. It is also to be noted that *U.S.* v. *Oregon*, 657 F. 2nd 1009 (9th Cir. 1981), is cited by the Circuit Court as a precedent for viewing depletion of a run as a violation of the treaty.

29. *U.S.* v. *Washington*, Phase II, 694 F2d 1374 (9th Cir. 1982), p. 1387.

30. Ibid., p. 1381.

31. Ibid., p. 1389.

32. Ibid., p. 1381.

33. Ibid., p. 1386.

34. "Plaintiff-Appellee Tribes Petition for Rehearing with Suggestion of Appropriateness of Rehearing En Banc," *U.S.* v. *Washington*, no. 81–3111, United States Court of Appeals for the Ninth Circuit, November 16, 1982, p. 13, citing *Condido Mutual Co., et. al.* v. *Federal Energy Regulatory Commission*, no. 79–7625, 80–7100 (November 2, 1982). Also see Joseph G. Jorgensen et al., *Native Americans and Energy Development* (Cambridge, Mass.: Anthropology Resource Center, 1978).

35. "Plaintiff Appellee Tribes Petition for Rehearing," p. 3.

36. Ibid., pp. 3–9.

37. Also called the Northwest Regional Power Act, Public Law 96–501, 94 Stat. 2697 (1980), codified at 16 U.S.C. para. 839–839h (Supp IV 1980). Also see "An Evaluation of the Columbia Basin Fish and Wildlife Program," Anadromous Fish Law Memo, Natural Resources Law Institute, July 1983.

38. Interview with Howard Harris, April 1983.

39. Interview with Joe Miyamoto, April 1983.

40. Donald C. Malins et al., "Chemical Contaminants and Abnormalities in Fish and Invertebrates from Puget Sound," NOAA Technical Memorandum OMPA–19 (NOAA Office of Marine Pollution Assessment, Boulder, Colo. 1982), p. XVIII. (Note that benthic refers to all submarine bottom-terrain, regardless of water depth and that portion of marine environment inhabited by marine organisms which live on or at the bottom. Pelagic refers to free-swimming or floating organisms of the sea not living in the bottom but living in the open sea or close to shore. See *Ocean Marine Dictionary*, Cornell Maritime Press, Centerville, Maryland, 1979.) It is also interesting that these reports were made to NOAA, Mr. Harris's agency.

41. P.M. Chapman et al. "Survey of Biological Effects of Toxicants

upon Puget Sound Biota: I. Broad-Scale Toxicity Survey," NOAA Technical Memorandum OMPA—25 (NOAA Office of Marine Pollution Assessment, Boulder, Colo., 1982), p. IX.

42. Lansing Jones, "Our Pristine State Is Being Fouled by Poisonous Waste," *Seattle Post-Intelligencer,* May 1, 1983, p. A1.

43. Daniel V. Thayer (fisheries biologist for Puyallup Tribe), personal communication, April 15, 1983.

44. Harper-Owes draft report, "Water Quality Assessment of the Duwamish Estuary," prepared for the Municipality of Metropolitan Seattle (Metro), October 1982, p. 4.

45. Ibid., p. VI.

46. PCBs are somewhat like chlorinated hydrocarbon pesticides, but are used in electrical capacitators, transformers, hydraulic fluids, in lubricants, and as plasticizers in waxes. They are no longer produced in the United States. They are exceptionally stable compounds and are persistent in the environment. See Edward A. Laws, *Aquatic Pollution* (New York: John Wiley and Sons, 1981), pp. 256–60. For a discussion of human health effects of PCBs, see K. Higuchi, ed., *PCB Poisoning and Pollution* (New York: Academic Press, 1976), and John M. Last, *Maxcy-Rosenau Public Health and Preventive Medicine* (11th ed; New York: Appleton-Century-Crofts, 1980), pp. 727–28.

47. Don Finney and Steve Elle, biologists for the Muckleshoot Indian Tribe, to Tom Hubbard, water quality planner for METRO, February 8, 1983.

48. Harper-Owes, "Water Quality Assessment," p. 113. For a report on PCBs exceeding FDA guidelines of 5 ppm found in salmon in the Great Lakes and other locales, see R. G. Martin, "PCBs—Polychlorinated Biphenyls," *Sport Fishing Institute Bulletin,* no. 288, September 1977, pp. 1–3.

49. Harper-Owes, "Water Quality Assessment," p. 116.

50. Robert H. Boyle and R. Alexander Boyle, *Acid Rain* (New York: Nick Lyons Books, 1983), p. 12.

51. A map of susceptible lakes and also a chart on effects on salmon can be found in Phil Weller and the Waterloo Public Interest Research Group, *Acid Rain: The Silent Crisis* (Kitchener, Ontario: Between the Lines, 1980), pp. 84 and 20 respectively. Information on the Douglas fir study is provided in Ross Harvard and Michael Perley, *Acid Rain: The North American Forecast* (Toronto: House of Anansi, 1980).

52. Boyle and Boyle, *Acid Rain,* pp. 64–65.

53. Larry Lange, "Acid Rain at a Critical Level Here, Study Says," *Seattle Post-Intelligencer,* September 28, 1983, p. A3.

54. *Still Waters,* Report of House of Commons (Canada) Subcommit-

tee on Acid Rain of the Standing Committee on Fisheries and Forestry, Ottawa, 1981, p. 11.

Chapter 10
WESTERN WASHINGTON TRIBES AND THE SALMON TODAY

1. This presentation focuses only on the *U.S.* v. *Washington* area. The Columbia River situation is discussed in chapter 8.

2. Interview with Michael Grayum, Northwest Indian Fisheries Commission, August 1, 1983.

3. Northwest Indian Fisheries Commission, *Annual Reports,* 1978, 1979, 1980, 1981, and 1982.

4. Interview with Cliff Bengston and Mike Hinton, Tulalip biologists, July 15, 1982. Also, if one looks at salmon *landed* in Washington state as a whole, the strength of the runs is also suggested by increasing poundage over the past three years: 33.8 million lbs. in 1980, valued at $39.8 million; 46.0 million lbs. in 1981, valued at $45.9 million; and 48.0 million lbs. in 1982, valued at $50.1 million. Statistics for 1980 and 1981 landings are from U.S. Department of Commerce, National Oceanic and Atmospheric Administration, *Fisheries of the United States 1981* (Current Fisheries Statistics no. 8200), April 1982, p. viii, and for 1982 from same publication no. 8300, published April 1983.

5. Interview with Harmon Sparr, June 7, 1980.

6. Interview with Carl Jones, July 15, 1982.

7. Interview with Walter Pacheco, Jr., July 24, 1980.

8. Interview with Ron Charles, July 7, 1979.

9. Russel L. Barsh, "The Economics of a Traditional Coastal Indian Salmon Fishery," *Human Organization* 41 (1982): 175.

10. Ibid., pp. 173–74.

11. *Statistical Abstract of the United States,* 1982–83 ed. (U.S. Department of Commerce, Bureau of the Census), p. 437. Both mean and median are statistical indicators of central tendency. The median family income is the amount above which and correspondingly below which 50 percent of the family incomes lie. The mean is the sum of all family incomes divided by the number of families.

12. Barsh, "Economics of a Traditional Fishery."

13. Such information would be very difficult to present because of the "moderate living" ceiling that the Supreme Court imposed upon the Indian catch. Since a "moderate living" has never been defined, tribes are concerned that any data on income at whatever level might be used by the state to argue for reducing the Indian share of the catch.

14. Skagit System Cooperative, *Annual Report,* 1981, p. 18.

15. "Tribes Deserve Credit for Hatchery Increases," *Seattle Times,* March 16, 1982, p. A14.

16. Point No Point Treaty Council *Annual Report,* 1980.

17. Don Hannula, "The Boldt Decision: Ten Years Later," *Seattle Times,* February 12, 1984. p. 16.

18. Interview with Linda Jones, July 1982.

19. Skagit System Cooperative, *Annual Report,* 1981, p. 3.

20. Interview with Rod Marrom, June 28, 1979.

21. If, for example, only less productive boats were sold, then the effect would be minimal.

22. Ross Anderson, "State and Tribes Settle Chinook Dispute," *Seattle Times,* March 30, 1982, p. B1; Brad O'Conner, "Fishermen Say They'll Live with Agreements," *Seattle Times,* March 30, 1982, p. D3.

23. *U.S.* v. *Washington,* 384 F. Supp. 392, p. 399.

24. "Indian Marchers Blast Measures on Steelhead," *Oregon Journal,* June 24, 1981.

25. Interview with Mason Morisset, July 1982.

26. Kenneth A. Henry, "International Salmon Interception," *Science, Politics and Fishing: A Series of Lectures,* Sea Grant College Program (Corvallis: Oregon State University, 1982).

27. Northwest Indian Fisheries Commission, *Annual Report,* 1983, p. 3.

28. Interview with Linda Jones, July 1982.

Chapter 11
WHAT SHALL ENDURE?

1. Interview with Harrison Sasche, December 1979.

2. Interview with Cecelia Carpenter, June 1980.

3. Interview with Bill Frank, Jr., July 1980.

4. 1982 was not a harvest year for pink salmon. In 1981, the catch was valued at $45 million caught and $108 processed. Valuation of the catch may vary according to different measures of value. Department of Fisheries, State of Washington, *Fisheries Statistical Report,* (Olympia, 1982) p. 7. It is interesting to note, however, that, as valuable as the fishing industry is, it represents a minor segment of the state's economy in comparison with aerospace and agricultural products.

5. Don Hannula, "The Boldt Decision: Ten Years Later," *Seattle Times,* February 12, 1984, p. A16.

6. See, for example; Reid Peyton Chambers, "Discharge of the Federal Trust Responsibility to Enforce Claims of Indian Tribes: Case Studies of Bureaucratic Conflict of Interest," in U.S. Senate, *A Study of Ad-*

ministrative Conflicts of Interest in the Protection of Indian Natural Resources (Washington, D.C.: U.S. Government Printing Office, 1971); U.S. Department of Justice, "Report on the Task Force on Indian Matters" (manuscript Washington, D.C., October 1975); William H. Veeder, "Federal Encroachment on Indian Water Rights and the Impairment of Reservation Development," *Toward Economic Development for Native American Communities,* Subcommittee on Economy in Government of the Joint Economic Committee, 91st Cong., 1st sess. (Washington, D.C.: U.S. Government Printing Office, 1969).

7. *Seminole* v. *United States,* 316 U.S. 286 (1942), pp. 296–97.

8. American Indian Policy Review Commission, *Final Report* (Washington, D.C.: U.S. Government Printing Office, 1977): 1: 12–13; also see chap. 4, Trust Responsibility. Note, however, that the Department of Interior tends to view trust responsibility more narrowly.

9. Harris Arthur, Preface, Joseph G. Jorgenson et al., *Native Americans and Energy Development* (Cambridge, Mass.: Anthropology Resource Center, 1978), p. 1.

10. Robert Bee, "To Get Something for the People: The Predicament of the American Indian Leader," *Human Organization* 38 (1979): 245.

11. "Boldt Ruling Liked by Few," *Seattle Times,* April 4, 1976; Education Research Systems and Jay Rockey Public Relations, public opinion survey results for the Pacific Northwest Indian Fisheries Commission, 1977.

12. Øystein Gaasholt and Fay Cohen, "In the Wake of the Boldt Decision: A Sociological Study," *American Indian Journal,* November 1980, pp. 9–17.

13. Ibid.

14. "Initiative to Renew Fish Fight," *Seattle Post-Intelligencer,* September 29, 1983, p. A7, Laura Parker, "Attempt to Overturn Boldt Fish Decision Splits Sportsmen's Groups," *Seattle Post-Intelligencer,* December 17, 1983, p. A4.

15. John DeYonge, "Fishing Initiative a Fruitless Protest," *Seattle Post-Intelligencer,* November 18, 1983, p. A19.

16. Laura Parker, "State Initiatives on Fishing and Budget Fail for Lack of Signatures," *Seattle Post-Intelligencer,* December 31, 1983, p. A3.

17. Initiative 456; also Official Summary on Petition. The official ballot title is "Shall Congress be petitioned to decommercialize steelhead, and state policies respecting Indian rights and management of natural resources be enacted?" It is interesting to note that the 1924 Snyder Act conferring citizenship upon Indians explicitly provided that Indian rights to tribal or other property were not affected by the legislation.

18. Pamphlet, *Nix 456,* published by the Committee to Nix 456; News Release, Washington Forest Protection Association, October 11, 1984.

19. Rita Hibbard, "Fishing Measure Passes but Abortion Ban Loses," *Seattle Post-Intelligencer,* November 7, 1984, p. A1. According to C. Montgomery Associates, the final count prior to tabulation of absentee ballots was 52.7 percent yes and 47.3 percent no (CMJA Assoc., "After Initiative 456, What Then?" November 12, 1984, p. 2).

20. Interstate Congress for Equal Rights and Responsibilities, *Are We Giving America Back to the Indians* (Winner, S.D., n.d.), front cover. Also see C. Herb Williams and Walt Neubrech, *Indian Treaties—American Nightmare* (Seattle: Outdoor Empire Publishing, 1976).

21. C. Montgomery Johnson Associates, "Three Surveys of the Attitudes, Perceptions, and Priorities of Citizens of Washington State Concerning the Native Indians of Washington State" (Olympia, 1978), p. 67. Of those surveyed, 30 percent disagreed and 20 percent were undecided.

22. This and the preceding section also draw upon the analysis of freedom and civil liberty by Thomas R. Berger, *Fragile Freedoms: Human Rights and Dissent in Canada* (Toronto: Clark, Irwin and Co., 1981).

23. Felix S. Cohen, "The Erosion of Indian Rights, 1950–1953: A Case Study in Bureaucracy," *Yale Law Review* 62 (1953): 390.

24. Allen Ankham, Columbia River Inter-Tribal Fish Commission, *CRITFC News* 7, no. 2 (March-April 1984): 7.

25. Bill Frank, Jr., January 5, 1985.

Index

works with Native American Rights Fund, 75; concern over contamination of Commencement Bay, 150–51

Puyallup River, 21, 30, 53, 67; encampment on, 80; chemical contamination of, 151

Puyallup Tribe v. *The Department of Game et al.*, 76–77, 81–82, 99, 107, 113, 138–39

Puyallup Trilogy. *See Puyallup Tribe* v. *The Department Game et al.*

Quackenbush, Judge Justin L., 146
Quileute Indian Tribe, 8, 21, 22–23, 37, 132, 163
Quinault Indian Tribe, 21, 66, 132; treaty with, 8, 37, 193n1; self-regulating, 13, 61–62, 84; and fishing activities at Queets, 162

Ray, Governor Dixy Lee: on implications of *U.S.* v. *Washington,* 139
Redds, 26, 146–47
Rehnquist, Justice William H., 114
Reservation policy, 35–36
Reserved rights doctrine: 4–5; defined in *U.S.* v. *Winans,* 56
Riley, Dr. Carroll, 6
Roosevelt, President Franklin D., 61

Salmon, 20, 22–29, 39, 155; chinook, 21, 25, 27, 28, 41, 93, 118–23 passim, 127, 174–75, 177; chum, 25, 27, 93; coho, 25, 27–28, 41, 93, 118, 123, 177; pink, 25, 27, 28, 157, 177; sockeye, 25, 27–28, 118, 119, 123, 177; life cycle, 25–28; smolts, 28; effect of change in technology of commercial preservation, 40; Boldt affirms treaty rights regarding, 178. *See also* Steelhead
Salmon and Steelhead Conservation Act of 1980, 154, 175, 181
Salmon sting, 133–34
Sandison, Gordon, 116
Sasche, Harrison, 179
Satiacum, Robert, 67, 73
Sauk-Suiattle Indian Tribe, 8, 21; op-

poses Copper Creek dam, 144; and Skagit System Cooperative, 168
Schwartz, Jack, 134
Schwartzer, Judge William, 131, 132, 135
Seattle City Light: and dams on Skagit, 144
Seattle First National Bank, 145–46
Seattle Post-Intelligencer, 116, 117, 181
Seattle Times, 11, 116, 117
Self-regulating tribes, 13. *See also under names of individual tribes*
Seufert Brothers v. *U.S.,* 56, 107
Shorelands Management Act, 140
Shoshone-Bannock Tribe, 130
Sierra Club, 140
Simcoe, F. L., 52, 53
Skagit Indian Tribe. *See* Upper Skagit Indian Tribe
Skagit River, xviii, 143–44, 172
Skagit System Cooperative, 144, 172–73; *Annual Report* of, 164; formation of, 168
Skokomish Indian Tribe, 8, 23, 24, 170; opposes Northern Tier Pipeline, 144; use of fish taxes, 161
Smith, Courtland, 45, 46
Smith, Hugh, 45
Smith, McKee A., 78
Smith, Marian, 21
Snake River, 118, 125
Sneed, Judge, 147–48
Sparr, Harmon, 158
Spellman, Governor John: rejects plans for Northern Tier Pipeline, 145
Sohappy, David, 78, 120, 133, 134
Sohappy, David, Jr., 134
Sohappy, Richard, 76, 78, 120, 133
Sohappy v. *Smith,* 21, 77, 78, 121, 133; consolidated with *U.S.* v. *Oregon,* for trial, 78, 120; on question of conservation regulations, 79
Squaxin Island Indian Tribe, 8, 172
State v. *Alexis,* 56–58
State v. *Satiacum,* 67–68
State v. *Towessnute,* 56–58
Steelhead-Salmon Protection Action for Washington Now (S/SPAWN), 184–86

Washington Environmental Council, 186

Washington et al. v. Washington State Commercial Passenger Fishing Vessel Association et al., Washington et al. v. U.S. et al., Puget Sound Gillnetters et al. v. U.S. District Court for Western District of Washington, 111–15

Washington Kelpers Association, 92

Washington Labor Council, 186

Washington Reefnet Owners Association, 7

Washington State Charter Boat Association, 186

Washington State Commercial Passenger Fishing Vessel Association v. Tollefson, 92, 99, 107; Supreme Court review of consolidated cases, 111–15

Washington State Fisheries Commission, 58

Washington State Sportsmen's Council, 7

Washington State Supreme Court,

107, 115–16; and cases related to fishing rights, 56–57, 67–68, 98, 99

Weyerhaeuser Company, 145–46

Wheeler-Howard Act. *See* Indian Reorganization Act (IRA)

Whitney, Dr. Richard, 96; appointed Technical Adviser to Boldt, 86; chairman of Fisheries Advisory Board, 94–95

Williams, Wayne, 72

Winans case. *See U.S. v. Winans*

Wolf, Hazel, 140

Yakima Nation. *See* Confederated Tribes and Bands of the Yakima Indian Nation

Yaryan, Canon John, 73

Yearlings. *See* Fry

Young, James, 67

Ziontz, Alvin, 68

Zone system: on Columbia River, 120–22